SUPER HOROSCOPE
PISCES

2010

FEBRUARY 19 – MARCH 20

B

BERKLEY BOOKS, NEW YORK

THE BERKLEY PUBLISHING GROUP
Published by the Penguin Group
Penguin Group (USA) Inc.
375 Hudson Street, New York, New York 10014, USA
Penguin Group (Canada), 90 Eglinton Avenue East, Suite 700, Toronto, Ontario M4P 2Y3, Canada
(a division of Pearson Penguin Canada Inc.)
Penguin Books Ltd., 80 Strand, London WC2R 0RL, England
Penguin Group Ireland, 25 St. Stephen's Green, Dublin 2, Ireland (a division of Penguin Books Ltd.)
Penguin Group (Australia), 250 Camberwell Road, Camberwell, Victoria 3124, Australia
(a division of Pearson Australia Group Pty. Ltd.)
Penguin Books India Pvt. Ltd., 11 Community Centre, Panchsheel Park, New Delhi—110 017, India
Penguin Group (NZ), 67 Apollo Drive, Rosedale, North Shore 0632, New Zealand
(a division of Pearson New Zealand Ltd.)
Penguin Books (South Africa) (Pty.) Ltd., 24 Sturdee Avenue, Rosebank, Johannesburg 2196,
South Africa

Penguin Books Ltd., Registered Offices: 80 Strand, London WC2R 0RL, England

2010 SUPER HOROSCOPE PISCES

The publishers regret that they cannot answer individual letters requesting personal horoscope information.

A Berkley Book / published by arrangement with the author

PRINTING HISTORY
Berkley trade paperback edition / July 2009

ISBN: 978-0-425-22662-9

Library of Congress Cataloging-in-Publication Data

ISSN: 1535-8984

PRINTED IN THE UNITED STATES OF AMERICA

10 9 8 7 6 5 4 3 2 1

CONTENTS

THE CUSP-BORN PISCES

Are you *really* a Pisces? If your birthday falls during the third week of February, at the beginning of Pisces, will you still retain the traits of Aquarius, the sign of the Zodiac before Pisces? And what if you were born late in March—are you more Aries than Pisces? Many people born at the edge, or cusp, of a sign have difficulty determining exactly what sign they are. If you are one of these people, here's how you can figure it out, once and for all.

Consult the cusp table on the facing page, then locate the year of your birth. The table will tell you the precise days on which the Sun entered and left your sign for the year of your birth. In that way you can determine if you are a true Pisces—or whether you are an Aquarius or Aries—according to the variations in cusp dates from year to year (see also page 17).

If you were born either at the beginning or the end of Pisces, yours is a lifetime reflecting a process of subtle transformation. Your life on Earth will symbolize a significant change in consciousness, for you are either about to enter a whole new way of living or are leaving one behind.

If you were born at the end of February you are newly hatched into the sign of the Fishes. You may want to read the horoscope book for Aquarius as well as Pisces, for Aquarius holds the key to your secret wishes, your private uncertainties and guilts—some of them—and the mystical means to your cosmic unfoldment.

Though you don't often know quite where to begin, you would like to find a place in life where you can be simply happy, surrounded by friends you love and who love you—for your true identity puzzles you and you long for simplicity.

When you are undisciplined and guilt-ridden, you can pursue pleasure or vice in an effort at self-destruction. When you accept your role in the world and the people around you, the freedom you are always seeking suddenly comes to you, and then you wake up to know what it means to be free.

If you were born the third week of March, you are a symbol of winter's end and faith must be your key word. You may want to read the horoscope book for Aries as well as Pisces, for through Aries you begin to make all your dreams happen. Your urges come alive, and you wake up to the world around you as your materialism is sparked.

You may get depressed and discouraged, defeated and saddened, by the tribulations of this life on Earth, but of all the Zodiac signs you symbolize the time when faith is the ultimate savior of all people. Forgiveness and compassion characterize your spirit, and you blend a gentle poetry with verve and dynamism. You can waver

4

between self-doubt and selfishness, but at best you are the symbol of the turning of the tide and spiritual regeneration.

THE CUSPS OF PISCES

DATES SUN ENTERS PISCES (LEAVES AQUARIUS)

February 19 every year from 1900 to 2010, except for the following:

February 18					February 20
1900	1954	1973	1989	2001	1917
21	57	74	90	2002	
25	58	77	91	2003	
29	61	78	93	2005	
33	62	81	94	2006	
37	65	82	95	2007	
41	66	85	97	2009	
45	69	86	98	2010	
49	70	87	99		
53					

DATES SUN LEAVES PISCES (ENTERS ARIES)

March 20 every year from 1900 to 2010, except for the following:

March 21				
1901	1911	1923	1938	1955
02	13	26	39	59
03	14	27	42	63
05	15	30	43	67
06	18	31	46	71
07	19	34	47	75
09	22	35	51	79
10				

THE ASCENDANT: PISCES RISING

Could you be a "double" Pisces? That is, could you have Pisces as your Rising sign as well as your Sun sign? The tables on pages 8–9 will tell you Pisces what your Rising sign happens to be. Just find the hour of your birth, then find the day of your birth, and you will see which sign of the Zodiac is your Ascendant, as the Rising sign is called. The Ascendant is called that because it is the sign rising on the eastern horizon at the time of your birth. For a more detailed discussion of the Rising sign and the twelve houses of the Zodiac, see pages 17–20.

The Ascendant, or Rising sign, is placed on the 1st house in a horoscope, of which there are twelve houses. The 1st house represents your response to the environment—your unique response. Call it identity, personality, ego, self-image, facade, come-on, body-mind-spirit—whatever term best conveys to you the meaning of the you that acts and reacts in the world. It is a you that is always changing, discovering a new you. Your identity started with birth and early environment, over which you had little conscious control, and continues to experience, to adjust, to express itself. The 1st house also represents how others see you. Has anyone ever guessed your sign to be your Rising sign? People may respond to that personality, that facade, that body type governed by your Rising sign.

Your Ascendant, or Rising sign, modifies your basic Sun sign personality, and it affects the way you act out the daily predictions for your Sun sign. If your Rising sign indeed is Pisces, what follows is a description of its effect on your horoscope. If your Rising sign is not Pisces, but some other sign of the Zodiac, you may wish to read the horoscope book for that sign as well.

With Pisces Rising, you have the planets Jupiter and Neptune, which are the co-rulers of Pisces, rising in the 1st house. Acting together here, Jupiter and Neptune give you a tremendous capacity for compassion and a highly developed visionary mind. Your chances of success in risky undertakings and in remote places are increased by the joint influences of these planets. Jupiter confers a measure of good fortune in health and disposition. Neptune bestows an inner strength and resourcefulness. But Neptune also gives you a restless, wandering mind and, at the same time, a fear of action, a dread of dangers, real or imagined, that block the nobility and freedom with which Jupiter impels you to act. You may then

6

waver in making choices, or, preferring secrecy, you could attract intrigue and enemies.

You have a strong need for, and love of, change. You seek change for change itself—not necessarily for the material comforts you could gain through it or for the escape from dangers it could allow. The search for challenging new environments suits your wanderlust. You are always looking for fresh experiences to stimulate your imagination. Travel and adventure, even if these pursuits are only intellectual or emotional voyages, are basic to your nature. From such excursions your dreams are born. And from your dreams you create visionary, utopian schemes of a bright, free world, for you have a definite social consciousness.

You are a creative symbol of that new world. Justice, fairness, equality are bywords for those of you with Pisces Rising. You are dedicated to sisterhood, brotherhood, peoplehood. You envision a free space without distinctions of age, race, sex, class. You tend to live your own life in these ideals, too, which could startle and antagonize many people around you. Defying convention, however, you may at times suffer by it. As a result, it is all too easy for you to cultivate secrecy or procrastination.

Impression and expression are twinned in your nature. If this sensory input and output are balanced, you can achieve artistic freedom and greatness. You will be generous with your gifts and talents; you can give yourself over to caring for others. But if impressions are denied you, you could turn in on yourself, wasting resources of thought and feeling, indulging your senses in limiting, even dangerous, experiences. And if your expressions are inhibited, you could become withdrawn and introverted, deeply pessimistic about human nature, preferring a hermit's existence.

There is always a touch of theatricality about you, even when you are in seclusion. Neptune, planet of mystery, shrouds you in tantalizing auras. Glamour may be a real part of your makeup, as all the arts have a great appeal for you, and sometime in your life you express yourself through an artistic medium. Emotion, rather than logic, lies at the core of your being. It allows you to master the craft of illusion, to create whatever persona or ambience suits an occasion. At the zenith of its development, emotion may make you a visionary. At its nadir, however, confusion reigns.

Compassion and expansiveness are the key words for those of you with Pisces Rising. Actualizing them, you can live a lifetime of creativity, fullness, service to others, as opposed to living in fear and discontent.

RISING SIGNS FOR PISCES

Hour of Birth*	Day of Birth		
	February 18–21	**February 22–29**	**March 1–5**
Midnight	Scorpio	Scorpio	Scorpio
1 AM	Scorpio	Sagittarius	Sagittarius
2 AM	Sagittarius	Sagittarius	Sagittarius
3 AM	Sagittarius	Sagittarius; Capricorn 2/25	Capricorn
4 AM	Capricorn	Capricorn	Capricorn
5 AM	Capricorn	Aquarius	Aquarius
6 AM	Aquarius	Aquarius	Aquarius; Pisces 3/3
7 AM	Pisces	Pisces	Pisces
8 AM	Pisces; Aries 2/20	Aries	Aries
9 AM	Aries	Taurus	Taurus
10 AM	Taurus	Taurus	Taurus; Gemini 3/2
11 AM	Gemini	Gemini	Gemini
Noon	Gemini	Gemini	Gemini; Cancer 3/2
1 PM	Cancer	Cancer	Cancer
2 PM	Cancer	Cancer	Cancer
3 PM	Cancer	Leo	Leo
4 PM	Leo	Leo	Leo
5 PM	Leo	Leo; Virgo 2/29	Virgo
6 PM	Virgo	Virgo	Virgo
7 PM	Virgo	Virgo	Virgo
8 PM	Virgo; Libra 2/20	Libra	Libra
9 PM	Libra	Libra	Libra
10 PM	Libra	Libra; Scorpio 2/28	Scorpio
11 PM	Scorpio	Scorpio	Scorpio

*Hour of birth given here is for Standard Time in any time zone. If your hour of birth was recorded in Daylight Saving Time, subtract on hour from it and consult that hour in the table above. For example, if you were born at 7 AM D.S.T., see 6 AM above.

Hour of Birth*	Day of Birth		
	March 6–9	March 10–15	March 16–21
Midnight	Scorpio; Sagittarius 3/7	Sagittarius	Sagittarius
1 AM	Sagittarius	Sagittarius	Sagittarius
2 AM	Sagittarius	Capricorn	Capricorn
3 AM	Capricorn	Capricorn	Capricorn
4 AM	Capricorn	Capricorn; Aquarius 3/11	Aquarius
5 AM	Aquarius	Aquarius	Aquarius
6 AM	Pisces	Pisces	Pisces
7 AM	Pisces; Aries 3/7	Aries	Aries
8 AM	Aries	Aries; Taurus 3/14	Taurus
9 AM	Taurus	Taurus	Taurus; Gemini 3/19
10 AM	Gemini	Gemini	Gemini
11 AM	Gemini	Gemini	Gemini; Cancer 3/18
Noon	Cancer	Cancer	Cancer
1 PM	Cancer	Cancer	Cancer
2 PM	Cancer; Leo 3/8	Leo	Leo
3 PM	Leo	Leo	Leo
4 PM	Leo	Leo	Virgo
5 PM	Virgo	Virgo	Virgo
6 PM	Virgo	Virgo	Virgo
7 PM	Virgo; Libra 3/7	Libra	Libra
8 PM	Libra	Libra	Libra
9 PM	Libra	Libra; Scorpio 3/15	Scorpio
10 PM	Scorpio	Scorpio	Scorpio
11 PM	Scorpio	Scorpio	Scorpio

*See note on facing page.

THE PLACE OF ASTROLOGY IN TODAY'S WORLD

Does astrology have a place in the fast-moving, ultra-scientific world we live in today? Can it be justified in a sophisticated society whose outriders are already preparing to step off the moon into the deep space of the planets themselves? Or is it just a hangover of ancient superstition, a psychological dummy for neurotics and dreamers of every historical age?

These are the kind of questions that any inquiring person can be expected to ask when they approach a subject like astrology which goes beyond, but never excludes, the materialistic side of life.

The simple, single answer is that astrology works. It works for many millions of people in the western world alone. In the United States there are 10 million followers and in Europe, an estimated 25 million. America has more than 4000 practicing astrologers, Europe nearly three times as many. Even down-under Australia has its hundreds of thousands of adherents. In the eastern countries, astrology has enormous followings, again, because it has been proved to work. In India, for example, brides and grooms for centuries have been chosen on the basis of their astrological compatibility.

Astrology today is more vital than ever before, more practicable because all over the world the media devotes much space and time to it, more valid because science itself is confirming the precepts of astrological knowledge with every new exciting step. The ordinary person who daily applies astrology intelligently does not have to wonder whether it is true nor believe in it blindly. He can see it working for himself. And, if he can use it—and this book is designed to help the reader to do just that—he can make living a far richer experience, and become a more developed personality and a better person.

Astrology and Relationships

Astrology is the science of relationships. It is not just a study of planetary influences on man and his environment. It is the study of man himself.

We are at the center of our personal universe, of all our relationships. And our happiness or sadness depends on how we act, how we relate to the people and things that surround us. The emotions that we generate have a distinct effect—for better or worse—on the world around us. Our friends and our enemies will confirm this. Just look in the mirror the next time you are angry. In other words, each of us is a kind of sun or planet or star radiating our feelings on the environment around us. Our influence on our personal universe, whether loving, helpful, or destructive, varies with our changing moods, expressed through our individual character.

Our personal "radiations" are potent in the way they affect our moods and our ability to control them. But we usually are able to throw off our emotion in some sort of action—we have a good cry, walk it off, or tell someone our troubles—before it can build up too far and make us physically ill. Astrology helps us to understand the universal forces working on us, and through this understanding, we can become more properly adjusted to our surroundings so that we find ourselves coping where others may flounder.

The Challenge of Love

The challenge of love lies in recognizing the difference between infatuation, emotion, sex, and, sometimes, the intentional deceit of the other person. Mankind, with its record of broken marriages, despair, and disillusionment, is obviously not very good at making these distinctions.

Can astrology help?

Yes. In the same way that advance knowledge can usually help in any human situation. And there is probably no situation as human, as poignant, as pathetic and universal, as the failure of man's love.

Love, of course, is not just between man and woman. It involves love of children, parents, home, and friends. But the big problems usually involve the choice of partner.

Astrology has established degrees of compatibility that exist between people born under the various signs of the Zodiac. Because people are individuals, there are numerous variations and modifications. So the astrologer, when approached on mate and marriage matters, makes allowances for them. But the fact remains that some groups of people are suited for each other and some are not, and astrology has expressed this in terms of characteristics we all can study and use as a personal guide.

No matter how much enjoyment and pleasure we find in the different aspects of each other's character, if it is not an overall compatibility, the chances of our finding fulfillment or enduring happiness in each other are pretty hopeless. And astrology can help us to find someone compatible.

Astrology and Science

Closely related to our emotions is the "other side" of our personal universe, our physical welfare. Our body, of course, is largely influenced by things around us over which we have very little control. The phone rings, we hear it. The train runs late. We snag our stocking or cut our face shaving. Our body is under a constant bombardment of events that influence our daily lives to varying degrees.

The question that arises from all this is, what makes each of us act so that we have to involve other people and keep the ball of activity and evolution rolling? This is the question that both science and astrology are involved with. The scientists have attacked it from different angles: anthropology, the study of human evolution as body, mind and response to environment; anatomy, the study of bodily structure; psychology, the science of the human mind; and so on. These studies have produced very impressive classifications and valuable information, but because the approach to the problem is fragmented, so is the result. They remain "branches" of science. Science generally studies effects. It keeps turning up wonderful answers but no lasting solutions. Astrology, on the other hand, approaches the question from the broader viewpoint. Astrology began its inquiry with the totality of human experience and saw it as an effect. It then looked to find the cause, or at least the prime movers, and during thousands of years of observation of man and his *universal* environment came up with the extraordinary principle of planetary influence—or astrology, which, from the Greek, means the science of the stars.

Modern science, as we shall see, has confirmed much of astrology's foundations—most of it unintentionally, some of it reluctantly, but still, indisputably.

It is not difficult to imagine that there must be a connection between outer space and Earth. Even today, scientists are not too sure how our Earth was created, but it is generally agreed that it is only a tiny part of the universe. And as a part of the universe, people on Earth see and feel the influence of heavenly bodies in almost every aspect of our existence. There is no doubt that the Sun has the greatest influence on life on this planet. Without it there would be no life, for without it there would be no warmth, no division into day and night, no cycles of time or season at all. This is clear and easy to see. The influence of the Moon, on the other hand, is more subtle, though no less definite.

There are many ways in which the influence of the Moon manifests itself here on Earth, both on human and animal life. It is a well-known fact, for instance, that the large movements of water on our planet—that is the ebb and flow of the tides—are caused by the Moon's gravitational pull. Since this is so, it follows that these water movements do not occur only in the oceans, but that all bodies of water are affected, even down to the tiniest puddle.

The human body, too, which consists of about 70 percent water, falls within the scope of this lunar influence. For example the menstrual cycle of most women corresponds to the 28-day lunar month; the period of pregnancy in humans is 273 days, or equal to nine lunar months. Similarly, many illnesses reach a crisis at the change of the Moon, and statistics in many countries have shown that the crime rate is highest at the time of the Full Moon. Even human sexual desire has been associated with the phases of the Moon. But it is in the movement of the tides that we get the clearest demonstration of planetary influence, which leads to the irresistible correspondence between the so-called metaphysical and the physical.

Tide tables are prepared years in advance by calculating the future positions of the Moon. Science has known for a long time that the Moon is the main cause of tidal action. But only in the last few years has it begun to realize the possible extent of this influence on mankind. To begin with, the ocean tides do not rise and fall as we might imagine from our personal observations of them. The Moon as it orbits around Earth sets up a circular wave of attraction which pulls the oceans of the world after it, broadly in an east to west direction. This influence is like a phantom wave crest, a loop of power stretching from pole to pole which passes over and around the Earth like an invisible shadow. It travels with equal effect across the land masses and, as scientists were recently amazed to observe, caused oysters placed in the dark in the middle of the United States where there is no sea to open their shells to receive the nonexistent tide. If the land-locked oysters react to this invisible signal, what effect does it have on us who not so long ago in evolutionary time came out of the sea and still have its salt in our blood and sweat?

Less well known is the fact that the Moon is also the primary force behind the circulation of blood in human beings and animals, and the movement of sap in trees and plants. Agriculturists have established that the Moon has a distinct influence on crops, which explains why for centuries people have planted according to Moon cycles. The habits of many animals, too, are directed by the movement of the Moon. Migratory birds, for instance, depart only at or near the time of the Full Moon. And certain sea creatures, eels in particular, move only in accordance with certain phases of the Moon.

Know Thyself—Why?

In today's fast-changing world, everyone still longs to know what the future holds. It is the one thing that everyone has in common: rich and poor, famous and infamous, all are deeply concerned about tomorrow.

But the key to the future, as every historian knows, lies in the past. This is as true of individual people as it is of nations. You cannot understand your future without first understanding your past, which is simply another way of saying that you must first of all know yourself.

The motto "know thyself" seems obvious enough nowadays, but it was originally put forward as the foundation of wisdom by the ancient Greek philosophers. It was then adopted by the "mystery religions" of the ancient Middle East, Greece, Rome, and is still used in all genuine schools of mind training or mystical discipline, both in those of the East, based on yoga, and those of the West. So it is universally accepted now, and has been through the ages.

But how do you go about discovering what sort of person you are? The first step is usually classification into some sort of system of types. Astrology did this long before the birth of Christ. Psychology has also done it. So has modern medicine, in its way.

One system classifies people according to the source of the impulses they respond to most readily: the muscles, leading to direct bodily action; the digestive organs, resulting in emotion; or the brain and nerves, giving rise to thinking. Another such system says that character is determined by the endocrine glands, and gives us such labels as "pituitary," "thyroid," and "hyperthyroid" types. These different systems are neither contradictory nor mutually exclusive. In fact, they are very often different ways of saying the same thing.

Very popular, useful classifications were devised by Carl Jung, the eminent disciple of Freud. Jung observed among the different faculties of the mind, four which have a predominant influence on character. These four faculties exist in all of us without exception, but not in perfect balance. So when we say, for instance, that someone is a "thinking type," it means that in any situation he or she tries to be rational. Emotion, which may be the opposite of thinking, will be his or her weakest function. This thinking type can be sensible and reasonable, or calculating and unsympathetic. The emotional type, on the other hand, can often be recognized by exaggerated language—everything is either marvelous or terrible—and in extreme cases they even invent dramas and quarrels out of nothing just to make life more interesting.

The other two faculties are intuition and physical sensation. The sensation type does not only care for food and drink, nice clothes and furniture; he or she is also interested in all forms of physical experience. Many scientists are sensation types as are athletes and nature-lovers. Like sensation, intuition is a form of perception and we all possess it. But it works through that part of the mind which is not under conscious control—consequently it sees meanings and connections which are not obvious to thought or emotion. Inventors and original thinkers are always intuitive, but so, too, are superstitious people who see meanings where none exist.

Thus, sensation tells us what is going on in the world, feeling (that is, emotion) tells us how important it is to ourselves, thinking enables us to interpret it and work out what we should do about it, and intuition tells us what it means to ourselves and others. All four faculties are essential, and all are present in every one of us. But some people are guided chiefly by one, others by another. In addition, Jung also observed a division of the human personality into the extrovert and the introvert, which cuts across these four types.

A disadvantage of all these systems of classification is that one cannot tell very easily where to place oneself. Some people are reluctant to admit that they act to please their emotions. So they deceive themselves for years by trying to belong to whichever type they think is the "best." Of course, there is no best; each has its faults and each has its good points.

The advantage of the signs of the Zodiac is that they simplify classification. Not only that, but your date of birth is personal—it is unarguably yours. What better way to know yourself than by going back as far as possible to the very moment of your birth? And this is precisely what your horoscope is all about, as we shall see in the next section.

WHAT IS A HOROSCOPE?

If you had been able to take a picture of the skies at the moment of your birth, that photograph would be your horoscope. Lacking such a snapshot, it is still possible to recreate the picture—and this is at the basis of the astrologer's art. In other words, your horoscope is a representation of the skies with the planets in the exact positions they occupied at the time you were born.

The year of birth tells an astrologer the positions of the distant, slow-moving planets Jupiter, Saturn, Uranus, Neptune, and Pluto. The month of birth indicates the Sun sign, or birth sign as it is commonly called, as well as indicating the positions of the rapidly moving planets Venus, Mercury, and Mars. The day and time of birth will locate the position of our Moon. And the moment—the exact hour and minute—of birth determines the houses through what is called the Ascendant, or Rising sign.

With this information the astrologer consults various tables to calculate the specific positions of the Sun, Moon, and other planets relative to your birthplace at the moment you were born. Then he or she locates them by means of the Zodiac.

The Zodiac

The Zodiac is a band of stars (constellations) in the skies, centered on the Sun's apparent path around the Earth, and is divided into twelve equal segments, or signs. What we are actually dividing up is the Earth's path around the Sun. But from our point of view here on Earth, it seems as if the Sun is making a great circle around our planet in the sky, so we say it is the Sun's apparent path. This twelve-fold division, the Zodiac, is a reference system for the astrologer. At any given moment the planets—and in astrology both the Sun and Moon are considered to be planets—can all be located at a specific point along this path.

Now where in all this are you, the subject of the horoscope? Your character is largely determined by the sign the Sun is in. So that is where the astrologer looks first in your horoscope, at your Sun sign.

The Sun Sign and the Cusp

There are twelve signs in the Zodiac, and the Sun spends approximately one month in each sign. But because of the motion of the Earth around the Sun—the Sun's apparent motion—the dates when the Sun enters and leaves each sign may change from year to year. Some people born near the cusp, or edge, of a sign have difficulty determining which is their Sun sign. But in this book a Table of Cusps is provided for the years 1900 to 2010 (page 5) so you can find out what your true Sun sign is.

Here are the twelve signs of the Zodiac, their ancient zodiacal symbol, and the dates when the Sun enters and leaves each sign for the year 2010. Remember, these dates may change from year to year.

ARIES	Ram	March 20–April 20
TAURUS	Bull	April 20–May 21
GEMINI	Twins	May 21–June 21
CANCER	Crab	June 21–July 22
LEO	Lion	July 22–August 23
VIRGO	Virgin	August 23–September 23
LIBRA	Scales	September 23–October 23
SCORPIO	Scorpion	October 23–November 22
SAGITTARIUS	Archer	November 22–December 21
CAPRICORN	Sea Goat	December 21–January 20
AQUARIUS	Water Bearer	January 20–February 18
PISCES	Fish	February 18–March 20

It is possible to draw significant conclusions and make meaningful predictions based simply on the Sun sign of a person. There are many people who have been amazed at the accuracy of the description of their own character based only on the Sun sign. But an astrologer needs more information than just your Sun sign to interpret the photograph that is your horoscope.

The Rising Sign and the Zodiacal Houses

An astrologer needs the exact time and place of your birth in order to construct and interpret your horoscope. The illustration on the next page shows the flat chart, or natural wheel, an astrologer uses. Note the inner circle of the wheel labeled 1 through 12. These 12 divisions are known as the houses of the Zodiac.

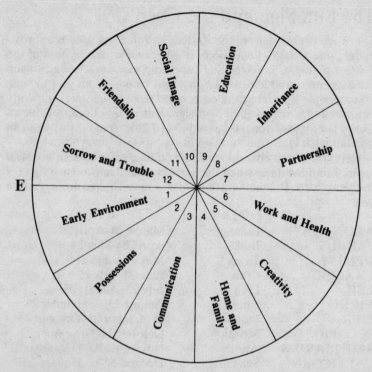

The 1st house always starts from the position marked E, which corresponds to the eastern horizon. The rest of the houses 2 through 12 follow around in a "counterclockwise" direction. The point where each house starts is known as a cusp, or edge.

The cusp, or edge, of the 1st house (point E) is where an astrologer would place your Rising sign, the Ascendant. And, as already noted, the exact time of your birth determines your Rising sign. Let's see how this works.

As the Earth rotates on its axis once every 24 hours, each one of the twelve signs of the Zodiac appears to be "rising" on the horizon, with a new one appearing about every 2 hours. Actually it is the turning of the Earth that exposes each sign to view, but in our astrological work we are discussing apparent motion. This Rising sign marks the Ascendant, and it colors the whole orientation of a horoscope. It indicates the sign governing the 1st house of the chart, and will thus determine which signs will govern all the other houses.

To visualize this idea, imagine two color wheels with twelve divisions superimposed upon each other. For just as the Zodiac is divided into twelve constellations that we identify as the signs, another twelvefold division is used to denote the houses. Now imagine one wheel (the signs) moving slowly while the other wheel (the houses) remains still. This analogy may help you see how the signs keep shifting the "color" of the houses as the Rising sign continues to change every two hours. To simplify things, a Table of Rising Signs has been provided (pages 8–9) for your specific Sun sign.

Once your Rising sign has been placed on the cusp of the 1st house, the signs that govern the rest of the 11 houses can be placed on the chart. In any individual's horoscope the signs do not necessarily correspond with the houses. For example, it could be that a sign covers part of two adjacent houses. It is the interpretation of such variations in an individual's horoscope that marks the professional astrologer.

But to gain a workable understanding of astrology, it is not necessary to go into great detail. In fact, we just need a description of the houses and their meanings, as is shown in the illustration above and in the table below.

THE 12 HOUSES OF THE ZODIAC

1st	Individuality, body appearance, general outlook on life	Personality house
2nd	Finance, possessions, ethical principles, gain or loss	Money house
3rd	Relatives, communication, short journeys, writing, education	Relatives house
4th	Family and home, parental ties, land and property, security	Home house
5th	Pleasure, children, creativity, entertainment, risk	Pleasure house
6th	Health, harvest, hygiene, work and service, employees	Health house
7th	Marriage and divorce, the law, partnerships and alliances	Marriage house
8th	Inheritance, secret deals, sex, death, regeneration	Inheritance house
9th	Travel, sports, study, philosophy and religion	Travel house
10th	Career, social standing, success and honor	Business house
11th	Friendship, social life, hopes and wishes	Friends house
12th	Troubles, illness, secret enemies, hidden agendas	Trouble house

The Planets in the Houses

An astrologer, knowing the exact time and place of your birth, will use tables of planetary motion in order to locate the planets in your horoscope chart. He or she will determine which planet or planets are in which sign and in which house. It is not uncommon, in an individual's horoscope, for there to be two or more planets in the same sign and in the same house.

The characteristics of the planets modify the influence of the Sun according to their natures and strengths.

Sun: Source of life. Basic temperament according to the Sun sign. The conscious will. Human potential.

Moon: Emotions. Moods. Customs. Habits. Changeable. Adaptive. Nurturing.

Mercury: Communication. Intellect. Reasoning power. Curiosity. Short travels.

Venus: Love. Delight. Charm. Harmony. Balance. Art. Beautiful possessions.

Mars: Energy. Initiative. War. Anger. Adventure. Courage. Daring. Impulse.

Jupiter: Luck. Optimism. Generous. Expansive. Opportunities. Protection.

Saturn: Pessimism. Privation. Obstacles. Delay. Hard work. Research. Lasting rewards after long struggle.

Uranus: Fashion. Electricity. Revolution. Independence. Freedom. Sudden changes. Modern science.

Neptune: Sensationalism. Theater. Dreams. Inspiration. Illusion. Deception.

Pluto: Creation and destruction. Total transformation. Lust for power. Strong obsessions.

Superimpose the characteristics of the planets on the functions of the house in which they appear. Express the result through the character of the Sun sign, and you will get the basic idea.

Of course, many other considerations have been taken into account in producing the carefully worked out predictions in this book: the aspects of the planets to each other; their strength according to position and sign; whether they are in a house of exaltation or decline; whether they are natural enemies or not; whether a planet occupies its own sign; the position of a planet in relation to its own house or sign; whether the sign is male or female; whether the sign is a fire, earth, water, or air sign. These are only a few of the colors on the astrologer's pallet which he or she must mix with the inspiration of the artist and the accuracy of the mathematician.

How To Use These Predictions

A person reading the predictions in this book should understand that they are produced from the daily position of the planets for a group of people and are not, of course, individually specialized. To get the full benefit of them our readers should relate the predictions to their own character and circumstances, coordinate them, and draw their own conclusions from them.

If you are a serious observer of your own life, you should find a definite pattern emerging that will be a helpful and reliable guide.

The point is that we always retain our free will. The stars indicate certain directional tendencies but we are not compelled to follow. We can do or not do, and wisdom must make the choice.

We all have our good and bad days. Sometimes they extend into cycles of weeks. It is therefore advisable to study daily predictions in a span ranging from the day before to several days ahead.

Daily predictions should be taken very generally. The word "difficult" does not necessarily indicate a whole day of obstruction or inconvenience. It is a warning to you to be cautious. Your caution will often see you around the difficulty before you are involved. This is the correct use of astrology.

In another section (pages 78–84), detailed information is given about the influence of the Moon as it passes through each of the twelve signs of the Zodiac. There are instructions on how to use the Moon Tables (pages 85–92), which provide Moon Sign Dates throughout the year as well as the Moon's role in health and daily affairs. This information should be used in conjunction with the daily forecasts to give a fuller picture of the astrological trends.

HISTORY OF ASTROLOGY

The origins of astrology have been lost far back in history, but we do know that reference is made to it as far back as the first written records of the human race. It is not hard to see why. Even in primitive times, people must have looked for an explanation for the various happenings in their lives. They must have wanted to know why people were different from one another. And in their search they turned to the regular movements of the Sun, Moon, and stars to see if they could provide an answer.

It is interesting to note that as soon as man learned to use his tools in any type of design, or his mind in any kind of calculation, he turned his attention to the heavens. Ancient cave dwellings reveal dim crescents and circles representative of the Sun and Moon, rulers of day and night. Mesopotamia and the civilization of Chaldea, in itself the foundation of those of Babylonia and Assyria, show a complete picture of astronomical observation and well-developed astrological interpretation.

Humanity has a natural instinct for order. The study of anthropology reveals that primitive people—even as far back as prehistoric times—were striving to achieve a certain order in their lives. They tried to organize the apparent chaos of the universe. They had the desire to attach meaning to things. This demand for order has persisted throughout the history of man. So that observing the regularity of the heavenly bodies made it logical that primitive peoples should turn heavenward in their search for an understanding of the world in which they found themselves so random and alone.

And they did find a significance in the movements of the stars. Shepherds tending their flocks, for instance, observed that when the cluster of stars now known as the constellation Aries was in sight, it was the time of fertility and they associated it with the Ram. And they noticed that the growth of plants and plant life corresponded with different phases of the Moon, so that certain times were favorable for the planting of crops, and other times were not. In this way, there grew up a tradition of seasons and causes connected with the passage of the Sun through the twelve signs of the Zodiac.

Astrology was valued so highly that the king was kept informed of the daily and monthly changes in the heavenly bodies, and the results of astrological studies regarding events of the future. Head astrologers were clearly men of great rank and position, and the office was said to be a hereditary one.

Omens were taken, not only from eclipses and conjunctions of the Moon or Sun with one of the planets, but also from storms and earthquakes. In the eastern civilizations, particularly, the reverence inspired by astrology appears to have remained unbroken since the very earliest days. In ancient China, astrology, astronomy, and religion went hand in hand. The astrologer, who was also an astronomer, was part of the official government service and had his own corner in the Imperial Palace. The duties of the Imperial astrologer, whose office was one of the most important in the land, were clearly defined, as this extract from early records shows:

> This exalted gentleman must concern himself with the stars in the heavens, keeping a record of the changes and movements of the Planets, the Sun and the Moon, in order to examine the movements of the terrestrial world with the object of prognosticating good and bad fortune. He divides the territories of the nine regions of the empire in accordance with their dependence on particular celestial bodies. All the fiefs and principalities are connected with the stars and from this their prosperity or misfortune should be ascertained. He makes prognostications according to the twelve years of the Jupiter cycle of good and evil of the terrestrial world. From the colors of the five kinds of clouds, he determines the coming of floods or droughts, abundance or famine. From the twelve winds, he draws conclusions about the state of harmony of heaven and earth, and takes note of good and bad signs that result from their accord or disaccord. In general, he concerns himself with five kinds of phenomena so as to warn the Emperor to come to the aid of the government and to allow for variations in the ceremonies according to their circumstances.

The Chinese were also keen observers of the fixed stars, giving them such unusual names as Ghost Vehicle, Sun of Imperial Concubine, Imperial Prince, Pivot of Heaven, Twinkling Brilliance, Weaving Girl. But, great astrologers though they may have been, the Chinese lacked one aspect of mathematics that the Greeks applied to astrology—deductive geometry. Deductive geometry was the basis of much classical astrology in and after the time of the Greeks, and this explains the different methods of prognostication used in the East and West.

Down through the ages the astrologer's art has depended, not so much on the uncovering of new facts, though this is important, as on the interpretation of the facts already known. This is the essence of the astrologer's skill.

But why should the signs of the Zodiac have any effect at all on the formation of human character? It is easy to see why people thought they did, and even now we constantly use astrological expressions in our everyday speech. The thoughts of "lucky star," "ill-fated," "star-crossed," "mooning around," are interwoven into the very structure of our language.

Wherever the concept of the Zodiac is understood and used, it could well appear to have an influence on the human character. Does this mean, then, that the human race, in whose civilization the idea of the twelve signs of the Zodiac has long been embedded, is divided into only twelve types? Can we honestly believe that it is really as simple as that? If so, there must be pretty wide ranges of variation within each type. And if, to explain the variation, we call in heredity and environment, experiences in early childhood, the thyroid and other glands, and also the four functions of the mind together with extroversion and introversion, then one begins to wonder if the original classification was worth making at all. No sensible person believes that his favorite system explains everything. But even so, he will not find the system much use at all if it does not even save him the trouble of bothering with the others.

In the same way, if we were to put every person under only one sign of the Zodiac, the system becomes too rigid and unlike life. Besides, it was never intended to be used like that. It may be convenient to have only twelve types, but we know that in practice there is every possible gradation between aggressiveness and timidity, or between conscientiousness and laziness. How, then, do we account for this?

A person born under any given Sun sign can be mainly influenced by one or two of the other signs that appear in their individual horoscope. For instance, famous persons born under the sign of Gemini include Henry VIII, whom nothing and no one could have induced to abdicate, and Edward VIII, who did just that. Obviously, then, the sign Gemini does not fully explain the complete character of either of them.

Again, under the opposite sign, Sagittarius, were both Stalin, who was totally consumed with the notion of power, and Charles V, who freely gave up an empire because he preferred to go into a monastery. And we find under Scorpio many uncompromising characters such as Luther, de Gaulle, Indira Gandhi, and Montgomery, but also Petain, a successful commander whose name later became synonymous with collaboration.

A single sign is therefore obviously inadequate to explain the differences between people; it can only explain resemblances, such as the combativeness of the Scorpio group, or the far-reaching devotion of Charles V and Stalin to their respective ideals—the Christian heaven and the Communist utopia.

But very few people have only one sign in their horoscope chart. In addition to the month of birth, the day and, even more, the hour to the nearest minute if possible, ought to be considered. Without this, it is impossible to have an actual horoscope, for the word horoscope literally means "a consideration of the hour."

The month of birth tells you only which sign of the Zodiac was occupied by the Sun. The day and hour tell you what sign was occupied by the Moon. And the minute tells you which sign was rising on the eastern horizon. This is called the Ascendant, and, as some astrologers believe, it is supposed to be the most important thing in the whole horoscope.

The Sun is said to signify one's heart, that is to say, one's deepest desires and inmost nature. This is quite different from the Moon, which signifies one's superficial way of behaving. When the ancient Romans referred to the Emperor Augustus as a Capricorn, they meant that he had the Moon in Capricorn. Or, to take another example, a modern astrologer would call Disraeli a Scorpion because he had Scorpio Rising, but most people would call him Sagittarius because he had the Sun there. The Romans would have called him Leo because his Moon was in Leo.

So if one does not seem to fit one's birth month, it is always worthwhile reading the other signs, for one may have been born at a time when any of them were rising or occupied by the Moon. It also seems to be the case that the influence of the Sun develops as life goes on, so that the month of birth is easier to guess in people over the age of forty. The young are supposed to be influenced mainly by their Ascendant, the Rising sign, which characterizes the body and physical personality as a whole.

It is nonsense to assume that all people born at a certain time will exhibit the same characteristics, or that they will even behave in the same manner. It is quite obvious that, from the very moment of its birth, a child is subject to the effects of its environment, and that this in turn will influence its character and heritage to a decisive extent. Also to be taken into account are education and economic conditions, which play a very important part in the formation of one's character as well.

People have, in general, certain character traits and qualities which, according to their environment, develop in either a positive or a negative manner. Therefore, selfishness (inherent selfishness, that is) might emerge as unselfishness; kindness and consideration as cruelty and lack of consideration toward others. In the same way, a naturally constructive person may, through frustration, become destructive, and so on. The latent characteristics with which people are born can, therefore, through environment and good or bad training, become something that would appear to be its opposite, and so give the lie to the astrologer's description of their character. But this is not the case. The true character is still there, but it is buried deep beneath these external superficialities.

Careful study of the character traits of various signs of the Zodiac are of immeasurable help, and can render beneficial service to the intelligent person. Undoubtedly, the reader will already have discovered that, while he is able to get on very well with some people, he just "cannot stand" others. The causes sometimes seem inexplicable. At times there is intense dislike, at other times immediate sympathy. And there is, too, the phenomenon of love at first sight, which is also apparently inexplicable. People appear to be either sympathetic or unsympathetic toward each other for no apparent reason.

Now if we look at this in the light of the Zodiac, we find that people born under different signs are either compatible or incompatible with each other. In other words, there are good and bad interrelating factors among the various signs. This does not, of course, mean that humanity can be divided into groups of hostile camps. It would be quite wrong to be hostile or indifferent toward people who happen to be born under an incompatible sign. There is no reason why everybody should not, or cannot, learn to control and adjust their feelings and actions, especially after they are aware of the positive qualities of other people by studying their character analyses, among other things.

Every person born under a certain sign has both positive and negative qualities, which are developed more or less according to our free will. Nobody is entirely good or entirely bad, and it is up to each of us to learn to control ourselves on the one hand and at the same time to endeavor to learn about ourselves and others.

It cannot be emphasized often enough that it is free will that determines whether we will make really good use of our talents and abilities. Using our free will, we can either overcome our failings or allow them to rule us. Our free will enables us to exert sufficient willpower to control our failings so that they do not harm ourselves or others.

Astrology can reveal our inclinations and tendencies. Astrology can tell us about ourselves so that we are able to use our free will to overcome our shortcomings. In this way astrology helps us do our best to become needed and valuable members of society as well as helpmates to our family and our friends. Astrology also can save us a great deal of unhappiness and remorse.

Yet it may seem absurd that an ancient philosophy could be a prop to modern men and women. But below the materialistic surface of modern life, there are hidden streams of feeling and thought. Symbology is reappearing as a study worthy of the scholar; the psychosomatic factor in illness has passed from the writings of the crank to those of the specialist; spiritual healing in all its forms is no longer a pious hope but an accepted phenomenon. And it is into this context that we consider astrology, in the sense that it is an analysis of human types.

Astrology and medicine had a long journey together, and only parted company a couple of centuries ago. There still remain in medical language such astrological terms as "saturnine," "choleric," and "mercurial," used in the diagnosis of physical tendencies. The herbalist, for long the handyman of the medical profession, has been dominated by astrology since the days of the Greeks. Certain herbs traditionally respond to certain planetary influences, and diseases must therefore be treated to ensure harmony between the medicine and the disease.

But the stars are expected to foretell and not only to diagnose.

Astrological forecasting has been remarkably accurate, but often it is wide of the mark. The brave person who cares to predict world events takes dangerous chances. Individual forecasting is less clear cut; it can be a help or a disillusionment. Then we come to the nagging question: if it is possible to foreknow, is it right to foretell? This is a point of ethics on which it is hard to pronounce judgment. The doctor faces the same dilemma if he finds that symptoms of a mortal disease are present in his patient and that he can only prognosticate a steady decline. How much to tell an individual in a crisis is a problem that has perplexed many distinguished scholars. Honest and conscientious astrologers in this modern world, where so many people are seeking guidance, face the same problem.

Five hundred years ago it was customary to call in a learned man who was an astrologer who was probably also a doctor and a philosopher. By his knowledge of astrology, his study of planetary influences, he felt himself qualified to guide those in distress. The world has moved forward at a fantastic rate since then, and yet people are still uncertain of themselves. At first sight it seems fantastic in the light of modern thinking that they turn to the most ancient of all studies, and get someone to calculate a horoscope for them. But is it really so fantastic if you take a second look? For astrology is concerned with tomorrow, with survival. And in a world such as ours, tomorrow and survival are the keywords for the twenty-first century.

SPECIAL OVERVIEW 2011–2020

The second decade of the twenty-first century opens on major planetary shifts that set the stage for challenge, opportunity, and change. The personal planets—notably Jupiter and Saturn—and the generational planets—Uranus, Neptune, and Pluto—have all moved forward into new signs of the zodiac. These fresh planetary influences act to shape unfolding events and illuminate pathways to the future.

Jupiter, the big planet that attracts luck, spends about one year in each zodiacal sign. It takes approximately twelve years for Jupiter to travel through all twelve signs of the zodiac in order to complete a cycle. In 2011 a new Jupiter cycle is initiated with Jupiter transiting Aries, the first sign of the zodiac. As each year progresses over the course of the decade, Jupiter moves forward into the next sign, following the natural progression of the zodiac. Jupiter visits Taurus in 2012, Gemini in 2013, Cancer in 2014, Leo in 2015, Virgo in 2016, Libra in 2017, Scorpio in 2018, Sagittarius in 2019, Capricorn in 2020. Then in late December 2020 Jupiter enters Aquarius just two weeks before the decade closes. Jupiter's vibrations are helpful and fruitful, a source of good luck and a protection against bad luck. Opportunity swells under Jupiter's powerful rays. Learning takes leaps of faith.

Saturn, the beautiful planet of reason and responsibility, spends about two and a half years in each zodiacal sign. A complete Saturn cycle through all twelve signs of the zodiac takes about twenty-nine to thirty years. Saturn is known as the lawgiver: setting boundaries and codes of conduct, urging self-discipline and structure within a creative framework. The rule of law, the role of government, the responsibility of the individual are all sourced from Saturn. Saturn gives as it takes. Once a lesson is learned, Saturn's reward is just and full.

Saturn transits Libra throughout 2011 until early autumn of 2012. Here Saturn seeks to harmonize, to balance, to bring order out of chaos. Saturn in Libra ennobles the artist, the judge, the high-minded, the honest. Saturn next visits Scorpio from autumn 2012 until late December 2014. With Saturn in Scorpio, tactic and strategy combine to get workable solutions and desired results. Saturn's problem-solving tools here can harness dynamic energy for the common good. Saturn in Sagittarius, an idealistic and humanistic transit that stretches from December 2014 into the last day of autumn 2017, promotes activism over mere dogma and debate. Saturn in Sagittarius can be a driving force for good. Saturn tours Capricorn, the sign that Saturn rules, from the first day of winter 2017 into early spring 2020. Saturn in Capricorn is a consolidating transit, bringing things forth and into fruition. Here a plan can be made right, made whole, then launched for success. Saturn starts to visit Aquarius, a sign that Saturn corules and a very good sign for Saturn to visit, in the very last year of the decade. Saturn in Aquarius fosters team spirit, the unity of effort amid diversity. The transit of Saturn in Aquarius until early 2023 represents a period of enlightened activism and unprecedented growth.

Uranus, Neptune, and Pluto spend more than several years in each sign. They produce the differences in attitude, belief, behavior, and taste that distinguish one generation from another—and so are called the generational planets.

Uranus, planet of innovation and surprise, is known as the awakener. Uranus spends seven to eight years in each sign. Uranus started a new cycle when it entered Aries, the first sign of the zodiac, in May 2010. Uranus tours Aries until May 2018. Uranus in Aries accents originality, freedom, independence, unpredictability. There can be a start-stop quality to undertakings given this transit. Despite contradiction and confrontation, significant invention and productivity mark this transit. Uranus next visits Taurus through the end of the decade into 2026. Strategic thinking and timely action characterize the transit of Uranus in Taurus. Here intuition is backed up by common sense, leading to fresh discoveries upon which new industries can be built.

Neptune spends about fourteen years in each sign. Neptune, the visionary planet, enters Pisces, the sign Neptune rules and the final sign of the zodiac, in early April 2011. Neptune journeys through Pisces until 2026 to complete the Neptune cycle of visiting all twelve zodiacal signs. Neptune's tour of Pisces ushers in a long period of great potentiality: universal understanding, universal good, universal love, universal generosity, universal forgiveness—the universal spirit affects all. Neptune in Pisces can oversee the fruition of such noble aims as human rights for all and liberation from all forms of tyranny. Neptune in Pisces is a pervasive influence that changes concepts, consciences, attitudes, actions. The impact of Neptune in Pisces is to illuminate and to inspire.

Pluto, dwarf planet of beginnings and endings, entered the earthy sign of Capricorn in 2008 and journeys there for sixteen years into late 2024. Pluto in Capricorn over the course of this extensive visit has the capacity to change the landscape as well as the humanscape. The transforming energy of Pluto combines with the persevering power of Capricorn to give depth and character to potential change. Pluto in Capricorn brings focus and cohesion to disparate, diverse creativities. As new forms arise and take root, Pluto in Capricorn organizes the rebuilding process. Freedom versus limitation, freedom versus authority is in the framework during this transit. Reasonableness struggles with recklessness to solve divisive issues. Pluto in Capricorn teaches important lessons about adversity, and the lessons will be learned.

THE SIGNS OF THE ZODIAC

Dominant Characteristics

Aries: March 21–April 20

The Positive Side of Aries

The Aries has many positive points to his character. People born under this first sign of the Zodiac are often quite strong and enthusiastic. On the whole, they are forward-looking people who are not easily discouraged by temporary setbacks. They know what they want out of life and they go out after it. Their personalities are strong. Others are usually quite impressed by the Ram's way of doing things. Quite often they are sources of inspiration for others traveling the same route. Aries men and women have a special zest for life that can be contagious; for others, they are a fine example of how life should be lived.

The Aries person usually has a quick and active mind. He is imaginative and inventive. He enjoys keeping busy and active. He generally gets along well with all kinds of people. He is interested in mankind, as a whole. He likes to be challenged. Some would say he thrives on opposition, for it is when he is set against that he often does his best. Getting over or around obstacles is a challenge he generally enjoys. All in all, Aries is quite positive and young-thinking. He likes to keep abreast of new things that are happening in the world. Aries are often fond of speed. They like things to be done quickly, and this sometimes aggravates their slower colleagues and associates.

The Aries man or woman always seems to remain young. Their whole approach to life is youthful and optimistic. They never say die, no matter what the odds. They may have an occasional setback, but it is not long before they are back on their feet again.

The Negative Side of Aries

Everybody has his less positive qualities—and Aries is no exception. Sometimes the Aries man or woman is not very tactful in communicating with others; in his hurry to get things done he is apt to be a little callous or inconsiderate. Sensitive people are likely to find him somewhat sharp-tongued in some situations. Often in his eagerness to get the show on the road, he misses the mark altogether and cannot achieve his aims.

At times Aries can be too impulsive. He can occasionally be stubborn and refuse to listen to reason. If things do not move quickly enough to suit the Aries man or woman, he or she is apt to become rather nervous or irritable. The uncultivated Aries is not unfamiliar with moments of doubt and fear. He is capable of being destructive if he does not get his way. He can overcome some of his emotional problems by steadily trying to express himself as he really is, but this requires effort.

Taurus: April 21–May 20

The Positive Side of Taurus

The Taurus person is known for his ability to concentrate and for his tenacity. These are perhaps his strongest qualities. The Taurus man or woman generally has very little trouble in getting along with others; it's his nature to be helpful toward people in need. He can always be depended on by his friends, especially those in trouble.

Taurus generally achieves what he wants through his ability to persevere. He never leaves anything unfinished but works on something until it has been completed. People can usually take him at his word; he is honest and forthright in most of his dealings. The Taurus person has a good chance to make a success of his life because of his many positive qualities. The Taurus who aims high seldom falls short of his mark. He learns well by experience. He is thorough and does not believe in shortcuts of any kind. The Bull's thoroughness pays off in the end, for through his deliberateness he learns how to rely on himself and what he has learned. The Taurus person tries to get along with others, as a rule. He is not

overly critical and likes people to be themselves. He is a tolerant person and enjoys peace and harmony—especially in his home life.

Taurus is usually cautious in all that he does. He is not a person who believes in taking unnecessary risks. Before adopting any one line of action, he will weigh all of the pros and cons. The Taurus person is steadfast. Once his mind is made up it seldom changes. The person born under this sign usually is a good family person—reliable and loving.

The Negative Side of Taurus

Sometimes the Taurus man or woman is a bit too stubborn. He won't listen to other points of view if his mind is set on something. To others, this can be quite annoying. Taurus also does not like to be told what to do. He becomes rather angry if others think him not too bright. He does not like to be told he is wrong, even when he is. He dislikes being contradicted.

Some people who are born under this sign are very suspicious of others—even of those persons close to them. They find it difficult to trust people fully. They are often afraid of being deceived or taken advantage of. The Bull often finds it difficult to forget or forgive. His love of material things sometimes makes him rather avaricious and petty.

Gemini: May 21–June 20

The Positive Side of Gemini

The person born under this sign of the Heavenly Twins is usually quite bright and quick-witted. Some of them are capable of doing many different things. The Gemini person very often has many different interests. He keeps an open mind and is always anxious to learn new things.

Gemini is often an analytical person. He is a person who enjoys making use of his intellect. He is governed more by his mind than by his emotions. He is a person who is not confined to one view; he can often understand both sides to a problem or question. He knows how to reason, how to make rapid decisions if need be.

He is an adaptable person and can make himself at home almost anywhere. There are all kinds of situations he can adapt to. He is a person who seldom doubts himself; he is sure of his talents and his ability to think and reason. Gemini is generally most satisfied when he is in a situation where he can make use of his intellect. Never short of imagination, he often has strong talents for invention. He is rather a modern person when it comes to life; Gemini almost always moves along with the times—perhaps that is why he remains so youthful throughout most of his life.

Literature and art appeal to the person born under this sign. Creativity in almost any form will interest and intrigue the Gemini man or woman.

The Gemini is often quite charming. A good talker, he often is the center of attraction at any gathering. People find it easy to like a person born under this sign because he can appear easygoing and usually has a good sense of humor.

The Negative Side of Gemini

Sometimes the Gemini person tries to do too many things at one time—and as a result, winds up finishing nothing. Some Twins are easily distracted and find it rather difficult to concentrate on one thing for too long a time. Sometimes they give in to trifling fancies and find it rather boring to become too serious about any one thing. Some of them are never dependable, no matter what they promise.

Although the Gemini man or woman often appears to be well-versed on many subjects, this is sometimes just a veneer. His knowledge may be only superficial, but because he speaks so well he gives people the impression of erudition. Some Geminis are sharp-tongued and inconsiderate; they think only of themselves and their own pleasure.

Cancer: June 21–July 20

The Positive Side of Cancer

The Moon Child's most positive point is his understanding nature. On the whole, he is a loving and sympathetic person. He would never go out of his way to hurt anyone. The Cancer man or woman is often very kind and tender; they give what they can to others. They hate to see others suffering and will do what they can to help someone in less fortunate circumstances than themselves. They are often very concerned about the world. Their interest in people generally goes beyond that of just their own families and close friends; they have a deep sense of community and respect humanitarian values. The Moon Child means what he says, as a rule; he is honest about his feelings.

The Cancer man or woman is a person who knows the art of patience. When something seems difficult, he is willing to wait until the situation becomes manageable again. He is a person who knows how to bide his time. Cancer knows how to concentrate on one thing at a time. When he has made his mind up he generally sticks with what he does, seeing it through to the end.

Cancer is a person who loves his home. He enjoys being surrounded by familiar things and the people he loves. Of all the signs, Cancer is the most maternal. Even the men born under this sign often have a motherly or protective quality about them. They like to take care of people in their family—to see that they are well loved and well provided for. They are usually loyal and faithful. Family ties mean a lot to the Cancer man or woman. Parents and in-laws are respected and loved. Young Cancer responds very well to adults who show faith in him. The Moon Child has a strong sense of tradition. He is very sensitive to the moods of others.

The Negative Side of Cancer

Sometimes Cancer finds it rather hard to face life. It becomes too much for him. He can be a little timid and retiring, when things don't go too well. When unfortunate things happen, he is apt to just shrug and say, "Whatever will be will be." He can be fatalistic to a fault. The uncultivated Cancer is a bit lazy. He doesn't have very much ambition. Anything that seems a bit difficult he'll gladly leave to others. He may be lacking in initiative. Too sensitive, when he feels he's been injured, he'll crawl back into his shell and nurse his imaginary wounds. The immature Moon Child often is given to crying when the smallest thing goes wrong.

Some Cancers find it difficult to enjoy themselves in environments outside their homes. They make heavy demands on others, and need to be constantly reassured that they are loved. Lacking such reassurance, they may resort to sulking in silence.

Leo: July 21–August 21

The Positive Side of Leo

Often Leos make good leaders. They seem to be good organizers and administrators. Usually they are quite popular with others. Whatever group it is that they belong to, the Leo man or woman is almost sure to be or become the leader. Loyalty, one of the Lion's noblest traits, enables him or her to maintain this leadership position.

Leo is generous most of the time. It is his best characteristic. He or she likes to give gifts and presents. In making others happy, the Leo person becomes happy himself. He likes to splurge when spending money on others. In some instances it may seem that the Lion's generosity knows no boundaries. A hospitable person, the Leo man or woman is very fond of welcoming people to his house and entertaining them. He is never short of company.

Leo has plenty of energy and drive. He enjoys working toward some specific goal. When he applies himself correctly, he gets what he wants most often. The Leo person is almost never unsure of himself. He has plenty of confidence and aplomb. He is a person who is direct in almost everything he does. He has a quick mind and can make a decision in a very short time.

He usually sets a good example for others because of his ambitious manner and positive ways. He knows how to stick to something once he's started. Although Leo may be good at making a joke, he is not superficial or glib. He is a loving person, kind and thoughtful.

There is generally nothing small or petty about the Leo man or woman. He does what he can for those who are deserving. He is a person others can rely upon at all times. He means what he says. An honest person, generally speaking, he is a friend who is valued and sought out.

The Negative Side of Leo

Leo, however, does have his faults. At times, he can be just a bit too arrogant. He thinks that no one deserves a leadership position except him. Only he is capable of doing things well. His opinion of himself is often much too high. Because of his conceit, he is sometimes rather unpopular with a good many people. Some Leos are too materialistic; they can only think in terms of money and profit.

Some Leos enjoy lording it over others—at home or at their place of business. What is more, they feel they have the right to. Egocentric to an impossible degree, this sort of Leo cares little about how others think or feel. He can be rude and cutting.

Virgo: August 22–September 22

The Positive Side of Virgo

The person born under the sign of Virgo is generally a busy person. He knows how to arrange and organize things. He is a good planner. Above all, he is practical and is not afraid of hard work.

Often called the sign of the Harvester, Virgo knows how to attain what he desires. He sticks with something until it is finished. He never shirks his duties, and can always be depended upon. The Virgo person can be thoroughly trusted at all times.

The man or woman born under this sign tries to do everything to perfection. He doesn't believe in doing anything halfway. He always aims for the top. He is the sort of a person who is always learning and constantly striving to better himself—not because he wants more money or glory, but because it gives him a feeling of accomplishment.

The Virgo man or woman is a very observant person. He is sensitive to how others feel, and can see things below the surface of a situation. He usually puts this talent to constructive use.

It is not difficult for the Virgo to be open and earnest. He believes in putting his cards on the table. He is never secretive or underhanded. He's as good as his word. The Virgo person is generally plainspoken and down to earth. He has no trouble in expressing himself.

The Virgo person likes to keep up to date on new developments in his particular field. Well-informed, generally, he sometimes has a keen interest in the arts or literature. What he knows, he knows well. His ability to use his critical faculties is well-developed and sometimes startles others because of its accuracy.

Virgos adhere to a moderate way of life; they avoid excesses. Virgo is a responsible person and enjoys being of service.

The Negative Side of Virgo

Sometimes a Virgo person is too critical. He thinks that only he can do something the way it should be done. Whatever anyone else does is inferior. He can be rather annoying in the way he quibbles over insignificant details. In telling others how things should be done, he can be rather tactless and mean.

Some Virgos seem rather emotionless and cool. They feel emotional involvement is beneath them. They are sometimes too tidy, too neat. With money they can be rather miserly. Some Virgos try to force their opinions and ideas on others.

Libra: September 23–October 22

The Positive Side of Libra

Libras love harmony. It is one of their most outstanding character traits. They are interested in achieving balance; they admire beauty and grace in things as well as in people. Generally speaking, they are kind and considerate people. Libras are usually very sympathetic. They go out of their way not to hurt another person's feelings. They are outgoing and do what they can to help those in need.

People born under the sign of Libra almost always make good friends. They are loyal and amiable. They enjoy the company of others. Many of them are rather moderate in their views; they believe in keeping an open mind, however, and weighing both sides of an issue fairly before making a decision.

Alert and intelligent, Libra, often known as the Lawgiver, is always fair-minded and tries to put himself in the position of the other person. They are against injustice; quite often they take up for the underdog. In most of their social dealings, they try to be tactful and kind. They dislike discord and bickering, and most Libras strive for peace and harmony in all their relationships.

The Libra man or woman has a keen sense of beauty. They appreciate handsome furnishings and clothes. Many of them are artistically inclined. Their taste is usually impeccable. They know how to use color. Their homes are almost always attractively arranged and inviting. They enjoy entertaining people and see to it that their guests always feel at home and welcome.

Libra gets along with almost everyone. He is well-liked and socially much in demand.

The Negative Side of Libra

Some people born under this sign tend to be rather insincere. So eager are they to achieve harmony in all relationships that they will even go so far as to lie. Many of them are escapists. They find facing the truth an ordeal and prefer living in a world of make-believe.

In a serious argument, some Libras give in rather easily even when they know they are right. Arguing, even about something they believe in, is too unsettling for some of them.

Libras sometimes care too much for material things. They enjoy possessions and luxuries. Some are vain and tend to be jealous.

Scorpio: October 23–November 22

The Positive Side of Scorpio

The Scorpio man or woman generally knows what he or she wants out of life. He is a determined person. He sees something through to the end. Scorpio is quite sincere, and seldom says anything he doesn't mean. When he sets a goal for himself he tries to go about achieving it in a very direct way.

The Scorpion is brave and courageous. They are not afraid of hard work. Obstacles do not frighten them. They forge ahead until they achieve what they set out for. The Scorpio man or woman has a strong will.

Although Scorpio may seem rather fixed and determined, inside he is often quite tender and loving. He can care very much for others. He believes in sincerity in all relationships. His feelings about someone tend to last; they are profound and not superficial.

The Scorpio person is someone who adheres to his principles no matter what happens. He will not be deterred from a path he believes to be right.

Because of his many positive strengths, the Scorpion can often achieve happiness for himself and for those that he loves.

He is a constructive person by nature. He often has a deep understanding of people and of life, in general. He is perceptive and unafraid. Obstacles often seem to spur him on. He is a positive person who enjoys winning. He has many strengths and resources; challenge of any sort often brings out the best in him.

The Negative Side of Scorpio

The Scorpio person is sometimes hypersensitive. Often he imagines injury when there is none. He feels that others do not bother to recognize him for his true worth. Sometimes he is given to excessive boasting in order to compensate for what he feels is neglect.

Scorpio can be proud, arrogant, and competitive. They can be sly when they put their minds to it and they enjoy outwitting persons or institutions noted for their cleverness.

Their tactics for getting what they want are sometimes devious and ruthless. They don't care too much about what others may think. If they feel others have done them an injustice, they will do their best to seek revenge. The Scorpion often has a sudden, violent temper; and this person's interest in sex is sometimes quite unbalanced or excessive.

Sagittarius: November 23–December 20

The Positive Side of Sagittarius

People born under this sign are honest and forthright. Their approach to life is earnest and open. Sagittarius is often quite adult in his way of seeing things. They are broad-minded and tolerant people. When dealing with others the person born under the sign of the Archer is almost always open and forthright. He doesn't believe in deceit or pretension. His standards are high. People who associate with Sagittarius generally admire and respect his tolerant viewpoint.

The Archer trusts others easily and expects them to trust him. He is never suspicious or envious and almost always thinks well of others. People always enjoy his company because he is so friendly and easygoing. The Sagittarius man or woman is often good-humored. He can always be depended upon by his friends, family, and co-workers.

The person born under this sign of the Zodiac likes a good joke every now and then. Sagittarius is eager for fun and laughs, which makes him very popular with others.

A lively person, he enjoys sports and outdoor life. The Archer is fond of animals. Intelligent and interesting, he can begin an animated

conversation with ease. He likes exchanging ideas and discussing various views.

He is not selfish or proud. If someone proposes an idea or plan that is better than his, he will immediately adopt it. Imaginative yet practical, he knows how to put ideas into practice.

The Archer enjoys sport and games, and it doesn't matter if he wins or loses. He is a forgiving person, and never sulks over something that has not worked out in his favor.

He is seldom critical, and is almost always generous.

The Negative Side of Sagittarius

Some Sagittarius are restless. They take foolish risks and seldom learn from the mistakes they make. They don't have heads for money and are often mismanaging their finances. Some of them devote much of their time to gambling.

Some are too outspoken and tactless, always putting their feet in their mouths. They hurt others carelessly by being honest at the wrong time. Sometimes they make promises which they don't keep. They don't stick close enough to their plans and go from one failure to another. They are undisciplined and waste a lot of energy.

Capricorn: December 21–January 19

The Positive Side of Capricorn

The person born under the sign of Capricorn, known variously as the Mountain Goat or Sea Goat, is usually very stable and patient. He sticks to whatever tasks he has and sees them through. He can always be relied upon and he is not averse to work.

An honest person, Capricorn is generally serious about whatever he does. He does not take his duties lightly. He is a practical person and believes in keeping his feet on the ground.

Quite often the person born under this sign is ambitious and knows how to get what he wants out of life. The Goat forges ahead and never gives up his goal. When he is determined about something, he almost always wins. He is a good worker—a hard worker. Although things may not come easy to him, he will not complain, but continue working until his chores are finished.

He is usually good at business matters and knows the value of money. He is not a spendthrift and knows how to put something away for a rainy day; he dislikes waste and unnecessary loss.

Capricorn knows how to make use of his self-control. He can apply himself to almost anything once he puts his mind to it. His ability to concentrate sometimes astounds others. He is diligent and does well when involved in detail work.

The Capricorn man or woman is charitable, generally speaking, and will do what is possible to help others less fortunate. As a friend, he is loyal and trustworthy. He never shirks his duties or responsibilities. He is self-reliant and never expects too much of the other fellow. He does what he can on his own. If someone does him a good turn, then he will do his best to return the favor.

The Negative Side of Capricorn

Like everyone, Capricorn, too, has faults. At times, the Goat can be overcritical of others. He expects others to live up to his own high standards. He thinks highly of himself and tends to look down on others.

His interest in material things may be exaggerated. The Capricorn man or woman thinks too much about getting on in the world and having something to show for it. He may even be a little greedy.

He sometimes thinks he knows what's best for everyone. He is too bossy. He is always trying to organize and correct others. He may be a little narrow in his thinking.

Aquarius: January 20–February 18

The Positive Side of Aquarius

The Aquarius man or woman is usually very honest and forthright. These are his two greatest qualities. His standards for himself are generally very high. He can always be relied upon by others. His word is his bond.

Aquarius is perhaps the most tolerant of all the Zodiac personalities. He respects other people's beliefs and feels that everyone is entitled to his own approach to life.

He would never do anything to injure another's feelings. He is never unkind or cruel. Always considerate of others, the Water Bearer is always willing to help a person in need. He feels a

very strong tie between himself and all the other members of mankind.

The person born under this sign, called the Water Bearer, is almost always an individualist. He does not believe in teaming up with the masses, but prefers going his own way. His ideas about life and mankind are often quite advanced. There is a saying to the effect that the average Aquarius is fifty years ahead of his time.

Aquarius is community-minded. The problems of the world concern him greatly. He is interested in helping others no matter what part of the globe they live in. He is truly a humanitarian sort. He likes to be of service to others.

Giving, considerate, and without prejudice, Aquarius have no trouble getting along with others.

The Negative Side of Aquarius

Aquarius may be too much of a dreamer. He makes plans but seldom carries them out. He is rather unrealistic. His imagination has a tendency to run away with him. Because many of his plans are impractical, he is always in some sort of a dither.

Others may not approve of him at all times because of his unconventional behavior. He may be a bit eccentric. Sometimes he is so busy with his own thoughts that he loses touch with the realities of existence.

Some Aquarius feel they are more clever and intelligent than others. They seldom admit to their own faults, even when they are quite apparent. Some become rather fanatic in their views. Their criticism of others is sometimes destructive and negative.

Pisces: February 19–March 20

The Positive Side of Pisces

Known as the sign of the Fishes, Pisces has a sympathetic nature. Kindly, he is often dedicated in the way he goes about helping others. The sick and the troubled often turn to him for advice and assistance. Possessing keen intuition, Pisces can easily understand people's deepest problems.

He is very broad-minded and does not criticize others for their faults. He knows how to accept people for what they are. On the whole, he is a trustworthy and earnest person. He is loyal to his friends and will do what he can to help them in time of need. Generous and good-natured, he is a lover of peace; he is often willing to help others solve their differences. People who have taken a wrong turn in life often interest him and he will do what he can to persuade them to rehabilitate themselves.

He has a strong intuitive sense and most of the time he knows how to make it work for him. Pisces is unusually perceptive and often knows what is bothering someone before that person, himself, is aware of it. The Pisces man or woman is an idealistic person, basically, and is interested in making the world a better place in which to live. Pisces believes that everyone should help each other. He is willing to do more than his share in order to achieve cooperation with others.

The person born under this sign often is talented in music or art. He is a receptive person; he is able to take the ups and downs of life with philosophic calm.

The Negative Side of Pisces

Some Pisces are often depressed; their outlook on life is rather glum. They may feel that they have been given a bad deal in life and that others are always taking unfair advantage of them. Pisces sometimes feel that the world is a cold and cruel place. The Fishes can be easily discouraged. The Pisces man or woman may even withdraw from the harshness of reality into a secret shell of his own where he dreams and idles away a good deal of his time.

Pisces can be lazy. He lets things happen without giving the least bit of resistance. He drifts along, whether on the high road or on the low. He can be lacking in willpower.

Some Pisces people seek escape through drugs or alcohol. When temptation comes along they find it hard to resist. In matters of sex, they can be rather permissive.

Sun Sign Personalities

ARIES: Hans Christian Andersen, Pearl Bailey, Marlon Brando, Wernher Von Braun, Charlie Chaplin, Joan Crawford, Da Vinci, Bette Davis, Doris Day, W. C. Fields, Alec Guinness, Adolf Hitler, William Holden, Thomas Jefferson, Nikita Khrushchev, Elton John, Arturo Toscanini, J. P. Morgan, Paul Robeson, Gloria Steinem, Sarah Vaughn, Vincent van Gogh, Tennessee Williams

TAURUS: Fred Astaire, Charlotte Brontë, Carol Burnett, Irving Berlin, Bing Crosby, Salvador Dali, Tchaikovsky, Queen Elizabeth II, Duke Ellington, Ella Fitzgerald, Henry Fonda, Sigmund Freud, Orson Welles, Joe Louis, Lenin, Karl Marx, Golda Meir, Eva Peron, Bertrand Russell, Shakespeare, Kate Smith, Benjamin Spock, Barbra Streisand, Shirley Temple, Harry Truman

GEMINI: Ruth Benedict, Josephine Baker, Rachel Carson, Carlos Chavez, Walt Whitman, Bob Dylan, Ralph Waldo Emerson, Judy Garland, Paul Gauguin, Allen Ginsberg, Benny Goodman, Bob Hope, Burl Ives, John F. Kennedy, Peggy Lee, Marilyn Monroe, Joe Namath, Cole Porter, Laurence Olivier, Harriet Beecher Stowe, Queen Victoria, John Wayne, Frank Lloyd Wright

CANCER: "Dear Abby," Lizzie Borden, David Brinkley, Yul Brynner, Pearl Buck, Marc Chagall, Princess Diana, Babe Didrikson, Mary Baker Eddy, Henry VIII, John Glenn, Ernest Hemingway, Lena Horne, Oscar Hammerstein, Helen Keller, Ann Landers, George Orwell, Nancy Reagan, Rembrandt, Richard Rodgers, Ginger Rogers, Rubens, Jean-Paul Sartre, O. J. Simpson

LEO: Neil Armstrong, James Baldwin, Lucille Ball, Emily Brontë, Wilt Chamberlain, Julia Child, William J. Clinton, Cecil B. De Mille, Ogden Nash, Amelia Earhart, Edna Ferber, Arthur Goldberg, Alfred Hitchcock, Mick Jagger, George Meany, Annie Oakley, George Bernard Shaw, Napoleon, Jacqueline Onassis, Henry Ford, Francis Scott Key, Andy Warhol, Mae West, Orville Wright

VIRGO: Ingrid Bergman, Warren Burger, Maurice Chevalier, Agatha Christie, Sean Connery, Lafayette, Peter Falk, Greta Garbo, Althea Gibson, Arthur Godfrey, Goethe, Buddy Hackett, Michael Jackson, Lyndon Johnson, D. H. Lawrence, Sophia Loren, Grandma Moses, Arnold Palmer, Queen Elizabeth I, Walter Reuther, Peter Sellers, Lily Tomlin, George Wallace

LIBRA: Brigitte Bardot, Art Buchwald, Truman Capote, Dwight D. Eisenhower, William Faulkner, F. Scott Fitzgerald, Gandhi, George Gershwin, Micky Mantle, Helen Hayes, Vladimir Horowitz, Doris Lessing, Martina Navratalova, Eugene O'Neill, Luciano Pavarotti, Emily Post, Eleanor Roosevelt, Bruce Springsteen, Margaret Thatcher, Gore Vidal, Barbara Walters, Oscar Wilde

SCORPIO: Vivien Leigh, Richard Burton, Art Carney, Johnny Carson, Billy Graham, Grace Kelly, Walter Cronkite, Marie Curie, Charles de Gaulle, Linda Evans, Indira Gandhi, Theodore Roosevelt, Rock Hudson, Katherine Hepburn, Robert F. Kennedy, Billie Jean King, Martin Luther, Georgia O'Keeffe, Pablo Picasso, Jonas Salk, Alan Shepard, Robert Louis Stevenson

SAGITTARIUS: Jane Austen, Louisa May Alcott, Woody Allen, Beethoven, Willy Brandt, Mary Martin, William F. Buckley, Maria Callas, Winston Churchill, Noel Coward, Emily Dickinson, Walt Disney, Benjamin Disraeli, James Doolittle, Kirk Douglas, Chet Huntley, Jane Fonda, Chris Evert Lloyd, Margaret Mead, Charles Schulz, John Milton, Frank Sinatra, Steven Spielberg

CAPRICORN: Muhammad Ali, Isaac Asimov, Pablo Casals, Dizzy Dean, Marlene Dietrich, James Farmer, Ava Gardner, Barry Goldwater, Cary Grant, J. Edgar Hoover, Howard Hughes, Joan of Arc, Gypsy Rose Lee, Martin Luther King, Jr., Rudyard Kipling, Mao Tse-tung, Richard Nixon, Gamal Nasser, Louis Pasteur, Albert Schweitzer, Stalin, Benjamin Franklin, Elvis Presley

AQUARIUS: Marian Anderson, Susan B. Anthony, Jack Benny, John Barrymore, Mikhail Baryshnikov, Charles Darwin, Charles Dickens, Thomas Edison, Clark Gable, Jascha Heifetz, Abraham Lincoln, Yehudi Menuhin, Mozart, Jack Nicklaus, Ronald Reagan, Jackie Robinson, Norman Rockwell, Franklin D. Roosevelt, Gertrude Stein, Charles Lindbergh, Margaret Truman

PISCES: Edward Albee, Harry Belafonte, Alexander Graham Bell, Chopin, Adelle Davis, Albert Einstein, Golda Meir, Jackie Gleason, Winslow Homer, Edward M. Kennedy, Victor Hugo, Mike Mansfield, Michelangelo, Edna St. Vincent Millay, Liza Minelli, John Steinbeck, Linus Pauling, Ravel, Renoir, Diana Ross, William Shirer, Elizabeth Taylor, George Washington

The Signs and Their Key Words

		POSITIVE	NEGATIVE
ARIES	self	courage, initiative, pioneer instinct	brash rudeness, selfish impetuosity
TAURUS	money	endurance, loyalty, wealth	obstinacy, gluttony
GEMINI	mind	versatility	capriciousness, unreliability
CANCER	family	sympathy, homing instinct	clannishness, childishness
LEO	children	love, authority, integrity	egotism, force
VIRGO	work	purity, industry, analysis	faultfinding, cynicism
LIBRA	marriage	harmony, justice	vacillation, superficiality
SCORPIO	sex	survival, regeneration	vengeance, discord
SAGITTARIUS	travel	optimism, higher learning	lawlessness
CAPRICORN	career	depth	narrowness, gloom
AQUARIUS	friends	human fellowship, genius	perverse unpredictability
PISCES	confinement	spiritual love, universality	diffusion, escapism

The Elements and Qualities of The Signs

Every sign has both an *element* and a *quality* associated with it. The element indicates the basic makeup of the sign, and the quality describes the kind of activity associated with each.

Element	Sign	Quality	Sign
FIRE	ARIES	CARDINAL	ARIES
	LEO		LIBRA
	SAGITTARIUS		CANCER
			CAPRICORN
EARTH	TAURUS		
	VIRGO		
	CAPRICORN	FIXED	TAURUS
			LEO
			SCORPIO
AIR	GEMINI		AQUARIUS
	LIBRA		
	AQUARIUS		
		MUTABLE	GEMINI
WATER	CANCER		VIRGO
	SCORPIO		SAGITTARIUS
	PISCES		PISCES

Signs can be grouped together according to their element and quality. Signs of the same element share many basic traits in common. They tend to form stable configurations and ultimately harmonious relationships. Signs of the same quality are often less harmonious, but they share many dynamic potentials for growth as well as profound fulfillment.

Further discussion of each of these sign groupings is provided on the following pages.

The Fire Signs

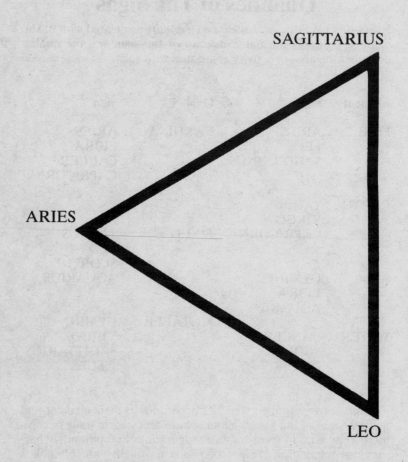

This is the fire group. On the whole these are emotional, volatile types, quick to anger, quick to forgive. They are adventurous, powerful people and act as a source of inspiration for everyone. They spark into action with immediate exuberant impulses. They are intelligent, self-involved, creative, and idealistic. They all share a certain vibrancy and glow that outwardly reflects an inner flame and passion for living.

The Earth Signs

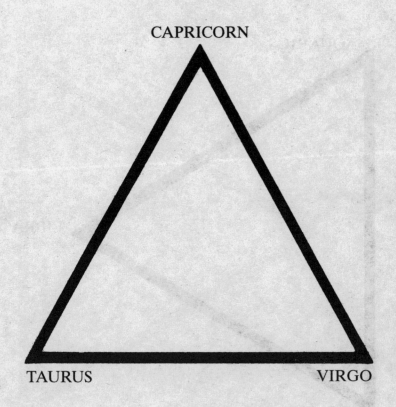

CAPRICORN

TAURUS   VIRGO

This is the earth group. They are in constant touch with the material world and tend to be conservative. Although they are all capable of spartan self-discipline, they are earthy, sensual people who are stimulated by the tangible, elegant, and luxurious. The thread of their lives is always practical, but they do fantasize and are often attracted to dark, mysterious, emotional people. They are like great cliffs overhanging the sea, forever married to the ocean but always resisting erosion from the dark, emotional forces that thunder at their feet.

The Air Signs

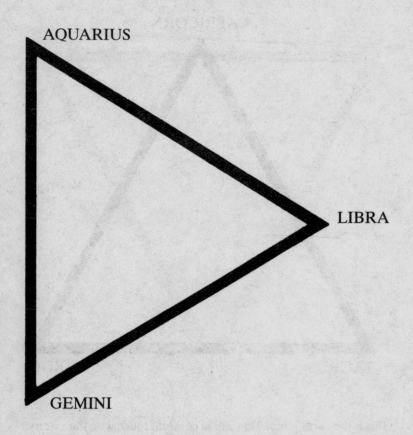

This is the air group. They are light, mental creatures desirous of contact, communication, and relationship. They are involved with people and the forming of ties on many levels. Original thinkers, they are the bearers of human news. Their language is their sense of word, color, style, and beauty. They provide an atmosphere suitable and pleasant for living. They add change and versatility to the scene, and it is through them that we can explore new territory of human intelligence and experience.

The Water Signs

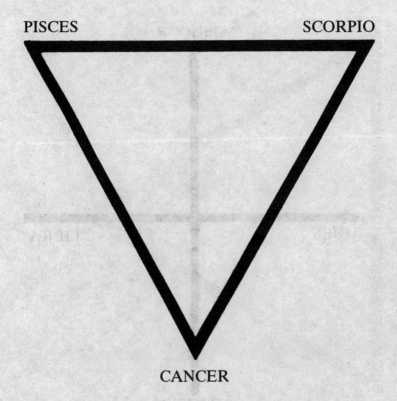

PISCES

SCORPIO

CANCER

This is the water group. Through the water people, we are all joined together on emotional, nonverbal levels. They are silent, mysterious types whose magic hypnotizes even the most determined realist. They have uncanny perceptions about people and are as rich as the oceans when it comes to feeling, emotion, or imagination. They are sensitive, mystical creatures with memories that go back beyond time. Through water, life is sustained. These people have the potential for the depths of darkness or the heights of mysticism and art.

The Cardinal Signs

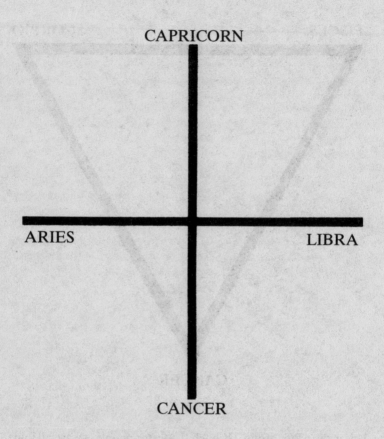

CAPRICORN

ARIES   LIBRA

CANCER

Put together, this is a clear-cut picture of dynamism, activity, tremendous stress, and remarkable achievement. These people know the meaning of great change since their lives are often characterized by significant crises and major successes. This combination is like a simultaneous storm of summer, fall, winter, and spring. The danger is chaotic diffusion of energy; the potential is irrepressible growth and victory.

The Fixed Signs

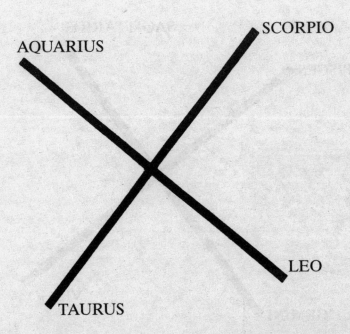

Fixed signs are always establishing themselves in a given place or area of experience. Like explorers who arrive and plant a flag, these people claim a position from which they do not enjoy being deposed. They are staunch, stalwart, upright, trusty, honorable people, although their obstinacy is well-known. Their contribution is fixity, and they are the angels who support our visible world.

The Mutable Signs

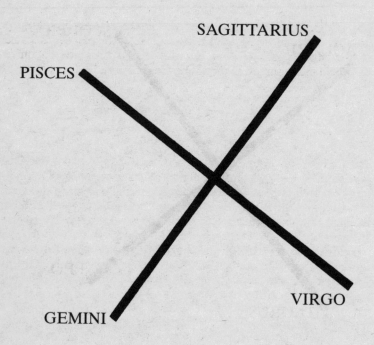

Mutable people are versatile, sensitive, intelligent, nervous, and deeply curious about life. They are the translators of all energy. They often carry out or complete tasks initiated by others. Combinations of these signs have highly developed minds; they are imaginative and jumpy and think and talk a lot. At worst their lives are a Tower of Babel. At best they are adaptable and ready creatures who can assimilate one kind of experience and enjoy it while anticipating coming changes.

THE PLANETS
OF THE SOLAR SYSTEM

This section describes the planets of the solar system. In astrology, both the Sun and the Moon are considered to be planets. Because of the Moon's influence in our day-to-day lives, the Moon is described in a separate section following this one.

The Planets and the Signs
They Rule

The signs of the Zodiac are linked to the planets in the following way. Each sign is governed or ruled by one or more planets. No matter where the planets are located in the sky at any given moment, they still rule their respective signs, and when they travel through the signs they rule, they have special dignity and their effects are stronger.

Following is a list of the planets and the signs they rule. After looking at the list, read the definitions of the planets and see if you can determine how the planet ruling *your* Sun sign has affected your life.

SIGNS	RULING PLANETS
Aries	Mars, Pluto
Taurus	Venus
Gemini	Mercury
Cancer	Moon
Leo	Sun
Virgo	Mercury
Libra	Venus
Scorpio	Mars, Pluto
Sagittarius	Jupiter
Capricorn	Saturn
Aquarius	Saturn, Uranus
Pisces	Jupiter, Neptune

Characteristics of the Planets

The following pages give the meaning and characteristics of the planets of the solar system. They all travel around the Sun at different speeds and different distances. Taken with the Sun, they all distribute individual intelligence and ability throughout the entire chart.

The planets modify the influence of the Sun in a chart according to their own particular natures, strengths, and positions. Their positions must be calculated for each year and day, and their function and expression in a horoscope will change as they move from one area of the Zodiac to another.

We start with a description of the sun.

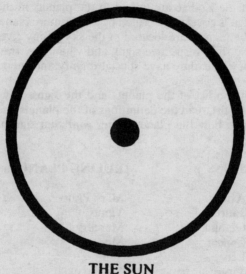

THE SUN

SUN

This is the center of existence. Around this flaming sphere all the planets revolve in endless orbits. Our star is constantly sending out its beams of light and energy without which no life on Earth would be possible. In astrology it symbolizes everything we are trying to become, the center around which all of our activity in life will always revolve. It is the symbol of our basic nature and describes the natural and constant thread that runs through everything that we do from birth to death on this planet.

To early astrologers, the Sun seemed to be another planet because it crossed the heavens every day, just like the rest of the bodies in the sky.

It is the only star near enough to be seen well—it is, in fact, a dwarf star. Approximately 860,000 miles in diameter, it is about ten times as wide as the giant planet Jupiter. The next nearest star is nearly 300,000 times as far away, and if the Sun were located as far away as most of the bright stars, it would be too faint to be seen without a telescope.

Everything in the horoscope ultimately revolves around this singular body. Although other forces may be prominent in the charts of some individuals, still the Sun is the total nucleus of being and symbolizes the complete potential of every human being alive. It is vitality and the life force. Your whole essence comes from the position of the Sun.

You are always trying to express the Sun according to its position by house and sign. Possibility for all development is found in the Sun, and it marks the fundamental character of your personal radiations all around you.

It is the symbol of strength, vigor, wisdom, dignity, ardor, and generosity, and the ability for a person to function as a mature individual. It is also a creative force in society. It is consciousness of the gift of life.

The underdeveloped solar nature is arrogant, pushy, undependable, and proud, and is constantly using force.

MERCURY

Mercury is the planet closest to the Sun. It races around our star, gathering information and translating it to the rest of the system. Mercury represents your capacity to understand the desires of your own will and to translate those desires into action.

In other words it is the planet of mind and the power of communication. Through Mercury we develop an ability to think, write, speak, and observe—to become aware of the world around us. It colors our attitudes and vision of the world, as well as our capacity to communicate our inner responses to the outside world. Some people who have serious disabilities in their power of verbal communication have often wrongly been described as people lacking intelligence.

Although this planet (and its position in the horoscope) indicates your power to communicate your thoughts and perceptions to the world, intelligence is something deeper. Intelligence is distributed throughout all the planets. It is the relationship of the planets to each other that truly describes what we call intelligence. Mercury rules speaking, language, mathematics, draft and design, students, messengers, young people, offices, teachers, and any pursuits where the mind of man has wings.

VENUS

Venus is beauty. It symbolizes the harmony and radiance of a rare and elusive quality: beauty itself. It is refinement and delicacy, softness and charm. In astrology it indicates grace, balance, and the aesthetic sense. Where Venus is we see beauty, a gentle drawing in of energy and the need for satisfaction and completion. It is a special touch that finishes off rough edges. It is sensitivity, and affection, and it is always the place for that other elusive phenomenon: love. Venus describes our sense of what is beautiful and loving. Poorly developed, it is vulgar, tasteless, and self-indulgent. But its ideal is the flame of spiritual love—Aphrodite, goddess of love, and the sweetness and power of personal beauty.

MARS

Mars is raw, crude energy. The planet next to Earth but outward from the Sun is a fiery red sphere that charges through the horoscope with force and fury. It represents the way you reach out for new adventure and new experience. It is energy and drive, initiative, courage, and daring. It is the power to start something and see it through. It can be thoughtless, cruel and wild, angry and hostile, causing cuts, burns, scalds, and wounds. It can stab its way through a chart, or it can be the symbol of healthy spirited adventure, well-channeled constructive power to begin and keep up the drive. If you have trouble starting things, if you lack the get-up-and-go to start the ball rolling, if you lack aggressiveness and self-confidence, chances are there's another planet influencing your Mars. Mars rules soldiers, butchers, surgeons, salesmen—any field that requires daring, bold skill, operational technique, or self-promotion.

JUPITER

This is the largest planet of the solar system. Scientists have recently learned that Jupiter reflects more light than it receives from the Sun. In a sense it is like a star itself. In astrology it rules good luck and good cheer, health, wealth, optimism, happiness, success, and joy. It is the symbol of opportunity and always opens the way for new possibilities in your life. It rules exuberance, enthusiasm, wisdom, knowledge, generosity, and all forms of expansion in general. It rules actors, statesmen, clerics, professional people, religion, publishing, and the distribution of many people over large areas.

Sometimes Jupiter makes you think you deserve everything, and you become sloppy, wasteful, careless and rude, prodigal and lawless, in the illusion that nothing can ever go wrong. Then there is the danger of overconfidence, exaggeration, undependability, and overindulgence.

Jupiter is the minimization of limitation and the emphasis on spirituality and potential. It is the thirst for knowledge and higher learning.

SATURN

Saturn circles our system in dark splendor with its mysterious rings, forcing us to be awakened to whatever we have neglected in the past. It will present real puzzles and problems to be solved, causing delays, obstacles, and hindrances. By doing so, Saturn stirs our own sensitivity to those areas where we are laziest.

Here we must patiently develop *method*, and only through painstaking effort can our ends be achieved. It brings order to a horoscope and imposes reason just where we are feeling least reasonable. By creating limitations and boundary, Saturn shows the consequences of being human and demands that we accept the changing cycles inevitable in human life. Saturn rules time, old age, and sobriety. It can bring depression, gloom, jealousy, and greed, or serious acceptance of responsibilities out of which success will develop. With Saturn there is nothing to do but face facts. It rules laborers, stones, granite, rocks, and crystals of all kinds.

THE OUTER PLANETS:
URANUS, NEPTUNE, PLUTO

Uranus, Neptune, Pluto are the outer planets. They liberate human beings from cultural conditioning, and in that sense are the law-breakers. In early times it was thought that Saturn was the last planet of the system—the outer limit beyond which we could never go. The discovery of the next three planets ushered in new phases of human history, revolution, and technology.

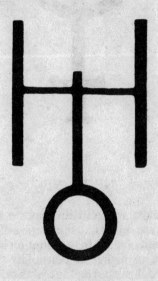

URANUS

Uranus rules unexpected change, upheaval, revolution. It is the symbol of total independence and asserts the freedom of an individual from all restriction and restraint. It is a breakthrough planet and indicates talent, originality, and genius in a horoscope. It usually causes last-minute reversals and changes of plan, unwanted separations, accidents, catastrophes, and eccentric behavior. It can add irrational rebelliousness and perverse bohemianism to a personality or a streak of unaffected brilliance in science and art. It rules technology, aviation, and all forms of electrical and electronic advancement. It governs great leaps forward and topsy-turvy situations, and *always* turns things around at the last minute. Its effects are difficult to predict, since it rules sudden last-minute decisions and events that come like lightning out of the blue.

NEPTUNE

Neptune dissolves existing reality the way the sea erodes the cliffs beside it. Its effects are subtle like the ringing of a buoy's bell in the fog. It suggests a reality higher than definition can usually describe. It awakens a sense of higher responsibility often causing guilt, worry, anxieties, or delusions. Neptune is associated with all forms of escape and can make things seem a certain way so convincingly that you are absolutely sure of something that eventually turns out to be quite different.

It is the planet of illusion and therefore governs the invisible realms that lie beyond our ordinary minds, beyond our simple factual ability to prove what is "real." Treachery, deceit, disillusionment, and disappointment are linked to Neptune. It describes a vague reality that promises eternity and the divine, yet in a manner so complex that we cannot really fathom it at all. At its worst Neptune is a cheap intoxicant; at its best it is the poetry, music, and inspiration of the higher planes of spiritual love. It has dominion over movies, photographs, and much of the arts.

PLUTO

Pluto lies at the outpost of our system and therefore rules finality in a horoscope—the final closing of chapters in your life, the passing of major milestones and points of development from which there is no return. It is a final wipeout, a closeout, an evacuation. It is a distant, subtle but powerful catalyst in all transformations that occur. It creates, destroys, then recreates. Sometimes Pluto starts its influence with a minor event or insignificant incident that might even go unnoticed. Slowly but surely, little by little, everything changes, until at last there has been a total transformation in the area of your life where Pluto has been operating. It rules mass thinking and the trends that society first rejects, then adopts, and finally outgrows.

Pluto rules the dead and the underworld—all the powerful forces of creation and destruction that go on all the time beneath, around, and above us. It can bring a lust for power with strong obsessions.

It is the planet that rules the metamorphosis of the caterpillar into a butterfly, for it symbolizes the capacity to change totally and forever a person's lifestyle, way of thought, and behavior.

THE MOON IN EACH SIGN

The Moon is the nearest planet to the Earth. It exerts more observable influence on us from day to day than any other planet. The effect is very personal, very intimate, and if we are not aware of how it works it can make us quite unstable in our ideas. And the annoying thing is that at these times we often see our own instability but can do nothing about it. A knowledge of what can be expected may help considerably. We can then be prepared to stand strong against the Moon's negative influences and use its positive ones to help us to get ahead. Who has not heard of going with the tide?

The Moon reflects, has no light of its own. It reflects the Sun—the life giver—in the form of vital movement. The Moon controls the tides, the blood rhythm, the movement of sap in trees and plants. Its nature is inconstancy and change so it signifies our moods, our superficial behavior—walking, talking, and especially thinking. Being a true reflector of other forces, the Moon is cold, watery like the surface of a still lake, brilliant and scintillating at times, but easily ruffled and disturbed by the winds of change.

The Moon takes about 27⅓ days to make a complete transit of the Zodiac. It spends just over 2¼ days in each sign. During that time it reflects the qualities, energies, and characteristics of the sign and, to a degree, the planet which rules the sign. When the Moon in its transit occupies a sign incompatible with our own birth sign, we can expect to feel a vague uneasiness, perhaps a touch of irritableness. We should not be discouraged nor let the feeling get us down, or, worse still, allow ourselves to take the discomfort out on others. Try to remember that the Moon has to change signs within 55 hours and, provided you are not physically ill, your mood will probably change with it. It is amazing how frequently depression lifts with the shift in the Moon's position. And, of course, when the Moon is transiting a sign compatible or sympathetic to yours, you will probably feel some sort of stimulation or just be plain happy to be alive.

In the horoscope, the Moon is such a powerful indicator that competent astrologers often use the sign it occupied at birth as the birth sign of the person. This is done particularly when the Sun is on the cusp, or edge, of two signs. Most experienced astrologers, however, coordinate both Sun and Moon signs by reading and confirming from one to the other and secure a far more accurate and personalized analysis.

For these reasons, the Moon tables which follow this section (see pages 86–92) are of great importance to the individual. They show the days and the exact times the Moon will enter each sign of the Zodiac for the year. Remember, you have to adjust the indicated times to local time. The corrections, already calculated for most of the main cities, are at the beginning of the tables. What follows now is a guide to the influences that will be reflected to the Earth by the Moon while it transits each of the twelve signs. The influence is at its peak about 26 hours after the Moon enters a sign. As you read the daily forecast, check the Moon sign for any given day and glance back at this guide.

MOON IN ARIES

This is a time for action, for reaching out beyond the usual self-imposed limitations and faint-hearted cautions. If you have plans in your head or on your desk, put them into practice. New ventures, applications, new jobs, new starts of any kind—all have a good chance of success. This is the period when original and dynamic impulses are being reflected onto Earth. Such energies are extremely vital and favor the pursuit of pleasure and adventure in practically every form. Sick people should feel an improvement. Those who are well will probably find themselves exuding confidence and optimism. People fond of physical exercise should find their bodies growing with tone and well-being. Boldness, strength, determination should characterize most of your activities with a readiness to face up to old challenges. Yesterday's problems may seem petty and exaggerated—so deal with them. Strike out alone. Self-reliance will attract others to you. This is a good time for making friends. Business and marriage partners are more likely to be impressed with the man and woman of action. Opposition will be overcome or thrown aside with much less effort than usual. CAUTION: Be dominant but not domineering.

MOON IN TAURUS

The spontaneous, action-packed person of yesterday gives way to the cautious, diligent, hardworking "thinker." In this period ideas will probably be concentrated on ways of improving finances. A great deal of time may be spent figuring out and going over schemes and plans. It is the right time to be careful with detail. People will find themselves working longer than usual at their desks. Or devoting more time to serious thought about the future. A strong desire to put order into business and financial arrangements may cause extra work. Loved ones may complain of being neglected and may fail to appreciate that your efforts are for their ultimate benefit. Your desire for system may extend to criticism of arrangements in the home and lead to minor upsets. Health may be affected through overwork. Try to secure a reasonable amount of rest and relaxation, although the tendency will be to "keep going" despite good advice. Work done conscientiously in this period should result in a solid contribution to your future security. CAUTION: Try not to be as serious with people as the work you are engaged in.

MOON IN GEMINI

The humdrum of routine and too much work should suddenly end. You are likely to find yourself in an expansive, quicksilver world of change and self-expression. Urges to write, to paint, to experience the freedom of some sort of artistic outpouring, may be very strong. Take full advantage of them. You may find yourself finishing something you began and put aside long ago. Or embarking on something new which could easily be prompted by a chance meeting, a new acquaintance, or even an advertisement. There may be a yearning for a change of scenery, the feeling to visit another country (not too far away), or at least to get away for a few days. This may result in short, quick journeys. Or, if you are planning a single visit, there may be some unexpected changes or detours on the way. Familiar activities will seem to give little satisfaction unless they contain a fresh element of excitement or expectation. The inclination will be toward untried pursuits, particularly those that allow you to express your inner nature. The accent is on new faces, new places. CAUTION: Do not be too quick to commit yourself emotionally.

MOON IN CANCER

Feelings of uncertainty and vague insecurity are likely to cause problems while the Moon is in Cancer. Thoughts may turn frequently to the warmth of the home and the comfort of loved ones. Nostalgic impulses could cause you to bring out old photographs and letters and reflect on the days when your life seemed to be much more rewarding and less demanding. The love and understanding of parents and family may be important, and, if it is not forthcoming, you may have to fight against bouts of self-pity. The cordiality of friends and the thought of good times with them that are sure to be repeated will help to restore you to a happier frame of mind. The desire to be alone may follow minor setbacks or rebuffs at this time, but solitude is unlikely to help. Better to get on the telephone or visit someone. This period often causes peculiar dreams and upsurges of imaginative thinking which can be helpful to authors of occult and mystical works. Preoccupation with the personal world of simple human needs can overshadow any material strivings. CAUTION: Do not spend too much time thinking— seek the company of loved ones or close friends.

MOON IN LEO
New horizons of exciting and rather extravagant activity open up. This is the time for exhilarating entertainment, glamorous and lavish parties, and expensive shopping sprees. Any merrymaking that relies upon your generosity as a host has every chance of being a spectacular success. You should find yourself right in the center of the fun, either as the life of the party or simply as a person whom happy people like to be with. Romance thrives in this heady atmosphere and friendships are likely to explode unexpectedly into serious attachments. Children and younger people should be attracted to you and you may find yourself organizing a picnic or a visit to a fun-fair, the movies, or the beach. The sunny company and vitality of youthful companions should help you to find some unsuspected energy. In career, you could find an opening for promotion or advancement. This should be the time to make a direct approach. The period favors those engaged in original research. CAUTION: Bask in popularity, not in flattery.

MOON IN VIRGO
Off comes the party cap and out steps the busy, practical worker. He wants to get his personal affairs straight, to rearrange them, if necessary, for more efficiency, so he will have more time for more work. He clears up his correspondence, pays outstanding bills, makes numerous phone calls. He is likely to make inquiries, or sign up for some new insurance and put money into gilt-edged investment. Thoughts probably revolve around the need for future security—to tie up loose ends and clear the decks. There may be a tendency to be "finicky," to interfere in the routine of others, particularly friends and family members. The motive may be a genuine desire to help with suggestions for updating or streamlining their affairs, but these will probably not be welcomed. Sympathy may be felt for less fortunate sections of the community and a flurry of some sort of voluntary service is likely. This may be accompanied by strong feelings of responsibility on several fronts and health may suffer from extra efforts made. CAUTION: Everyone may not want your help or advice.

MOON IN LIBRA

These are days of harmony and agreement and you should find yourself at peace with most others. Relationships tend to be smooth and sweet-flowing. Friends may become closer and bonds deepen in mutual understanding. Hopes will be shared. Progress by cooperation could be the secret of success in every sphere. In business, established partnerships may flourish and new ones get off to a good start. Acquaintances could discover similar interests that lead to congenial discussions and rewarding exchanges of some sort. Love, as a unifying force, reaches its optimum. Marriage partners should find accord. Those who wed at this time face the prospect of a happy union. Cooperation and tolerance are felt to be stronger than dissension and impatience. The argumentative are not quite so loud in their bellowings, nor as inflexible in their attitudes. In the home, there should be a greater recognition of the other point of view and a readiness to put the wishes of the group before selfish insistence. This is a favorable time to join an art group. CAUTION: Do not be too independent—let others help you if they want to.

MOON IN SCORPIO

Driving impulses to make money and to economize are likely to cause upsets all around. No area of expenditure is likely to be spared the ax, including the household budget. This is a time when the desire to cut down on extravagance can become near fanatical. Care must be exercised to try to keep the aim in reasonable perspective. Others may not feel the same urgent need to save and may retaliate. There is a danger that possessions of sentimental value will be sold to realize cash for investment. Buying and selling of stock for quick profit is also likely. The attention turns to organizing, reorganizing, tidying up at home and at work. Neglected jobs could suddenly be done with great bursts of energy. The desire for solitude may intervene. Self-searching thoughts could disturb. The sense of invisible and mysterious energies in play could cause some excitability. The reassurance of loves ones may help. CAUTION: Be kind to the people you love.

MOON IN SAGITTARIUS

These are days when you are likely to be stirred and elevated by discussions and reflections of a religious and philosophical nature. Ideas of faraway places may cause unusual response and excitement. A decision may be made to visit someone overseas, perhaps a person whose influence was important to your earlier character development. There could be a strong resolution to get away from present intellectual patterns, to learn new subjects, and to meet more interesting people. The superficial may be rejected in all its forms. An impatience with old ideas and unimaginative contacts could lead to a change of companions and interests. There may be an upsurge of religious feeling and metaphysical inquiry. Even a new insight into the significance of astrology and other occult studies is likely under the curious stimulus of the Moon in Sagittarius. Physically, you may express this need for fundamental change by spending more time outdoors: sports, gardening, long walks appeal. CAUTION: Try to channel any restlessness into worthwhile study.

MOON IN CAPRICORN
Life in these hours may seem to pivot around the importance of gaining prestige and honor in the career, as well as maintaining a spotless reputation. Ambitious urges may be excessive and could be accompanied by quite acquisitive drives for money. Effort should be directed along strictly ethical lines where there is no possibility of reproach or scandal. All endeavors are likely to be characterized by great earnestness, and an air of authority and purpose which should impress those who are looking for leadership or reliability. The desire to conform to accepted standards may extend to sharp criticism of family members. Frivolity and unconventional actions are unlikely to amuse while the Moon is in Capricorn. Moderation and seriousness are the orders of the day. Achievement and recognition in this period could come through community work or organizing for the benefit of some amateur group. CAUTION: Dignity and esteem are not always self-awarded.

MOON IN AQUARIUS
Moon in Aquarius is in the second last sign of the Zodiac where ideas can become disturbingly fine and subtle. The result is often a mental "no-man's land" where imagination cannot be trusted with the same certitude as other times. The dangers for the individual are the extremes of optimism and pessimism. Unless the imagination is held in check, situations are likely to be misread, and rosy conclusions drawn where they do not exist. Consequences for the unwary can be costly in career and business. Best to think twice and not speak or act until you think again. Pessimism can be a cruel self-inflicted penalty for delusion at this time. Between the two extremes are strange areas of self-deception which, for example, can make the selfish person think he is actually being generous. Eerie dreams which resemble the reality and even seem to continue into the waking state are also possible. CAUTION: Look for the fact and not just for the image in your mind.

MOON IN PISCES

Everything seems to come to the surface now. Memory may be crystal clear, throwing up long-forgotten information which could be valuable in the career or business. Flashes of clairvoyance and intuition are possible along with sudden realizations of one's own nature, which may be used for self-improvement. A talent, never before suspected, may be discovered. Qualities not evident before in friends and marriage partners are likely to be noticed. As this is a period in which the truth seems to emerge, the discovery of false characteristics is likely to lead to disenchantment or a shift in attachments. However, when qualities are accepted, it should lead to happiness and deeper feeling. Surprise solutions could bob up for old problems. There may be a public announcement of the solving of a crime or mystery. People with secrets may find someone has "guessed" correctly. The secrets of the soul or the inner self also tend to reveal themselves. Religious and philosophical groups may make some interesting discoveries. CAUTION: Not a time for activities that depend on secrecy.

NOTE: When you read your daily forecasts, use the Moon Sign Dates that are provided in the following section of Moon Tables. Then you may want to glance back here for the Moon's influence in a given sign.

MOON TABLES

CORRECTION FOR NEW YORK TIME, FIVE HOURS
WEST OF GREENWICH

Atlanta, Boston, Detroit, Miami, Washington, Montreal,
Ottawa, Quebec, Bogota, Havana, Lima, Santiago ... Same time
Chicago, New Orleans, Houston, Winnipeg, Churchill,
Mexico City .... Deduct 1 hour
Albuquerque, Denver, Phoenix, El Paso, Edmonton,
Helena .... Deduct 2 hours
Los Angeles, San Francisco, Reno, Portland,
Seattle, Vancouver .... Deduct 3 hours
Honolulu, Anchorage, Fairbanks, Kodiak .... Deduct 5 hours
Nome, Samoa, Tonga, Midway .... Deduct 6 hours
Halifax, Bermuda, San Juan, Caracas, La Paz,
Barbados .... Add 1 hour
St. John's, Brasilia, Rio de Janeiro, Sao Paulo,
Buenos Aires, Montevideo .... Add 2 hours
Azores, Cape Verde Islands .... Add 3 hours
Canary Islands, Madeira, Reykjavik .... Add 4 hours
London, Paris, Amsterdam, Madrid, Lisbon,
Gibraltar, Belfast, Raba .... Add 5 hours
Frankfurt, Rome, Oslo, Stockholm, Prague,
Belgrade .... Add 6 hours
Bucharest, Beirut, Tel Aviv, Athens, Istanbul, Cairo,
Alexandria, Cape Town, Johannesburg .... Add 7 hours
Moscow, Leningrad, Baghdad, Dhahran,
Addis Ababa, Nairobi, Teheran, Zanzibar .... Add 8 hours
Bombay, Calcutta, Sri Lanka .... Add 10½ hours
Hong Kong, Shanghai, Manila, Peking, Perth .... Add 13 hours
Tokyo, Okinawa, Darwin, Pusan .... Add 14 hours
Sydney, Melbourne, Port Moresby, Guam .... Add 15 hours
Auckland, Wellington, Suva, Wake .... Add 17 hours

2010 MOON SIGN DATES—
NEW YORK TIME

JANUARY		FEBRUARY		MARCH	
Day Moon Enters		**Day Moon Enters**		**Day Moon Enters**	
1. Leo	9:42 pm	1. Virgo		1. Libra	7:32 pm
2. Leo		2. Libra	8:43 am	2. Libra	
3. Virgo	9:54 pm	3. Libra		3. Scorp.	9:12 pm
4. Virgo		4. Scorp.	11:57 am	4. Scorp.	
5. Libra	11:59 pm	5. Scorp.		5. Scorp.	
6. Libra		6. Sagitt.	7:05 pm	6. Sagitt.	1:37 am
7. Libra		7. Sagitt.		7. Sagitt.	
8. Scorp.	5:01 am	8. Sagitt.		8. Capric.	12:14 pm
9. Scorp.		9. Capric.	5:45 am	9. Capric.	
10. Sagitt.	1:11 pm	10. Capric.		10. Capric.	
11. Sagitt.		11. Aquar.	6:25 pm	11. Aquar.	12:43 am
12. Capric.	11:55 pm	12. Aquar.		12. Aquar.	
13. Capric.		13. Aquar.		13. Pisces	1:45 pm
14. Capric.		14. Pisces	7:24 am	14. Pisces	
15. Aquar.	12:18 pm	15. Pisces		15. Pisces	
16. Aquar.		16. Aries	7:31 pm	16. Aries	1:33 am
17. Aquar.		17. Aries		17. Aries	
18. Pisces	1:18 am	18. Aries		18. Taurus	11:30 am
19. Pisces		19. Taurus	5:56 am	19. Taurus	
20. Aries	1:37 pm	20. Taurus		20. Gemini	7:29 pm
21. Aries		21. Gemini	1:48 pm	21. Gemini	
22. Taurus	11:41 pm	22. Gemini		22. Gemini	
23. Taurus		23. Cancer	6:30 pm	23. Cancer	1:17 am
24. Taurus		24. Cancer		24. Cancer	
25. Gemini	6:12 am	25. Leo	8:09 pm	25. Leo	4:40 am
26. Gemini		26. Leo		26. Leo	
27. Cancer	9:02 am	27. Virgo	7:53 pm	27. Virgo	5:58 am
28. Cancer		28. Virgo		28. Virgo	
29. Leo	9:11 am			29. Libra	6:22 am
30. Leo				30. Libra	
31. Virgo	8:24 am			31. Scorp.	7:42 am

Daylight saving time to be considered where applicable.

2010 MOON SIGN DATES—
NEW YORK TIME

APRIL
Day Moon Enters
1. Scorp.
2. Sagitt. 11:54 am
3. Sagitt.
4. Capric. 8:08 pm
5. Capric.
6. Capric.
7. Aquar. 7:52 am
8. Aquar.
9. Pisces 8:49 pm
10. Pisces
11. Pisces
12. Aries 8:32 am
13. Aries
14. Taurus 5:56 pm
15. Taurus
16. Taurus
17. Gemini 1:09 am
18. Gemini
19. Cancer 6:40 am
20. Cancer
21. Leo 10:43 am
22. Leo
23. Virgo 1:25 pm
24. Virgo
25. Libra 3:18 pm
26. Libra
27. Scorp. 5:30 pm
28. Scorp.
29. Sagitt. 9:37 pm
30. Sagitt.

MAY
Day Moon Enters
1. Sagitt.
2. Capric. 5:01 am
3. Capric.
4. Aquar. 3:53 pm
5. Aquar.
6. Aquar.
7. Pisces 4:35 am
8. Pisces
9. Aries 4:30 pm
10. Aries
11. Aries
12. Taurus 1:49 am
13. Taurus
14. Gemini 8:19 am
15. Gemini
16. Cancer 12:47 pm
17. Cancer
18. Leo 4:07 pm
19. Leo
20. Virgo 6:59 pm
21. Virgo
22. Libra 9:51 pm
23. Libra
24. Libra
25. Scorp. 1:18 am
26. Scorp.
27. Sagitt. 6:17 am
28. Sagitt.
29. Capric. 1:45 pm
30. Capric.
31. Capric.

JUNE
Day Moon Enters
1. Aquar. 12:09 am
2. Aquar.
3. Pisces 12:35 pm
4. Pisces
5. Pisces
6. Aries 12:51 am
7. Aries
8. Taurus 10:42 am
9. Taurus
10. Gemini 5:12 pm
11. Gemini
12. Cancer 8:51 pm
13. Cancer
14. Leo 10:55 pm
15. Leo
16. Leo
17. Virgo 12:42 am
18. Virgo
19. Libra 3:14 am
20. Libra
21. Scorp. 7:15 am
22. Scorp.
23. Sagitt. 1:11 pm
24. Sagitt.
25. Capric. 9:22 pm
26. Capric.
27. Capric.
28. Aquar. 7:53 am
29. Aquar.
30. Pisces 8:11 pm

Daylight saving time to be considered where applicable.

2010 MOON SIGN DATES— NEW YORK TIME

JULY Day Moon Enters		AUGUST Day Moon Enters		SEPTEMBER Day Moon Enters	
1. Pisces		1. Aries		1. Gemini	
2. Pisces		2. Taurus	3:14 am	2. Gemini	
3. Aries	8:45 am	3. Taurus		3. Cancer	1:52 am
4. Aries		4. Gemini	11:55 am	4. Cancer	
5. Taurus	7:30 pm	5. Gemini		5. Leo	4:46 am
6. Taurus		6. Cancer	4:51 pm	6. Leo	
7. Taurus		7. Cancer		7. Virgo	4:54 am
8. Gemini	2:52 am	8. Leo	6:24 pm	8. Virgo	
9. Gemini		9. Leo		9. Libra	4:02 am
10. Cancer	6:39 am	10. Virgo	6:02 pm	10. Libra	
11. Cancer		11. Virgo		11. Scorp.	4:22 am
12. Leo	7:55 am	12. Libra	5:44 pm	12. Scorp.	
13. Leo		13. Libra		13. Sagitt.	7:53 am
14. Virgo	8:16 am	14. Scorp.	7:27 pm	14. Sagitt.	
15. Virgo		15. Scorp.		15. Capric.	3:31 pm
16. Libra	9:25 am	16. Scorp.		16. Capric.	
17. Libra		17. Sagitt.	12:35 am	17. Capric.	
18. Scorp.	12:43 pm	18. Sagitt.		18. Aquar.	2:36 am
19. Scorp.		19. Capric.	9:18 am	19. Aquar.	
20. Sagitt.	6:50 pm	20. Capric.		20. Pisces	3:16 pm
21. Sagitt.		21. Aquar.	8:38 pm	21. Pisces	
22. Sagitt.		22. Aquar.		22. Pisces	
23. Capric.	3:40 am	23. Aquar.		23. Aries	3:48 am
24. Capric.		24. Pisces	9:12 am	24. Aries	
25. Aquar.	2:39 pm	25. Pisces		25. Taurus	3:18 pm
26. Aquar.		26. Aries	9:50 pm	26. Taurus	
27. Aquar.		27. Aries		27. Taurus	
28. Pisces	3:01 am	28. Aries		28. Gemini	1:12 am
29. Pisces		29. Taurus	9:36 am	29. Gemini	
30. Aries	3:43 pm	30. Taurus		30. Cancer	8:47 am
31. Aries		31. Gemini	7:20 pm		

Daylight saving time to be considered where applicable.

2010 MOON SIGN DATES—
NEW YORK TIME

OCTOBER		NOVEMBER		DECEMBER	
Day Moon Enters		**Day Moon Enters**		**Day Moon Enters**	
1. Cancer		1. Virgo		1. Libra	
2. Leo	1:22 pm	2. Virgo		2. Scorp.	9:45 am
3. Leo		3. Libra	12:20 am	3. Scorp.	
4. Virgo	3:01 pm	4. Libra		4. Sagitt.	1:00 pm
5. Virgo		5. Scorp.	1:17 am	5. Sagitt.	
6. Libra	2:53 pm	6. Scorp.		6. Capric.	6:17 pm
7. Libra		7. Sagitt.	3:29 am	7. Capric.	
8. Scorp.	2:53 pm	8. Sagitt.		8. Capric.	
9. Scorp.		9. Capric.	8:38 am	9. Aquar.	2:32 am
10. Sagitt.	5:10 pm	10. Capric.		10. Aquar.	
11. Sagitt.		11. Aquar.	5:33 pm	11. Pisces	1:42 pm
12. Capric.	11:18 pm	12. Aquar.		12. Pisces	
13. Capric.		13. Aquar.		13. Pisces	
14. Capric.		14. Pisces	5:25 am	14. Aries	2:16 am
15. Aquar.	9:25 am	15. Pisces		15. Aries	
16. Aquar.		16. Aries	6:00 pm	16. Taurus	1:50 pm
17. Pisces	9:53 pm	17. Aries		17. Taurus	
18. Pisces		18. Aries		18. Gemini	10:38 pm
19. Pisces		19. Taurus	5:05 am	19. Gemini	
20. Aries	10:24 am	20. Taurus		20. Gemini	
21. Aries		21. Gemini	1:47 pm	21. Cancer	4:23 am
22. Taurus	9:31 pm	22. Gemini		22. Cancer	
23. Taurus		23. Cancer	8:15 pm	23. Leo	7:52 am
24. Taurus		24. Cancer		24. Leo	
25. Gemini	6:49 am	25. Cancer		25. Virgo	10:15 am
26. Gemini		26. Leo	1:02 am	26. Virgo	
27. Cancer	2:15 pm	27. Leo		27. Libra	12:39 pm
28. Cancer		28. Virgo	4:35 am	28. Libra	
29. Leo	7:40 pm	29. Virgo		29. Scorp.	3:51 pm
30. Leo		30. Libra	7:16 am	30. Scorp.	
31. Virgo	10:52 pm			31. Sagitt.	8:22 pm

Daylight saving time to be considered where applicable.

2010 PHASES OF THE MOON— NEW YORK TIME

New Moon	First Quarter	Full Moon	Last Quarter
Dec. 15 ('09)	Dec. 24 ('09)	Dec. 31 ('09)	Jan. 7
Jan. 15	Jan. 23	Jan. 30	Feb. 5
Feb. 13	Feb. 21	Feb. 28	March 7
March 15	March 23	March 29	April 6
April 14	April 21	April 28	May 5
May 13	May 20	May 27	June 4
June 12	June 18	June 26	July 4
July 11	July 18	July 25	August 3
August 9	August 16	August 24	Sept. 1
Sept. 8	Sept. 15	Sept. 23	Sept. 30
Oct. 7	Oct. 14	Oct. 22	Oct. 30
Nov. 6	Nov. 13	Nov. 21	Nov. 28
Dec. 5	Dec. 13	Dec. 21	Dec. 27

Each phase of the Moon lasts approximately seven to eight days, during which the Moon's shape gradually changes as it comes out of one phase and goes into the next.

There will be a solar eclipse during the New Moon phase on January 15 and July 11.

There will be a lunar eclipse during the Full Moon phase on June 26 and December 21.

2010 FISHING GUIDE

	Good	Best
January	3-4-16-28-29-30-31	2-6-23-27
February	1-2-13-21-26-27-28	5-25
March	1-7-15-27-28-29	2-3-24-30-31
April	13-22-24-29	1-2-3-8-26-27-28
May	1-7-14-20-27-28-29	25-26-30
June	12-24-25-28-29	4-19-26-27
July	4-22-26-27	11-17-23-24-28
August	10-16-21-22-23-27-28	3-24-25
September	1-8-14-19-20-23-24-25	21-22-26
October	21-22-23-25-26-30	1-7-14-19-24
November	13-17-18-22-23-28	6-19-20-24
December	5-19-20-21-23-24	13-17-22-28

2010 PLANTING GUIDE

	Aboveground Crops	Root Crops
January	18-19-23-24-28	1-6-7-8-9-13-14
February	15-16-20-24	2-3-4-5-9-10
March	19-20-23-24	2-3-4-5-9-10-14-30-31
April	15-16-19-20-26-27	1-5-6-10-11-28
May	17-23-24-25-26	2-3-7-8-13-30-31
June	13-14-19-20-21-22	4-9-10-26-27
July	17-18-19-20-23-24	1-2-6-28-29
August	13-14-15-16-20-21	3-7-8-25-26-30-31
September	9-10-11-12-16-17-21	3-4-26-27
October	7-8-9-13-14-18-19	1-7-24-28
November	10-11-15-16-19-20	3-4-5-24-25-30
December	7-8-12-13-17-18	1-2-3-22-28-29-30-31

	Pruning	Weeds and Pests
January	1-8-9	2-3-4-5-11-12-30-31
February	5-6	1-7-8-12-28
March	4-5-15	6-7-11-12
April	1-10-11-28-29	3-4-8-9-13-30
May	7-8	1-5-6-10-28
June	4	1-2-6-7-11-29-30
July	1-2-28-29	3-4-8-26-27-31
August	7-8-25-26	1-5-9-27-28
September	3-4	1-2-5-6-7-23-24-28-29
October	1-28	3-4-5-26-30-31
November	24-25	1-2-22-23-26-27-28-29
December	3-4-22-30-31	5-24-25-26

MOON'S INFLUENCE OVER PLANTS

Centuries ago it was established that seeds planted when the Moon is in signs and phases called Fruitful will produce more growth than seeds planted when the Moon is in a Barren sign.

Fruitful Signs: Taurus, Cancer, Libra, Scorpio, Capricorn, Pisces
Barren Signs: Aries, Gemini, Leo, Virgo, Sagittarius, Aquarius
Dry Signs: Aries, Gemini, Sagittarius, Aquarius

Activity	Moon In
Mow lawn, trim plants	**Fruitful sign:** 1st & 2nd quarter
Plant flowers	**Fruitful sign:** 2nd quarter; best in Cancer and Libra
Prune	**Fruitful sign:** 3rd & 4th quarter
Destroy pests; spray	**Barren sign:** 4th quarter
Harvest potatoes, root crops	**Dry sign:** 3rd & 4th quarter; Taurus, Leo, and Aquarius

MOON'S INFLUENCE OVER YOUR HEALTH

ARIES   Head, brain, face, upper jaw
TAURUS   Throat, neck, lower jaw
GEMINI   Hands, arms, lungs, shoulders, nervous system
CANCER   Esophagus, stomach, breasts, womb, liver
LEO   Heart, spine
VIRGO   Intestines, liver
LIBRA   Kidneys, lower back
SCORPIO   Sex and eliminative organs
SAGITTARIUS   Hips, thighs, liver
CAPRICORN   Skin, bones, teeth, knees
AQUARIUS   Circulatory system, lower legs
PISCES   Feet, tone of being

Try to avoid work being done on that part of the body when the Moon is in the sign governing that part.

MOON'S INFLUENCE OVER DAILY AFFAIRS

The Moon makes a complete transit of the Zodiac every 27 days 7 hours and 43 minutes. In making this transit the Moon forms different aspects with the planets and consequently has favorable or unfavorable bearings on affairs and events for persons according to the sign of the Zodiac under which they were born.

When the Moon is in conjunction with the Sun it is called a New Moon; when the Moon and Sun are in opposition it is called a Full Moon. From New Moon to Full Moon, first and second quarter—which takes about two weeks—the Moon is increasing or waxing. From Full Moon to New Moon, third and fourth quarter, the Moon is decreasing or waning.

Activity	Moon In
Business: buying and selling new, requiring public support	Sagittarius, Aries, Gemini, Virgo 1st and 2nd quarter
meant to be kept quiet	3rd and 4th quarter
Investigation	3rd and 4th quarter
Signing documents	1st & 2nd quarter, Cancer, Scorpio, Pisces
Advertising	2nd quarter, Sagittarius
Journeys and trips	1st & 2nd quarter, Gemini, Virgo
Renting offices, etc.	Taurus, Leo, Scorpio, Aquarius
Painting of house/apartment	3rd & 4th quarter, Taurus, Scorpio, Aquarius
Decorating	Gemini, Libra, Aquarius
Buying clothes and accessories	Taurus, Virgo
Beauty salon or barber shop visit	1st & 2nd quarter, Taurus, Leo, Libra, Scorpio, Aquarius
Weddings	1st & 2nd quarter

Pisces

PISCES
Character Analysis

People born under the sign of Pisces are dreamy, romantic, and idealistic. Emotional and changeable, Pisces are responsive and impressionable. Theirs is a sensitive nature. They approach life in a serious yet somewhat unrealistic way.

The sign of Pisces is symbolized by the two Fishes, one swimming one way and the other the opposite way, and indicates a double nature. Indeed, there often seems to be more to someone born under this twelfth sign of the Zodiac than meets the eye. Their behavior is often a riddle to other people.

Pisces may seem secretive about the smallest, most unimportant thing yet open in important matters when perhaps secrecy would be warranted. Chances are Pisces are kind and gentle people who never would do anything to injure someone's feelings. Although the Fishes can be purposeful when necessary, they sometimes seem unable to grapple with life's routine problems. They can appear to be a bit helpless and lacking in self-confidence. Uncertain, Pisces may take an extraordinarily long time to make up his or her mind about the smallest thing.

Pisces individuals are generally well liked. They can be trusted. They are conscientious in all that they undertake. People can depend on the Fishes no matter what situation arises. Their word is their bond. Likable and pleasant, the Pisces man or woman makes other people feel comfortable and understood. Because Pisces seek peace and quiet in any environment, their personality usually projects a calm, even-tempered quality that allows companions to relax and let their hair down.

Because Pisces men and women are so easygoing, an opportunist might try to take advantage of their inherent goodness. Pisces are not fighters by nature. If someone abuses their generosity and openness, they are not likely to put up a fight or cause a scene. They may not always speak up or speak out when they should. Pisces are very sensitive, and their feelings are easily hurt. Sometimes they take offense when none is intended.

Pisces individuals are usually methodical, although they may seem a bit lazy or passive to the casual observer. But they will live up to their responsibilities at home or at work if they see that it is necessary for keeping peace and order. They can take life as it comes. Moreover, they can easily adapt to whatever situation arises. They will not complain idly about the situation. They will try to do something about it.

Pisces men and women are not afraid of change. In fact, they welcome change, especially if other people can benefit from it. Anything that Pisces individuals feel will make the world a better place in which to live is something they will support.

Pisces men and women readily sympathize with anyone who is in dire straits. They are always prepared to help someone in need or in trouble if they can. In a rather uncanny way, Pisces seems to know how other people are feeling before such people even say anything.

Blessed with great perceptive and intuitive powers, the Fishes are familiar with the problems of the world. Their dreams and schemes often center around bettering the world situation, either on a grand scale or closer to home and neighborhood. But sometimes the Pisces man or woman is too much of a dreamer to put their plans and hopes into action. They may lack that driving force to turn plans into reality.

When they do go about revising their habits, finishing their work, and completing their plans, Pisces usually can make a very important contribution to the world. They are generous, sometimes to a fault. They think more of the other person, at times, than they do of themselves. They can be quite self-sacrificing, denying themselves many material comforts in order to serve the good of humanity.

Imagination and creativity are basic to the Pisces nature. These men and women are usually interested in the arts. In the fields of music, painting, and poetry Pisces can plunge to their heart's content and forget about the hard realities of life. Mysterious and mystical things attract the Fishes. Unknown realms seem to lure them on. At the same time this kind of interest clashes with their basic personality, making it difficult to adjust to the hard, stubborn facts of life.

When Pisces men and women take up an interest, they go all the way. They are very susceptible. Subjects that appeal to them have a complete hold until they know the subject inside out. Theories, religious doctrines, and spiritual beliefs captivate Pisces. Although they may learn a great deal about such a subject, they may become somewhat saddened, for they feel that their knowledge cuts them off from other people. Some Pisces feel superior in their intellectual isolation.

The Pisces man or woman can be moody. They can go from feeling high to low, and back again, in a remarkably short time. This emotional turbulence is reflected in the zodiacal symbol of the Fishes swimming both ways. At times Pisces individuals feel sorry for themselves, a self-pity born from believing that their talents are not really appreciated. The strong Pisces, however, knows how to put such thoughts out of mind and to forge ahead.

Inspiration and faith are also basic to the Pisces nature. While remaining in the background of things, the Pisces man or woman can inspire other people to great heights. Sometimes the Pisces hesitation to step into the fray comes from fear and frustration. They can be somewhat afraid of conflict and so will do their best to avoid it. They will take themselves out of the action while encouraging other people to go on.

When forced to face harsh reality, Pisces can be at loose ends. It is too much to bear. They would rather hear a pleasant lie than the cold, hard truth. If things become too difficult to manage, Pisces may try to escape from everyday responsibilities.

Pisces men and women do best when in the company of a strong, purposeful individual. Alone, they may give in to their fears. But when encouraged by loved ones, friends, and associates, Pisces will try harder to realize goals, hopes, and plans.

Health

The average Pisces man or woman may not look very strong or healthy. However, their constitution is usually quite good and they can recover from an illness fairly quickly. In general, their health is good. The great outdoors is likely to be good for Pisces. They need plenty of sunshine and fresh air in order to feel fit. They should also get plenty of exercise. On the other hand, they should not do anything that might cause stress or strain.

Quite often a Pisces man or woman looks younger than he or she really is. Their build or physique is deceptive. Pisces may appear slim and delicate, but they contain a wiry strength. Many of the world's best dancers are born under this sign. The eyes and the feet are usually the weak points of the Pisces anatomy. These men and women also must guard against chills and cold, which affect the extremities.

Pisces individuals should be moderate in their behavior. Overindulgence is apt to be bad for their constitution. A well-balanced diet, with plenty of green vegetables and fresh fruit, will help to maintain good physique and fitness.

Pisces men and women may have a weakness for substances that are known to be physical stimulants. Good health can be abused by the use of alcohol or drugs, so it is important to avoid these substances. Pisces who know what is needed to protect their health will generally live to a ripe old age.

Some Pisces individuals are stubborn, however, and do the things that please them most without giving much thought to the consequences. If they do become addicted to drugs or to alcohol, they may have a difficult time trying to break the habit. Their emotional, psychological dependency can be stronger than their willpower.

Sometimes Pisces want pity, so they put on their best act to appear sorrowful, martyred, or victimized.

Occupation

Pisces men and women do well in any kind of work that involves helping and healing. This is their main interest in life. They like doing what they can for people. The sick and needy can always depend on Pisces for compassion, advice, and actual aid.

Pisces individuals make good doctors, psychiatrists, teachers, and ministers. Social work in all areas is another profession that attracts the Fishes. Sympathetic and intuitive, Pisces men and women often know what is wrong with someone before the person is aware of it. Anyone in trouble or in need will turn to Pisces because they can easily put themselves in the person's place and offer genuine help.

Pisces men and women contain a magical charm, and so do well in any profession that relies on persuasion and convincing. Diplomatic work, public relations, and selling fields appeal.

The Pisces strong point is insight, the ability to understand people and their problems. When choosing a job or career, these men and women should try to make use of their innate gifts. Generally well liked by associates and colleagues, Pisces are easy to get along with and always ready to listen to someone's troubles.

Pisces men and women are flexible. They can take on many different roles if need be. The two sides of Pisces mean they usually have many interests. Like their zodiacal symbol of the Fishes, they can move in any direction with equal skill.

Their flexible personality coupled with their imaginative powers fit Pisces ideally for a career in the world of theater and film. They usually have remarkable dramatic talents both as actors and writers. They understand human nature, they are expressive, and they know how best to portray a character on stage or screen.

Whatever they do, Pisces individuals are happiest when given a chance to exercise their many interests. They like and need variety in their work. In the right position, they are not afraid of encountering frustration or opposition, for they are well equipped to deal with it.

Work that requires a great deal of concentration and attention to small details seldom interests Pisces. But they can apply themselves to anything that completely absorbs their imagination and creative spirit. As workers they can always be depended on to do their best in a methodical, industrious way. Often they cleverly think up ways of cutting the work time in half, much to the delight of their co-workers and teammates.

Some Pisces do not have much faith in themselves or what they can achieve. Sometimes they do not really know what they want in life and find it hard to direct themselves toward a particular goal. If they meet with the slightest upset, they are ready to call it quits. Confusion is a danger. When confronted with frustration, they can become disorganized and have difficulty putting their thoughts in order, as well as putting things in order.

The Pisces man or woman can be a sensualist. They like to pamper themselves with comforts and material things that ease their pain or frustration. Money does not interest Pisces for what it is but for what it can do. They need the security money can bring.

Many Pisces are afraid of growing old, and they want a nest egg they can draw on when they become senior citizens. If they do not have as much money as they think they need, they may worry about it constantly. They may worry so much that it prevents them from making the headway they desperately desire.

Chances are the average Pisces will never become a millionaire. These men and woman want only enough money to adequately provide for themselves and those they care for. Pisces, always trying to help people, may become too generous with money. They sometimes spend money, or give it away, to help someone when they should be helping themselves. If Pisces individuals come into a lot of money unexpectedly, there probably will be opportunists around trying to take it away. Pisces will never say no to a hand-out, especially if someone is in dire need.

Once Pisces men and women find their niche in life, they can go far on sheer will and determination. The strong Pisces has a good sense of direction and will work hard to attain goals and to make dreams come true. Some Pisces individuals are lucky and attain financial success without having to work hard. The well-heeled Pisces would be wise to invest money in something secure, perhaps real estate or gilt-edge stocks and bonds. A lucky streak notwithstanding, Pisces should avoid risks as much as possible.

Pisces men and women are good in business even though they may not have a very competitive nature. In fact, their spirit of cooperation is the quality that enables them sometimes to extend their business base by networking, merger, and other linkup. In a partnership, they can do well as long as the partner possesses business qualities they lack or that complement theirs.

Home and Family

Pisces men and women are very susceptible to their environment. If they are to succeed, they have to be in an environment that encourages success. They like a home where they can relax in comfort—a place where their imagination can roam. Home and family are important to the Pisces who wants to go far in life. It provides the stability and haven they need.

Pisces is a home lover by nature. The warm and peaceful atmosphere of a comfortable home is a great motivator. Pisces tastes are eclectic, blending the old-fashioned with the modern. The home may contain some beautiful and meaningful art objects. Art plays an important part in the lives of Pisces men and woman. At times, art means more to them than so-called practical things.

A home in the country would please Pisces individuals. They like wide open spaces where they can wander around freely without having to be disturbed by traffic or crowds. The countryside, especially a place near the shore, gives Pisces a chance to relax and let their imagination run free.

People enjoy visiting the Pisces man or woman because he or she knows how to make guests feel at home. Pisces is a good conversationalist. When someone is seriously talking or confiding something, Pisces is never bored but listens carefully, interrupting every now and again to make a helpful suggestion.

Pisces is a true romantic. Marriage appeals to these men and women because it gives them a chance to explore both the idealistic and sensual sides of their nature. A happy home is where Pisces can be most imaginative and creative.

Social Relationships

Pisces individuals are perhaps the most sensitive people in existence. They are gentle, considerate, and kind. They are earnest in expressing their affections and look for affection to be reciprocated. Pisces men and women never want to hurt anyone, and they also try to protect themselves from injury, especially emotional insult. They do not like anyone who is mean or petty.

Pisces standards for friendship and companionship are quite high. They choose someone who is enlightened and humane, someone who is well-groomed and intelligent, someone who probably has as great an interest in the arts as they do. But Pisces men and women are realistic when it comes to looking for a friend or a companion. The happy Pisces is one who can take a person for what he or she is and not long for perfection.

At times, Pisces may shuttle from one mood to another without warning, which is apt to puzzle their friends and loved ones. Pisces can be passionate one moment and cool the next, for no apparent reason. The people who love Pisces must learn to accept this.

It is sometimes difficult for even the most intimate friend to really know how a Pisces feels. A lover may find reason to doubt Pisces' love even when they profess it profusely. It can be hard to know whether or not Pisces men and women really mean what they say in times of stress or struggle.

Sincere Pisces individuals take stock of themselves and try to do something about their weak points. They try to correct personality quirks and extreme emotional sensitivity. Pisces may even try to appear tougher than they really are as a protection against anyone who would take advantage of their kind nature.

Pisces may fool many with this facade, but not anyone who really knows these men and women. While exhibiting a hard-bitten exterior, Pisces is likely to be as soft as cotton candy inside. Friends and loved ones will accept Pisces for all their qualities—both the good and the bad. True friends will not be put off by the mask of toughness.

Alone, Pisces can become disheartened and disillusioned. Whims and fancies are not a suitable substitute for fulfilling social relationships. Although the private side of the Pisces nature can be tapped in an artistic way, these men and women need people and do best in a strong relationship.

Pisces men and women are adaptable and can easily take on the character of anyone with whom they associate. So it is very important to mix with the right people. People who know their own mind, who are positive thinkers with a firm grip on reality are right for Pisces. In association with such people, these qualities rub off on Pisces and serve to build their confidence and strengthen their purpose.

Love and Marriage

Pisces men and women feel deeply. When they give their love, it usually is for keeps. They don't play with anyone's affections. Love is too important for that. They must be on guard against an aggressive pursuer. If someone makes consistent and obvious advances, Pisces may be too weak to resist. Then they become trapped in a love affair they neither wished nor willed.

Weak Pisces individuals do not really know what they want in romance. They may flee from one affair to another not knowing how to make up their mind. Pisces can be a dreamy lover, fantasizing more about the kind of romance they want but doing little to make it a reality.

When they do find the person of their dreams, they may become possessive and jealous. They may suspect a loved one of infidelity when there really are no grounds for such a belief. Intense jealousy can ruin Pisces emotionally, as well as destroy the relationship.

The romantic Pisces man or woman often has very high ideals. If the right person is behind them, they are bound to go far. They need someone who understands their emotional turbulence and moodiness as well as their great capacity to endure life's ceaseless struggles. Pisces individuals need love, and without it life may seem useless and empty.

Naturally affectionate, Pisces wants a lover who is equally free in expressing affection. These men and women need to be reassured that a loved one really loves them. They need to be complimented, too, to be praised as a lover or as a provider. Flattery is music to Pisces ears.

Oversensitivity and overemotionalism may cause Pisces to end an affair. They may imagine that they have been slighted when that is not the case at all. Strong Pisces guard against becoming a victim of this illusion. They do what they can to keep the romance alive and healthy.

Romance after marriage means a lot to Pisces. Lovemaking should maintain the glow and glamour of the early days. Pisces men and women are very considerate mates and do all they can to see that a partner is comfortable and provided for. Home also means a lot to Pisces. It is a place where they can relax in comfort and be themselves without fear of being taken advantage of.

Romance and the Pisces Woman

Of all the women of the Zodiac, Pisces is the most sensitive and the most loving. She is very giving by nature and does what she can to make those she loves happy and content. Marriage means a lot to her. She is sincere and affectionate. The man who wins her is a lucky fellow.

She is usually interested in a sensitive man, someone who is intelligent and has an understanding and appreciation of the arts. She cannot abide a man who is mean or petty. She likes someone who is expansive and strong, someone she can depend on at all times. She may find it difficult to make up her own mind at times. So it is important for her to have someone who knows what he wants in life, someone she can lean on and ask for advice when she needs it.

Some Pisces women really don't know what they want in a man and may drift from one romance to another. She is a true romantic and may spend her waking hours daydreaming about the kind of love life she would like. But then she may just keep it a dream, afraid to go out and do something about it. She likes her loved one to make a fuss over her, to tell her how lovely and desirable she is. She has to be assured that her man really loves her. Small gifts and compliments keep her spirits up.

The Pisces woman is sensitive and may imagine that someone has insulted her when she has no real reason for thinking so. She can become very jealous at times. If she suspects her lover of being unfaithful, it could mean the end of the relationship. Although her lover may be innocent of the accusation, he may find it impossible to convince his Pisces partner that this is so. The strong Pisces woman acknowledges this weakness and does her best to brush imagined jealousy out of her mind.

She is a good wife and likes taking care of things at home. She may not have much patience for financial accounting, so she can be disdainful of the figures and spend money carelessly or unreasonably.

She loves children and makes a tender and permissive mother. Her tendency is to spoil children. She may give them too much love and attention when a firmer hand is needed. There is always a strong tie between a Pisces mother and her child.

Romance and the Pisces Man

The Pisces man is a romantic. He is sincere in his affections and does not tend to move from one romance to another. He believes in being true to just one woman. He likes an artistic and intelligent woman, someone with whom he can discuss his interests as an equal. He likes a woman who will fuss over him. He likes being flattered even if there is not a grain of truth in what is said. He has to be constantly reassured. He has to have a woman who is kind and considerate, someone who is able to put up with his changing moods.

A woman who has a strong character is well-suited to the Pisces man. He must not have someone who is weaker than himself. He is the kind of a man who has to be in love. Without love, he feels lonely and unwanted. He may try to make up for this by drinking heavily or abusing his health in other ways. However, too strong or forceful a woman may be too much for him. He may find it impossible to avoid her advances and then will cheat with someone he does not really love.

He likes to know where his loved one is every moment of the day. He can be possessive even before marriage. His loved one may find some of his demands excessive at times. Jealousy could easily destroy him and his romance. The wise Pisces man knows how to put foolish thoughts out of his head and to trust the woman he loves when he has no reason to do otherwise.

His love is deep. When he marries and settles down, it's usually for good. He makes a faithful husband. He does what he can to provide for his family. A happy, well-run home is important to him. He does what he can to make his wife and children feel loved and needed. Security is also important to him, and he will always do what he can to keep his home together.

Children love him. He may be too easygoing as a father, letting his children do as they please. It is fine if his wife is a bit firmer in handling the youngsters, for then they have a chance of developing their potential.

Woman—Man

PISCES WOMAN
ARIES MAN

Although it's possible that a Pisces woman could find happiness with a man born under the sign of the Ram, it's uncertain as to how long that happiness would last.

An Aries who has made his mark in the world and is somewhat steadfast in his outlook and attitude could be quite a catch for you. On the other hand, Rams are impulsive and in a hurry. Their industrious mannerisms may fail to impress you, especially if you feel that much of their get-up-and-go often leads nowhere.

When it comes to a fine romance, you want someone with a nice, broad shoulder to lean on. A relationship with someone who doesn't like to stay put for too long can be somewhat upsetting.

Aries may have a little trouble in understanding you, too, at least in the beginning of the relationship. He may find you a bit too shy and moody. Aries men speak their minds frankly. He will not soften his criticism or be diplomatic.

You may find the Aries man too demanding. He may give you the impression that he expects you to be at his constant beck and call. You have a lot of patience at your disposal, and he may try every last bit of it. He is not as thorough as you in everything he does. In order to achieve success or a goal quickly, he will overlook small but important details—then regret it when it is far too late.

Being married to an Aries does not mean that you'll have a secure and safe life as far as finances are concerned. Not all Aries are rash with cash, but they lack the sound head you perhaps have for putting away something for that inevitable rainy day. He'll do his best, however, to see that you're adequately provided for—even though his efforts may leave something to be desired as far as you're concerned.

With an Aries man for a mate, you'll find yourself constantly among people. Aries generally have many friends, and you may not heartily approve of them all. Aries are often more interested in interesting people than they are in influential ones. Although there may be a family squabble from time to time, you are forgiving enough to be able to take it in your stride.

The Aries father is young at heart and will spoil children every chance he gets. His ability to jump fron thing one to another will delight the kids and keep them active. His quick mind and energetic behavior appeal to the young, who will follow his every footstep. Make sure they are not going in too many directions at once.

PISCES WOMAN
TAURUS MAN

Some Taurus men are strong and silent. They do all they can to protect and provide for the women they love. The Taurus man will never let you down. He's steady, sturdy, and reliable. He's pretty honest and practical, too. He says what he means and means what he says. He never indulges in deceit and will always put his cards on the table.

Taurus is a very affectionate man. Being loved, appreciated, and understood is very important for his well-being. Like you, he is also looking for peace and security in life. If you both work toward these goals together, they can be easily attained.

If you should marry a Taurus man, you can be sure that the wolf will never darken your door. They are notoriously good providers, and do everything they can to make their families comfortable and happy.

He'll appreciate the way you have of making a home warm and inviting. Good food, good music, good art are essential ingredients in making your Taurus husband happy at the end of the workday. Although he may be a big lug of a guy, he's fond of gentleness and soft things. If you puff up his pillow and tuck him in at night, he won't complain. He'll eat it up and ask for more.

You probably won't complain about his friends. Taurus tends to seek out friends who are successful or prominent. You admire people, too, who work hard and achieve what they set out for. It helps to reassure your way of life and the way you look at things.

The Taurus man doesn't care too much for change. He's a stay-at-home of the first order. Chances are that the house you move into after you're married will be the house you'll live in for the rest of your life.

Taurus is easy to get along with. It's unlikely that you'll have many quarrels or arguments. Although he'll be gentle and tender with you, your Taurus man is far from being a sensitive type. He's a man's man. Chances are he loves sports from fishing to football. He can be earthy as well as down to earth.

The Taurus father has much affection for the children and has no trouble demonstrating his love and warmth. He does everything he can not to spoil the children. But he can be a disciplinarian when he wants the kids to behave properly. The youngsters will be polite and poised, with a healthy respect for tradition.

PISCES WOMAN
GEMINI MAN

The Gemini man is quite a catch. Many a woman has set her cap for him and failed to bag him. Generally, Gemini men are intelligent, witty, and outgoing. Many of them are versatile with many interests.

On the other hand, some Geminis seem to lack the common sense you set so much store in. Their tendencies to start a half-dozen projects, then toss them up in the air out of boredom, may exasperate you.

One thing that causes a Twin's mind and affection to wander is a bore. But Pisces has as many interests and talents as Gemini. Both of you are double signs, with lots going for you. The Gemini man who has caught your heart will admire you for your ideas and intellect and talents perhaps even more than for your good looks.

A strong-willed woman could easily fill the role of rudder for her Gemini's ship-without-a-sail. The intelligent Gemini is often aware of his shortcomings and doesn't mind if someone with better bearings gives him a shove in the right direction, when it's needed. The average Gemini doesn't have serious ego hang-ups and will even accept a well-deserved chewing out from his mate or lover.

A successful and serious-minded Gemini could make you a very happy woman if you gave him half the chance. Although he may give you the impression that he has a hole in his head, the Gemini man generally has a good head on his shoulders and can make efficient use of it when he wants. Some of them, who have learned the art of being steadfast, have risen to great heights in their professions.

Once you convince yourself that not all people born under the sign of the Twins are witless grasshoppers, you won't mind dating a few—to test your newborn conviction. If you do wind up walking down the aisle with one, accept the fact that married life with him will mean your taking the bitter with the sweet.

Life with a Gemini man can be more fun than a barrel of clowns. You'll never experience a dull moment. Don't leave money matters to him, or you'll both wind up behind the eight ball.

Gemini men are always attractive to the opposite sex. You'll perhaps have to allow him an occasional harmless flirtation. It will seldom amount to more than that.

The Gemini father loves the children so much he usually lets them do what they want. He believes that youngsters should explore the variety of life because experience is the best teacher. He will help to develop the children's logical and verbal skills at an early age. If he overemphasizes the role of reason, you are there to encourage the full emotional development of the youngsters.

PISCES WOMAN
CANCER MAN

The Cancer man may very well be the one after your own heart. You are both water signs who understand the ebb and flow of emotions. Cancer nevertheless is steady and practical, interested in security and a stable relationship.

Despite their seemingly grouchy exterior, men born under the sign of the Crab are sensitive and kind. They are almost always hard workers and are very interested in making successes of themselves in business as well as socially. His conservative outlook on many things often agrees with yours. He'll be a man on whom you can depend come rain or come shine. He'll never shirk his responsibilities as a provider, and he'll always see to it that his wife and family never want.

Your patience will come in handy if you decide it is a Cancer you want for a mate. He isn't the type that rushes headlong into romance. He wants to be as sure about love as you do. If after the first couple of months of dating, he suggests that you take a walk with him down lovers' lane, don't jump to the conclusion that he's about to make his "great play." Chances are he'll only hold your hand and seriously observe the stars. Don't let his coolness fool you, though. Beneath his starched reserve lies a very warm heart. He's just not interested in showing off as far as affection is concerned. Don't think his interest is wandering if he doesn't kiss you goodnight at the front door; that just isn't his style. For him, affection should only be displayed for two sets of eyes—yours and his. He's passionate only in private.

He will never step out of line. He's too much of a gentleman for that. When you're all alone with him and there's no chance of you being disturbed or spied upon, he'll pull out an engagement ring (that used to belong to his grandmother) and slip it on your trembling finger.

Speaking of relatives, you'll have to get pretty much used to the fact that Cancer men are overly fond of their mothers. When he says his mother's the most wonderful woman in the world, you'd better agree with him—that is, if you want to become his wife.

He'll always be a faithful husband. Cancers never pussyfoot around after they've taken that marriage vow. They don't take marriage responsibilities lightly. He'll see to it that everything in the house runs smoothly and that bills are paid promptly—never put aside. He's likely to take all kinds of insurance policies out on his family and property. He'll arrange it so that when retirement time rolls around, you'll both be very well off.

The Cancer father is proud, patient, and protective. But he can be a little too protective. His sheltering instincts can interfere with a youngster's desire to test the waters outside the home. Still, the Cancer father doesn't want to see the kids learning about life from the streets. Your faith in the youngsters' good sense will help allay his fears and allow the children the necessary leeway to explore and learn.

PISCES WOMAN
LEO MAN

To know a man born under the sign of the Lion is not necessarily to love him, even though the temptation may be great. When he fixes most women with his leonine double-whammy, it causes their hearts to pitter-pat and their minds to soar.

You are impressionable enough to be bowled over by a regal strut and a roar. There's no denying that Leo has a way with women. Still, you are no pushover for romantic charm—especially if you feel it's all show, which you quickly see through.

He'll wine you and dine you in the fanciest places. He'll croon to you under the moon and shower you with diamonds if he can get a hold of them. Still, it would be wise to find out just how long that shower is going to last before consenting to be his wife.

Lions in love are hard to ignore, let alone brush off. Your resistance will have a way of nudging him on until he feels he has you completely under his spell. Once mesmerized by this romantic powerhouse, you will most likely find yourself doing things you never dreamed of. Leos can be vain pussycats, needing constant pampering and petting. This may not be your cup of tea exactly. But if you cater to Leo's creativity and sense of theatricality, you'll make him purr.

Although he may be big and magnanimous while trying to win you, he'll caterwaul if he thinks he's not getting the tender love and care he feels is his due. If you keep him well supplied with affection, you can be sure his eyes will never look for someone else and his heart will never wander.

Leo men often tend to be authoritarian. They are bound to lord it over others in one way or another it seems. If he is the top banana at his firm, he'll most likely do everything he can to stay on top. If he's not number one, he's most likely working on it and will be sitting on the throne before long.

You'll have more security than you can use if he is in a position to support you in the manner to which he feels you should be accustomed. He is apt to be too lavish, though, at least by your standards.

You'll always have plenty of friends when you have a Leo for a mate. He's a natural-born wheeler-dealer and entertainer. He just loves to let his hair down at parties.

The Leo father has a tendency to spoil the children, but only up to a point. If the children pay little attention to the rules Leo has set up, he feels neglected and dismissed as a parent. Then he will become the drillmaster and insist that everything go his way. A little of the Pisces compassion will go a long way in keeping the youngsters happy.

PISCES WOMAN
VIRGO MAN
In the astrological scheme of things, Pisces and Virgo are true zodiacal partners—as well as zodiacal opposites. One of you is ruled by emotion, the other by logic.

Although the Virgo man may be a fussbudget at times, his seriousness and common sense will enable you to overlook his tendency to be overly critical and find fault with minor things.

Virgo men are often quiet, respectable types who set great store in conservative behavior and levelheadedness. He'll admire you for your depth and intuition, perhaps even more than for your good looks. He's seldom bowled over by a glamour-puss.

When he gets his courage up, he turns to a serious woman for romance. He'll be far from a Valentino while dating. In fact, you may wind up making all the passes. Once he does get his motor running, however, he can be a warm and wonderful fellow to the right partner.

He's gradual about love. Chances are your romance with him will start out like an ordinary friendship. Once he's sure you're no fly-by-night flirt and have no intention of taking him for a ride, he'll open up and spread sunshine in your heart.

Virgo men tend to marry late in life. He believes in holding out until he's met the right lover. He may not have many names in his little black book; in fact, he may not even have a black book. He's not interested in playing the field, leaving that to men of the more flamboyant signs.

The Virgo man is so particular that he may remain romantically inactive for a long period. His lover has to be perfect or it's no go. If you feel weak-kneed for a Virgo, do your best to convince him that perfection is not so important when it comes to love. Help him to realize that he's missing out on a great deal by not considering the near-perfect or whatever it is you consider yourself to be. With your magical touch, you will enchant him and he'll reciprocate your romantic interest.

The Virgo man is no block of ice. He'll respond to what he feels to be the right feminine flame. Once your love life with a Virgo man starts to bubble, don't give it a chance to fall flat. You may never have a second chance at winning his heart.

If you should ever split with him, forget about patching it up. He'd prefer to let the pieces lie scattered. Once married, though, he'll stay that way—even if it hurts. He's too conscientious to try to back out of a legal deal of any sort.

The Virgo man is as neat as a pin. He's thumbs down on sloppy housekeeping. Keep everything bright, neat, and shiny, and that goes for the children, too.

The Virgo father appreciates good manners and courtesy. He will instill a sense of order in the household and teach the children all about the facts of life. He is usually worried about the kids' health and safety, so he may be strict on occasion. If he sometimes ignores the youngsters' emotional needs, they will turn to you for deep understanding and the healing touch.

PISCES WOMAN
LIBRA MAN

You may find many a Libra man too wrapped up in his own private dreams to be really interesting as far as love and romance are concerned. Quite often, it is difficult to bring him down to earth. It is hard for him to face reality at times.

Although he may be very cautious about weighing both sides of an argument, he may never really come to a reasonable decision about anything. Decision making often makes the Libra man uncomfortable. He'd rather leave that job to someone else. Don't ask him why, for he probably doesn't know himself.

Qualities such as permanence and constancy are important to you in a love relationship. The Libra man may be quite a puzzlement. One moment he comes on hard and strong with declarations of his love; the next moment he's left you like yesterday's mashed potatoes. It does no good to wonder what went wrong. Chances are nothing, really. It's just one of Libra's strange ways.

He is not exactly what you would call an ambitious person. You are perhaps looking for a mate or friend with more drive and fidelity. You are interested in making some headway in the areas that interest you. Libra is often content just to drift along. He does have drive, however, but it's not the long-range, practical kind.

He's interested in material things. He appreciates luxuries and the like, but he may not be willing to work hard enough to obtain them. Beauty and harmony interest him. He'll dedicate a lot of time to arranging things so that they are aesthetically pleasing. It would be difficult to accuse the Libra man of being practical; nine times out of ten, he isn't.

If you do begin a relationship with a Libra man, you will have to coax him now and again to face various situations in a realistic manner. You'll have your hands full, that's for sure. But if you love him, you'll undoubtedly do your best to understand him—no matter how difficult this may be.

If you take up with a Libra man, either temporarily or permanently, you'd better take over the task of managing his money. Often he has little understanding of financial matters. He tends to spend without thinking, following his whims.

The Libra father is patient, gentle, and fair. He can be firm without exercising undue strictness or discipline. Although he can be a harsh judge at times, with the kids he will radiate harmony and tact. Sometimes he is so tactful he may hide a few unpleasant facts of life from them. With your faith in their basic goodness, the children will grow up knowing right from wrong.

PISCES WOMAN
SCORPIO MAN

Some people have a hard time understanding the man born under the sign of Scorpio. Few, however, are able to resist his fiery charm. When angered, he can act like an overturned wasps' nest. His sting can leave an almost permanent mark. If you find yourself interested in the Scorpio man, you'd better learn how to keep on his good side.

Scorpio is straight to the point. He can be as sharp as a razor blade and just as cutting to anyone who crosses him. The Scorpio man can be quite blunt when he chooses. At times, he may seem rather hard-hearted. He can be touchy every now and then, and this is apt to get on your nerves after a while. When you feel like you can't take it anymore, you'd better tiptoe away from the scene rather than chance an explosive confrontation.

If he finds fault with you, he'll let you know. He might misinterpret your patience and think it a sign of indifference. Still you can adapt to almost any sort of relationship or circumstance if you put your heart and mind to it.

Scorpio men are all quite perceptive and intelligent. In some respects, they know how to use their brains more effectively than most. They believe in winning, in whatever they do; second place holds no interest for them. In business, they usually achieve the position they want through drive and use of intellect.

Your interest in home life is not likely to be shared by him. No matter how comfortable you've managed to make the house, it will have very little influence on him with regard to making him aware of his family responsibilities. He does not like to be tied down, generally, and would rather be out on the battlefield of life, belting away at what he feels to be a just and worthy cause. Don't try to keep the homefires burning too brightly while you wait for him to come home from work.

The Scorpio man is passionate in all things, including love. Most women are easily attracted to him, and you are perhaps no exception. Those who allow themselves to be swept off their feet by a Scorpio man soon find that they're dealing with a carton of romantic fireworks. The Scorpio man is intensely sexual and intent on sex.

The Scorpio father likes large families, perhaps because he enjoys the challenge of tapping different talents and abilities in each child. Sometimes, though, he fails to live up to his responsibilities as a parent. When he takes his fatherly duties seriously, he is a powerful teacher. He prepares his youngsters for life's adversities and complexities.

PISCES WOMAN
SAGITTARIUS MAN

The woman who has set her cap for a man born under the sign of Sagittarius may have to apply a lot of strategy before she can get him to drop down on bended knee. Although some Sagittarius may be marriage-shy, they're not ones to skitter away from romance. A high-spirited woman may find a relationship with a Sagittarius— whether a fling or the real thing—a very enjoyable experience.

As a rule, Sagittarius are bright, happy, and healthy. They have a strong sense of fair play. Often they're a source of inspiration to others. They're full of ideas and drive.

You'll be taken by the Archer's infectious grin and his light-hearted, friendly nature. If you do wind up being the woman in his life, he's apt to treat you more like a buddy than the love of his life. It's just his way. Sagittarius are often chummy instead of romantic.

You'll admire his broad-mindedness in most matters, including those of the heart. If, while dating you, he claims that he still wants to play the field, he'll expect you to enjoy the same liberty. Once he's promised to love, honor, and obey, however, he does just that. Marriage for him, once he's taken that big step, is very serious business.

A woman who has a keen imagination and a great love of freedom will not be disappointed if she does tie up with a Sagittarius. The Sagittarius man has a genuine interest in equality. He hates prejudice and injustice.

If he does insist on a night out with the boys, he won't scowl if you decide to let him shift for himself in the kitchen while you pursue your own interests. He believes in fairness.

He's not much of a homebody. Quite often he's occupied with faraway places either in his dreams or in reality. He enjoys, just as you do, being on the go or on the move. He refuses to sit still for long stretches at a time. Humdrum routine—especially at home—bores him. At the drop of a hat, he may ask you to jet off to an exotic location. He likes surprising people.

He'll take great pride in showing you off to his friends. He'll always be a considerate mate. He will never embarrass or disappoint you intentionally. He's very tolerant when it comes to friends, and you'll most likely spend a lot of time entertaining people.

The Sagittarius father will dote on any newborn son or daughter, though he might feel clumsy handling the infant. He usually becomes comfortable with children once they have passed through the baby stage. As soon as the youngsters are old enough to walk and talk, the Sagittarius father encourages each and every sign of talent and skill.

PISCES WOMAN
CAPRICORN MAN

A with-it, hip woman is likely to find the average Capricorn man a bit of a drag. The man born under the sign of the Goat is often a closed person and difficult to get to know. Even if you do get to know him, you may not find him very interesting. In romance, Capricorn men are reserved and cautious. You'll probably have to make all the passes.

You may find his plodding manner irritating and his conservative, traditional ways maddening. He's not one to take chances on anything. If it was good enough for his father, it's good enough for him. He follows a way that is tried and true. Whenever adventure rears its tantalizing head, the Goat will turn the other way; he's interested in safety.

The Capricorn man is very ambitious, but his ways of accomplishing his aims are subterranean or at least seem so. He operates from the background a good deal of the time. At a gathering you may never even notice him, but he's there, taking in everything, sizing everyone up, planning his next careful move.

Although Capricorns may be intellectual and well-educated, it is not the kind of intuitive intelligence you appreciate. He may not be as quick or as deep as you. His understanding from an emotional level may be inhibited.

If you do decide to take up with a man born under this sign, you should be pretty good in the cheering up department. The Capricorn man often acts as though he's constantly being followed by a cloud of gloom.

The Capricorn man is most at ease when in the comfort and privacy of his own home. The security possible within four walls can make him a happy man. He'll spend as much time as he can at home. If he is loaded down with extra work, he'll bring it home instead of working overtime at the office.

You'll most likely be frequently confronted by his relatives. Family is very important to the Capricorn—his family, that is. They better have an important place in your life, too, if you want to keep your home a happy one.

Although his caution in most matters may drive you up the wall, his concerned way with money is justified most of the time. He'll plan everything right down to the last penny.

The Capricorn father is loving and dutiful, although he may not understand the children's carefree ways. He believes there are goals to be achieved, and there is the right way to achieve them. The Capricorn father can be quite a scold when it comes to disciplining the youngsters. Your faith in them and your compassionate manner will ease their growing pains.

PISCES WOMAN
AQUARIUS MAN

You will find the Aquarius man the most broad-minded man you have ever met. On the other hand, you will find him the most impractical. Often he's more of a dreamer than a doer. But you can understand a man whose heart and mind are in the stars and whose head is almost always up in the clouds. Your Aquarius date will surely capture your fancy.

He's no dumbbell; make no mistake about that. He can be busy making some very complicated and idealistic plans when he's got that out-to-lunch look in his eyes. But more than likely, he'll never execute them. He will share all of his progressive ideas with you, and even you may think he's too way-out. But don't go jumping to conclusions. There's a saying that Aquarius are a half-century ahead of everybody else in the thinking department.

If you decide to marry him, you'll find out how right his zany whims are on or about your 50th anniversary. Maybe the waiting will be worth it. Could be that you have an Einstein on your hands—and heart.

Life with an Aquarius won't be one of total despair if you can learn to temper his airiness with your understanding of real life. He won't gripe if you do. Aquarius always maintains an open mind. He'll entertain the ideas and opinions of everybody, though he may not agree with all of them. Don't go tearing your hair out when you find that it's almost impossible to hold a normal conversation with your Aquarius friend at times. Always try to keep in mind that he means well.

His broad-mindedness doesn't stop when it comes to you and your personal freedom. You won't have to give up any of your hobbies or projects after you're married. He'll encourage you to continue in your interests.

He'll be a kind and generous husband. He'll never quibble over petty things. Keep track of the money you both spend. He can't. Money burns a hole in his pocket.

At times, you may feel like calling it quits. Chances are, though, that you'll always give him another chance.

The Aquarius father is a good family man. He can be a fine role model for the children because he sees them as individuals in their own right, not as extensions of himself. Kids love him and vice versa. He'll be as tolerant with them as he is with adults. He understands that youngsters need the freedom to experiment and experience many facets of life.

PISCES WOMAN
PISCES MAN

The Pisces man is a dreamer, a romantic like you. Together you flow through a sea of emotion and idealism. With mutual understanding and quiet acceptance, you can love each other from near or far. You are both believers.

The Pisces man is easygoing and seems to take things in stride. He'll entertain all kinds of views and opinions from anyone, and give the impression that he's with them one hundred percent while that may not be the case at all. His attitude may be why bother when he's confronted with someone who stubbornly holds on to a wrong idea. The Pisces man will seldom speak his mind if he thinks he'll be rigidly opposed.

The Pisces man is oversensitive at times. He's afraid his feelings will be hurt. He'll sometimes imagine a personal affront when none's been made. You know better than most how a sense of inadequacy, an inferiority complex can wreck true love. You can share the escapism for a while. Then you will bring him back to face reality.

One thing you'll admire is his concern for people who are sickly or troubled. He'll make his shoulder available to anyone in the mood for a good cry. He can listen to one hard-luck story after another without seeming to tire. When his advice is asked, he is capable of coming across with some words of wisdom. He often knows what is bothering someone before that person is aware of it. It's almost intuitive with Pisces.

Still, at the end of the day, this man will want some peace and quiet. If you've got a problem when he comes home, don't unload it in his lap. If you do, you will find him short-tempered. He's a good listener but he can only take so much.

Pisces are not aimless although they may seem so at times. The positive Pisces man is quite often successful in his profession and is likely to wind up rich and influential. Material gain, however, is never a direct goal for Pisces. The weaker Pisces are usually content to stay on the level where they find themselves. They won't complain too much if the roof leaks or if the fence is in need of repair.

The Pisces father truly believes in live and let live, so he is immensely popular with children of all ages. For youngsters Pisces plays the double role of confidant and playmate. It will never enter his mind to discipline a child, no matter how spoiled or incorrigible that child becomes.

Man—Woman

PISCES MAN
ARIES WOMAN

The Aries woman may be a little too bossy and busy for you. Aries are ambitious creatures. They can become impatient with people who are more thorough and deliberate than they are, especially if they feel they're taking too much time.

The Aries woman is a fast worker. Sometimes she's so fast she forgets to look where she's going. When she stumbles or falls, it would be nice if you were there to catch her. Aries are proud women. They don't like to be criticized when they err. Tongue lashings can turn them into blocks of ice. Don't think that the Aries woman frequently gets tripped up in her plans. She is capable of taking aim and hitting the bull's-eye. You'll be flabbergasted at times by her accuracy as well as by her ambition. On the other hand, you're apt to spot a flaw in your Aries plans before she does.

You are perhaps somewhat slower than Aries in attaining your goals. Still, you are not apt to make mistakes along the way. You're almost always well-prepared.

The Aries woman can be sensitive at times. She likes gentleness and respect. Let her know that you love her for her brains as well as for her good looks. Never give her cause to become jealous. When your Aries date sees green, you'd better forget about sharing a rosy future together. Treat her with tender loving care, and she's yours.

The Aries woman can be giving if she feels her partner is deserving. She is no iceberg; she responds to the proper masculine flame. She needs a man she can look up to and feel proud of. If the shoe fits, put it on. If not, quietly tiptoe out of her sight. She can cause you plenty of heartache if you've made up your mind about her but she hasn't made up hers about you.

Aries women are very demanding at times. Some of them tend to be high-strung. They can be difficult if they feel their independence is being hampered.

The cultivated Aries woman makes a wonderful homemaker and hostess. You'll find she's very clever in decorating and using color. Your house will be tastefully furnished and will radiate harmony. The Aries wife knows how to make guests feel at home.

Although the Aries mother may not be keen on burdensome responsibilities, she is fond of children and the joy they bring. She is skilled at juggling both career and motherhood, so her kids will never feel that she is an absentee parent. In fact, as the youngsters grow older, they might want a little more of the freedom that is so important to her.

PISCES MAN
TAURUS WOMAN

A Taurus woman could perhaps understand you better than most women. She is very considerate and loving. She is thorough and methodical in whatever she does. She knows how to take her time in doing things because she is anxious to avoid mistakes. She is a careful person. She never skips over things even if they seem unimportant. She goes over everything with a fine-tooth comb.

Home is very important to the Taurus woman. She is an excellent homemaker. Although your home may not be a palace, it will become, under her care, a comfortable and happy abode. She'll love it when friends drop by for the evening. She is a good cook and enjoys feeding people well. No one will ever go away from your house with an empty stomach.

The Taurus woman is serious about love and affection. When she has taken a tumble for someone, she'll stay by him—for good, if possible. She will try to be practical in romance, to some extent. When she sets her cap for a man, she keeps after him.

The Taurus woman is a passionate and sensuous lover, though she may appear otherwise at first glance. She is on the lookout for someone who can return her affection fully. Taurus are sometimes given to fits of jealousy and possessiveness. They expect fair play in the area of marriage. When it doesn't come about, they can be bitingly sarcastic and mean.

The Taurus woman is generally easygoing. She's fond of keeping peace. She won't argue unless she has to. She'll do her best to keep your love relationship on an even keel.

Marriage is generally a one-time thing for Taurus. Once they've made the serious step, they seldom try to back out of it. Marriage is for keeps. They are fond of love and warmth. With the right man, they turn out to be ideal wives.

The Taurus mother seldom puts up with nonsense from her children. She is not so much strict as concerned. She wants her children to be well-behaved and dutiful. Nothing pleases a Taurus mother more than a compliment from a neighbor or teacher about her child's behavior. Although some children may inwardly resent the iron hand of a Taurus mother, in later life they are often thankful that they were brought up in such an orderly and conscientious way.

PISCES MAN
GEMINI WOMAN

You may find a romance with a woman born under the sign of the Twins a many-splendored thing. In her you can find the intellectual companionship you often look for in a friend or mate. A Gemini woman can appreciate your aims and desires because she travels pretty much the same road as you do intellectually. She may share your interests but she will lack your emotional understanding.

She suffers from itchy feet. She can be here, there, all over the place and at the same time, or so it would seem. Her eagerness to be on the move may make you dizzy. Still, you'll enjoy and appreciate her liveliness and mental agility.

Geminis often have sparkling personalities. You'll be attracted by her warmth and grace. While she's on your arm, you'll probably notice that many male eyes are drawn to her. She may even return a gaze or two, but don't let that worry you. All Geminis have nothing against a harmless flirt once in a while. They enjoy this sort of attention. If she feels she is already spoken for, however, she will never let it get out of hand.

Although she may not be as handy as you'd like in the kitchen, you'll never go hungry for a filling and tasty meal. Gemini is always in a rush. She won't feel like she's cheating by breaking out the instant mashed potatoes or the frozen peas. She may not spend much time cooking, but she is clever. With a dash of this and a suggestion of that, she can make an impromptu dinner taste like a gourmet meal. Maybe you've struck it rich and have a Gemini lover who finds complicated recipes a challenge to her intellect. If so, you'll find every meal a tantalizing and mouth-watering surprise.

When you're beating your brains out over a tough crossword puzzle and find yourself stuck, just ask your Gemini. She'll give you all the right answers without batting an eyelash.

Like you, she loves all kinds of people. You may even find that you're a bit more particular than she. Often all that a Gemini requires is that her friends be interesting—and stay interesting. One thing she's not able to abide is a dullard.

Leave the party organizing to your Gemini sweetheart or mate, and you'll never have a chance to know what a dull moment is. She'll bring out the swinger in you if you give her half the chance.

A Gemini mother enjoys her children, and her love is communicated to them in a variety of ways. Like the kids, she is often restless, adventurous, and easily bored. She will never complain about their fleeting interests because she understands the changes they will go through as they mature.

PISCES MAN
CANCER WOMAN

The Cancer woman needs to be protected from the cold, cruel world. She'll love you for your masculine, yet gentle manner; you make her feel safe and secure. You don't have to pull any he-man or heroic stunts to win her heart; that's not what interests her. She's more likely to be impressed by your romantic idealism, the way you make her feel that she's the only girl in the world. When she's feeling glum, you have the knack of saying just the right thing. You know how to calm her fears, no matter how silly some of them may seem.

The Cancer woman has her ups and downs. You have a talent for smoothing out the ruffles in her sea of life. She'll most likely worship the ground you walk on or put you on a terribly high pedestal. Don't disappoint her if you can help it. She'll never disappoint you.

She will take great pleasure in devoting the rest of her natural life to you. She'll darn your socks, mend your overalls, scrub floors, wash windows, shop, cook, and do just about anything short of murder in order to please you and to let you know that she loves you. Sounds like that legendary good old-fashioned girl, doesn't it? Contrary to popular belief, there are still a good number of them around—and many of them are Cancers.

There's one thing you should be warned about: never be unkind to your mother-in-law. It will be the only golden rule your Cancer wife will probably expect you to live up to. No mother-in-law jokes please; they'll go over like a lead balloon. Mother is special to Cancer, so treat your mother-in-law like she's one of the landed gentry. Sometimes this may be difficult to swallow, but if you want to keep your home together and your wife happy, you'd better learn to grin and bear it.

Treat your Cancer wife like a queen, and she'll treat you like a king.

Of all the signs of the Zodiac, Cancer women are the most maternal. In caring for and bringing up children, they know just how to combine the right amount of tenderness with the proper dash of discipline. A child couldn't ask for a better mother. The Cancer mother is sympathetic, affectionate, and patient with her children.

PISCES MAN
LEO WOMAN

The Leo woman can make most men roar like lions. If any woman in the Zodiac has that indefinable something that can make men lose their heads and find their hearts, it's the Leo woman.

She's got more than a fair share of charm and glamour. She knows how to make the most of her assets, especially when she's in the company of the opposite sex. Jealous men are apt to lose their cool or their sanity when trying to woo a woman born under the sign of the Lion.

She likes to kick up her heels and doesn't care who knows it. She often makes heads turn and tongues wag. You don't have to believe any of what you hear. It's most likely jealous gossip or wishful thinking. Needless to say, other women in her vicinity turn green with envy and will try anything in order to put her out of the running.

Although this vamp makes the blood rush to your head and makes you momentarily forget all the things you thought were important and necessary in your life, you may feel differently when you come back down to earth and the stars are out of your eyes. You may feel that she isn't the kind of girl you planned to marry. Although the Leo woman may do her best to be a good wife for you, chances are she'll fall short of your idea of what a good wife should be like.

If the Leo woman has you flipping your lid, you'd better be financially equipped for some very expensive dating. Be prepared to shower her with expensive gifts and to take her dining and dancing to the smartest spots in town. Promise her the moon if you're in a position to go that far. Luxury and glamour are two things that are bound to lower a Leo's resistance. She's got expensive tastes, and you'd better cater to them if you expect to get to first base.

If you've got an important business deal to clinch and you have doubts as to whether you can swing it or not, bring your Leo lover along to the business luncheon. Chances are that with her on your arm, you'll be able to win any business battle with both hands tied. She won't have to say or do anything—just being there at your side is enough. The grouchiest oil magnate can be transformed into a gushing, obedient schoolboy if there's a charming Leo woman in the room.

The Leo mother is sometimes blind to the faults of her children.

She can spoil them no end. But when she wants them to learn something or follow her rules, she can be a strict yet patient teacher. Easygoing and friendly, the Leo mother loves to pal around with the kids while proudly showing them off.

PISCES MAN
VIRGO WOMAN

Although Virgo is your zodiacal partner as well as your zodiacal opposite, you may at first be more aware of the differences between you—the opposites that sharply contrast. The Virgo woman may be difficult for you to understand. She is mysterious. Even when you think you know her, don't bet on it.

She is capable of keeping things hidden in the recesses of her soul—things she'll only release when she's sure you're the man she's been looking for. It may take her some time to come to this decision. Virgos are finicky about almost everything. Everything has to be letter-perfect before they're satisfied. Many of them believe that the only people who can do things right are Virgos.

Nothing offends a Virgo woman more than slovenly dress, sloppy character, or a careless display of affection. Make sure your tie is not crooked and your shoes sport a bright shine before you go calling on this lady. Take her arm when crossing the street. Don't rush the romance. Trying to corner her in the back of a cab may be one way of striking out. Never criticize the way she looks. In fact, the best policy would be to agree with her as much as possible.

Still, there's just so much a man can take; all those dos and don'ts you'll have to observe if you want to get to first base with a Virgo may be just a little too much to ask of you. After a few dates, you may come to the conclusion that she just isn't worth all that trouble. However, the Virgo woman is mysterious enough to keep her men running back for more. Chances are you'll be intrigued by her airs and graces.

If lovemaking means a lot to you, you'll be disappointed at first in the cool ways of your Virgo lover. However, under her glacial facade there lies a hot cauldron of seething excitement. If you're patient and artful in your romantic approach, you'll find that all that caution was well worth the trouble. When Virgos love, they don't stint. It's all or nothing as far as they're concerned. Once they're convinced that they love you, they go all the way, tossing all cares to the wind.

One thing a Virgo woman can't stand in love is hypocrisy. She doesn't give a hoot what the neighbors say. If her heart tells her to go ahead, she listens. Virgo is very concerned with human truths. So if her heart stumbles on another fancy, she will be true to the new heartthrob and leave you standing in the rain. She's honest to her heart and will be as true to you as you are with her. Do her wrong once, however, and it's farewell.

The Virgo mother has high expectations for her children, and she will strive to bring out the very best in them. She is more tender than strict, so she might nag rather than discipline. But Pisces-Virgo parents maintain unconditional love for the youngsters, who will develop outstanding traits in an environment of faith and encouragement.

PISCES MAN
LIBRA WOMAN

Libra invented the notion that it's a woman's prerogative to change her mind. Libra's changeability, in spite of its undeniable charm, could actually drive even a man of your patience up the wall. She's capable of smothering you with love and kisses one day, and the next avoid you like the plague.

If you have unlimited faith and endurance, then perhaps you can tolerate her sometime-ness without suffering too much. However, if you own up to the fact that you're a mere mortal who can only take so much, then you'd better fasten your attention on a woman who's somewhat more constant.

But don't get the wrong idea. A love affair with a Libra is not bad at all. In fact, it can have a lot of pluses to it. Libra women are soft, very feminine, and warm. She doesn't have to vamp all over the place in order to gain a man's attention. Her delicate presence is enough to warm any man's heart. One smile and you're putty in her hand.

She can be fluffy and affectionate and gracious. On the other hand, her indecision about which dress to wear, what to cook for dinner, or whether to redecorate could make you tear your hair out. What will perhaps be more exasperating is her flat denial of the accusation that she cannot make even the simplest decision. The trouble is that she wants to be fair or just in all matters. She'll spend hours weighing pros and cons. Don't make her rush into a decision; that will only irritate her.

The Libra woman likes to be surrounded by beautiful things. Money is no object when beauty is concerned. There will always be plenty of flowers in the house. She'll know how to arrange them tastefully, too. Libra women are fond of stylish clothes and fine furnishings, especially antiques. They will run up bills without batting an eye if given the chance.

Once she's cottoned to you, the Libra woman will do everything in her power to make you happy. She'll wait on you hand and foot when you're sick and bring you breakfast in bed on Sundays. She'll be very thoughtful and devoted. If anyone dares suggest you're not the grandest man in the world, your Libra wife will give that person a good sounding-out.

The Libra mother works wonders with children. She is sensitive and intuitive, understanding what a child needs. Gentle persuasion and affection are qualities that work in bringing up the children. Her youngsters will never lack for anything that could make their lives easier and richer.

PISCES MAN
SCORPIO WOMAN

When the Scorpio woman chooses to be sweet, all's right with the world. When her temper flies, so will everything else that isn't bolted down. She can be as hot as a tamale or as cool as a cucumber when she wants. Whatever mood she's in, you can be sure it's for real. She doesn't believe in poses or hypocrisy.

The Scorpio woman is often seductive and sultry. Her femme fatale charm can pierce through the hardest of hearts like a laser ray. She doesn't have to look like Mata Hari (many of them resemble the tomboy next door), but once you've looked into those tantalizing eyes, you're a goner.

The Scorpio woman can be a whirlwind of passion. Life with her will not be all smiles and smooth sailing. If you think you can handle a spitfire, then try your luck. Your deeply compassionate nature will most likely have a calming effect on her. You're the kind of man she can trust and rely on. But never cross her, even on the smallest thing. If you do, you'd better tell Fido to make room for you in the doghouse; you'll be his guest for the next couple of days.

Generally, the Scorpio woman will keep family battles within the walls of your home. When company visits, she's apt to give the impression that married life with you is one big joyride. It's just her way of expressing her loyalty to you, at least in front of others. She believes that family matters are and should stay private. She'll certainly see to it that others have a high opinion of you both. She'll be right behind you whatever it is you want to do.

Although she's an individualist, after she has married, she'll put her own interests aside for those of the man she loves. With a woman like this behind you, you can't help but go far. She'll never try to take over your role as boss of the family. She'll give you all the support you need in order to fulfill that role. She won't complain if the going gets rough. She is a courageous woman. She's as anxious as you to find that place in the sun for you both.

The Scorpio mother will not spoil the children or put them on a pedestal. Protective and encouraging, she is eager to see them develop their various talents. What she lacks in overt affection she makes up for in devotion. Under her skillful guidance the youngsters will learn how to cope with life's extremes. She'll teach the children to be courageous and steadfast.

PISCES MAN
SAGITTARIUS WOMAN

You'll most likely never come across a more good-natured woman than the one born under the sign of Sagittarius. She is full of bounce and good cheer. Her sunny disposition seems almost permanent and can be relied upon even on the rainiest of days.

Sagittarius women are almost never malicious. If ever they seem to be, it is unintentional. Archers are often a little short on tact and say literally anything that comes into their heads, no matter what the occasion. Sometimes the words that tumble out of their mouths seem downright cutting and cruel. Still, no matter what she says, she means well. The Sagittarius woman is quite capable of losing some of her friends—and perhaps even some of yours—through a careless slip of the lip.

On the other hand, you will appreciate her honesty and good intentions. To you, qualities of this sort play an important part in life. With a little patience and practice, you can probably help cure your Sagittarius of her loose tongue and blunt speech. She'll give in to your better judgment and try to follow your advice.

Chances are, she'll be the outdoor-type of partner. Long hikes, fishing trips, and white-water canoeing will most likely appeal to her. She's a busy person; no one could ever call her a slouch. She sets great store in mobility. She won't sit still for one minute if she doesn't have to.

She is great company most of the time and, generally, lots of fun. Even if your buddies drop by for poker and beer, she won't have any trouble fitting in.

On the whole, she is a very kind and sympathetic woman. If she feels she's made a mistake, she'll be the first to call your attention to it. She's not afraid to own up to her own faults and shortcomings.

After she's seen how upset her shortsightedness has made you, she'll do her best to straighten up.

The Sagittarius woman is not the kind who will pry into your business affairs. But she'll always be there, ready to offer advice if you need it.

The Sagittarius woman is seldom suspicious. Your word will almost always be good enough for her.

The Sagittarius mother is a wonderful and loving friend to her children. She will consistently encourage them in their studies and sports. With her enthusiasm for knowledge, and your faith in the future, the children will grow up to be eager, adventurous young adults.

PISCES MAN
CAPRICORN WOMAN

The Capricorn woman may not be the most romantic of the Zodiac, but she's far from frigid when she meets the right man. She believes in true love. She doesn't appreciate getting involved in flings. To her, they're just a waste of time. She's looking for a man who means business—in life as well as in love.

Although she can be very affectionate with her boyfriend or mate, she tends to let her head govern her heart. That is not to say she is a cool, calculating cucumber. On the contrary, she just feels she can be more honest about love if she consults her brain first. She wants to size up the situation before throwing her heart in the ring. She wants to make sure it won't get stepped on.

The Capricorn woman is faithful, dependable, and systematic in just about everything she undertakes. She is quite concerned with security and sees to it that every penny she spends is spent wisely. She is very economical about using her time, too. She does not believe in whittling away her energy on a scheme that is bound not to pay off.

Ambitious themselves, Capricorns are quite often attracted to ambitious men, men who are interested in getting somewhere in life. If a man of this sort wins her heart, she'll stick by him and do all she can to help him get to the top.

The Capricorn woman is almost always diplomatic. She makes an excellent hostess. She can be very influential when your business acquaintances come to dinner.

The Capricorn woman is likely to be very concerned, if not downright proud, about her family tree. Relatives are important to her, particularly if they're socially prominent. Never say a cross word about her family members. That can really go against her grain, and she'll punish you by not talking to you for days.

She's generally thorough in whatever she does: handling a career, homemaking, and generally being successful in both. Capricorn women are well-mannered and gracious, no matter what their backgrounds. They excel at entertaining whether as a guest or a hostess. They have it in their natures always to behave properly. They have a built-in sense of what is right.

If you should marry a Capricorn woman, you need never worry about her going on a wild shopping spree. She understands the value of money better than most women. If you turn over your paycheck to her at the end of the week, you can be sure that a good hunk of it will wind up in the bank.

The Capricorn mother is very ambitious for her children. She wants them to have every advantage and to benefit from things she perhaps lacked as a child. She is loving and correct. She will teach her youngsters to respect the family and to build honorable codes of conduct. She will prepare children to take their place in society.

PISCES MAN
AQUARIUS WOMAN

If you fall head over heels for a woman born under the sign of the Water Bearer, you'd better fasten your safety belt. It may take you quite a while to actually discover what she is like. Even then, you may have nothing to go on but a string of vague hunches. The Aquarius female is like a rainbow, full of bright and shining hues. There is something elusive about her, something difficult to put your finger on.

The Aquarius woman can be odd and eccentric at times. Some say this is the source of her mysterious charm. You will appreciate her idealism and you will share many of her dreams. But you may be bewildered by her unpredictability.

Aquarius women by nature are unpredictable and often unconventional. They have their own ideas about how the world should be run. Chances are they're a bit too progressive. It is said that the way Aquarius thinks, so will the world in 50 years.

If you find that she's too much mystery and charm for you to handle, just talk it out with her and say that you think it would be better to call it quits. She'll most likely want to remain friends. Aquarius women are like that. Perhaps you'll both find it easier to get along in a friendship than in a romance.

It is not difficult for her to remain buddy-buddy with an ex-lover. For Aquarius people, the line between friendship and romance is a fuzzy one.

She is not a jealous person. While you're romancing her, she won't expect you to be, either. You'll find her a free spirit most of the time. Just when you think you know her inside out, you'll discover that you don't really know her at all.

She's a very sympathetic and warm person. She is often helpful to those in need of assistance and advice. She'll most likely be the most tolerant and open-minded woman you've ever encountered.

She'll seldom be suspicious, even when she has every right to be. If the man she loves makes a little slip, she's likely to forgive it and forget it.

The Aquarius mother is generous and seldom refuses her children anything. Her open-minded attitude is easily transmitted to the youngsters. They have every chance of growing up to be tolerant, kind individuals who can cope with life's complexities.

PISCES MAN
PISCES WOMAN

Many a man dreams of an alluring Pisces woman. As a Pisces your-self, you delight in joining your emotions with another whose feel-ings run as deep as yours. If one of you is strong and decisive enough to cope with the everyday realities, you can be happy together for a long time.

The Pisces woman will let you be the brains of the family. She will, though, play a behind-the-scenes role in order to help you achieve your goals. The illusion that you are the master of the household is the kind of magic the Pisces woman is adept at creating.

She can be very ladylike and proper. Your business associates and friends will be dazzled by her warmth and femininity. Although she's a charmer, there is a lot more to her than just a pretty exterior. There is a brain ticking away behind that soft, womanly facade. You may never become aware of it—until you're married to her. It's no cause for alarm. She'll never use it against you, only to help you and possibly set you on a more successful path.

If she feels you're botching up your married life through careless behavior or if she feels you could be earning more money than you do, she'll tell you about it. But any wife would, really. She will never try to usurp your position as head and breadwinner of the family.

No one had better dare say one uncomplimentary word about you in her presence. It's likely to cause her to break into tears. Pisces women are usually very sensitive beings. Their reaction to adversity, frustration, or anger is just a plain, good, old-fashioned cry. They can weep buckets when inclined.

She can do wonders with a house. She is very fond of dramatic and beautiful things. There will always be plenty of fresh-cut flowers around the house. She will choose charming artwork and antiques, if they are affordable. She'll see to it that the house is decorated in a dazzling yet welcoming style.

She'll have an extra special dinner prepared for you when you come home from an important business meeting. Don't dwell on the boring details of the meeting, though. But if you need that grand vision, the big idea, to seal a contract or make a conquest, your Pisces woman is sure to confide a secret that will guarantee your success. She is canny and shrewd with money, and once you are on her wavelength you can manage the intricacies on your own.

Treat her with tenderness and generosity and your relationship will be an enjoyable one. She's most likely fond of chocolates. A bunch of beautiful flowers will never fail to make her eyes light up. See to it that you never forget her birthday or your anniversary. These things are very important to her.

If you are patient and kind, you can keep a Pisces woman happy for a lifetime. She, however, is not without her faults. Her sensitivity may get on your nerves after a while. You may find her lacking in practicality and good old-fashioned stoicism. You may even feel that she uses her tears as a method of getting her own way.

The Pisces mother totally believes in her children, and her faith never wavers. Her unconditional love for them makes her a strong, self-sacrificing mother who can deny herself in order to fulfill their needs. She will teach youngsters the value of service to the community while not letting them lose their individuality.

PISCES
LUCKY NUMBERS 2010

Lucky numbers and astrology can be linked through the movements of the Moon. Each phase of the thirteen Moon cycles vibrates with a sequence of numbers for your Sign of the Zodiac over the course of the year. Using your lucky numbers is a fun system that connects you with tradition.

New Moon	First Quarter	Full Moon	Last Quarter
Dec. 15 ('09)	Dec. 24 ('09)	Dec. 31 ('09)	Jan. 7
3 6 8 1	1 0 5 0	1 8 9 3	3 9 8 2
Jan. 15	Jan. 23	Jan. 30	Feb. 5
4 9 8 7	9 9 2 6	7 4 5 3	1 8 5 1
Feb. 13	Feb. 21	Feb. 28	March 7
1 4 7 3	3 9 5 4	7 8 6 4	2 8 7 9
March 15	March 23	March 29	April 6
9 9 1 3	2 6 0 9	1 9 8 6	4 1 0 9
April 14	April 21	April 28	May 5
3 3 5 7	2 6 2 5	6 5 3 9	7 7 6 9
May 13	May 20	May 27	June 4
2 5 4 8	3 0 7 6	4 2 9 6	5 5 8 1
June 12	June 18	June 26	July 4
3 7 7 2	5 0 6 4	8 6 3 2	5 5 7 9
July 11	July 18	July 25	August 3
4 2 8 2	3 0 8 5	5 2 1 9	4 6 8 3
August 9	August 16	August 24	Sept. 1
7 6 1 2	9 7 5 2	1 5 8 0	3 7 2 5
Sept. 8	Sept. 15	Sept. 23	Sept. 30
5 0 6 4	4 2 9 6	5 9 2 4	8 3 6 7
Oct. 7	Oct. 14	Oct. 22	Oct. 30
1 1 5 3	9 1 7 6	9 2 5 7	2 6 9 1
Nov. 6	Nov. 13	Nov. 21	Nov. 28
8 8 6 4	0 1 9 3	5 5 7 5	9 3 4 2
Dec. 5	Dec. 13	Dec. 21	Dec. 27
9 6 7 4	3 3 6 8	0 5 9 5	1 9 7 5

PISCES
YEARLY FORECAST 2010

Forecast for 2010 Concerning Business
and Financial Affairs, Job Prospects,
Travel, Health, Romance and Marriage
for Persons Born with the Sun
in the Zodiacal Sign of Pisces.
February 19–March 20

For those born under the influence of the Sun in the zodiacal sign of Pisces, ruled by Jupiter, planet of faith and hope, and also by inspirational Neptune, 2010 promises to be a year of growth, good fortune and personal achievement if effort is applied. With expansion as a theme, discipline and self-control will also be required. The accent is on financial stability throughout 2010. Learning the art of money management and remaining focused on goals are the lessons and rewards of the coming year.

As 2010 begins, more energy will be exerted than received. That is because both your rulers, Jupiter and Neptune, reside in Aquarius, your twelfth house of secrets, limitations, and private matters. On January 17 Jupiter moves to your sign of Pisces, lighting up your first house. Then from June 6 to September 8 Jupiter will be in Aries, your second house of money. From then through year's end Jupiter will be back in your sign and your first house. Jupiter in Pisces is a lucky position, and growth in many areas of your life should be experienced. Most impacted will be your personality and physical body. You can expect an influx of vim and vitality. But moderation will be the key for success or for downfall. If willpower is lacking, it may be more difficult to stay within limits. Unless vigilance is applied, self-indulgent tendencies may increase and so will your waistline. As your physical energies ebb and flow, you need to withdraw and take time out for rest, relaxation, and solitude.

Venus begins the year in Capricorn and your solar eleventh house of friends, hopes, and wishes. Pluto, Mercury, and the Sun also reside in Capricorn at the outset of 2010. Creative urges and imagination remain strong, but a desire to launch into artistic ventures could be squashed by obligations to family and life circumstances. For some Pisces involvement with groups and associations as well as with friends could become an emotional lifeline. Some group members might take the place of absent or detached family members. The wider community may also draw you away from family. Finding a balance between work, family, and external involvements may be difficult to achieve. Because so much time and energy could go into a variety of activities, the attached Pisces might have to work harder making quality time for your partner.

The desire to succeed is accentuated because all year Pluto transits Capricorn, your house of friends and long-term goals. Issues regarding friends could come to a head, and there will be people moving in and out of your friendship circle during 2010. Career changes could be implemented as your ambitions rise and your life purpose becomes clearer. You may be put in touch with folks who become helpful contacts in the future. The self-employed Pisces could find that you are now in a stronger position of power, more assertive, and ready to steadily focus on life goals.

Pisces folks can expect a roller coaster of a ride over the next few years with money matters. Higher paid employment, a promotion, or a new business venture are potential events that will make your bank balance grow. But savings could be tapped if income dips due to changes in working hours or cutbacks on overtime. Some Pisces may take maternity leave or go on a long vacation without pay. It will be essential to maintain a regular savings plan to cover the highs and lows of income flow throughout 2010.

Uranus has been transiting your sign of Pisces for several years. April 28 Uranus will move into Aries, your house of money matters and self-worth. So look for changes in finances and the generation of income from this time onward. Uranus is the planet of unexpected and chaotic occurrences, and will make a big impact on your financial situation. You will need to view long-range financial goals in a different light. This Uranus transit will make sure that you are not complacent about your money and your material possessions. Pisces on a limited income should endeavor to curb impulsive purchases and to conserve resources while there is any uncertainty surrounding your cash flow. On June 7 energetic planet Mars moves into Virgo, your partnership house, and money matters should become more manageable then.

All year taskmaster Saturn is in Libra, your solar eighth house of joint assets and of a partner's income. Hiring a professional to provide guidance with money management could be worthwhile. Joint funds, investments, and your credit limits could be a concern. If you are someone who doesn't handle financial details efficiently, obtain the services of a bookkeeper or accountant to do the books, file taxes, and minimize your liabilities. Problems with debt could occur unless a responsible approach to fiscal security is maintained. Be careful with credit cards. Invest in low-risk areas. Make sure health, home, and vehicle insurance is kept current. The purchase of real estate is a likely scenario for some Pisces, a good way to build a financial nest egg as long as mortgage payments are affordable. Be very careful with renovations of living quarters, and don't overvalue your property.

Ties to professional partners can be strengthened if that is what you want. Arrangements that are no longer serving a purpose might need to be dissolved. Changes that occur could push you to examine where you are heading. Pisces who haven't made a will should attend to this task. Pisces in business are advised to avoid extravagance and seek good advice. Speculation in the stock market or in games of chance shouldn't play a large part in your financial strategies throughout 2010. From early October until mid-November, business Pisces might have extra worries or delays with financial payments as well as issues around import and export of goods, travel, or legal proceedings.

As far as your health goes, this shouldn't be a very testing year as long as you are careful with personal safety. Mighty Mars begins the year in Leo, your sixth house of health, service, and work, and remains in Leo until mid-June. Mars here charges up daily activities, making you raring to go. This is an excellent time to get physical, burn up the calories, and dispel hidden frustration and stress. Changing long-standing bad habits and negative patterns of behavior can also be more successful at this time. This Mars transit can be a potentially exhausting period, with deadlines to meet and people making more demands on your time. If you are working harder and staying on the job longer, it is essential to add downtime to your schedule and to pace activities to avoid burnout. In early August and again in early December Mars forms patterns with planets that can increase the chances of accidents and injuries. So be extra cautious. Falls, burns, or electrical shocks can be avoided if you are alert. An innovative approach to your health care and fitness regime can work wonders. Consider taking courses in self-improvement. Continue to upgrade all your skills and expertise for maximum fulfillment.

Travel abroad for business, study, or vacation is foreseen in the autumn months. A holiday romance could become quite serious. If money is tighter than usual, July is a month when the self-employed Pisces should proceed with care taking trips for business expansions or viewing commercial real estate for purchase. Vacations taken near water are very beneficial. Massage, meditation, dance, and music can be a revitalizing energy source for Pisces. Soothing hobbies and pastimes can also recharge run-down batteries. Spending leisure periods with loved ones can also increase emotional comfort. Those of you who have been through a rocky patch in a committed union could find that more time together helps to put the zing back into your relationship.

For the solo Pisces there will be numerous occasions to fall in love, to find a partner, and to enter a committed union. Seeking adventure, taking risks, and exploring avenues through groups and affiliated associations can also lead to promising romantic encounters. Expect an increase in parties and celebrations. Some of you may receive an unexpected wedding proposal. Expansion of the family circle is also likely. The arrival of a baby will be a happy occasion for many Fish. From June 6 to September 8 while Jupiter is in Aries, your personal money house, spending will be an immense source of pleasure. It will be terrific if you can afford to splurge but not so fine if you are on a strict budget or limited income. Because you won't want to deprive yourself or family of the goodies in life, the challenge is to avoid running up debt.

The message from your two rulers is clear this year. Learning to distinguish between what you want and what you need will be a test throughout 2010. With coruler Jupiter expect hefty expenses. Conversely, an improvement in income is foreseen as well as more luck with money matters. Coruler Neptune is the other key player in the life of a Pisces. Throughout 2010 Neptune continues the journey through Aquarius, your twelfth house of spiritual inclinations, secrets, and solitude. If you are in an established union, steer clear of becoming involved in a romantic fling, as you are bound to be caught out. Your ability to tap into creative, intuitive, and healing abilities remains enhanced. This is a year to open yourself up to who you really are and what it is you really want.

Pisces, you can be conservative and realistic while still looking toward the future with faith and optimism. With courage and persistence to obtain cherished goals and dreams, the chances of success are greatly enhanced.

PISCES
DAILY FORECAST

January–December 2010

JANUARY

1. FRIDAY. Happy New Year! The party is likely to continue for the social Fish as 2010 dawns. Having fun, spreading joy, and spending time with loved ones and children can occupy much of your day. With the Cancer Moon touring your house of pleasure, leisure, and treasure, take advantage of the time to do whatever gives you the most happiness. Although you may have big plans in mind for the coming year, it would be wise to put these on the back burner for a few more days and enjoy the holiday period, especially while Mercury remains in retrograde motion. Wind down activities by early evening and have an early night to avoid the possibility of dramatics spoiling your good mood.

2. SATURDAY. Unsettled. If work is not on your agenda, opt to sleep late this morning. You may feel at odds with the world for much of the day. Old value systems are dissolving, and new ones might not yet be sufficiently developed to know what it is you want. Don't rush; mistakes are more easily made when confusion reigns. Avoid making any major monetary decisions. If you are heading to the January sales, check that intended purchases are really bargains so that you don't experience discontent with the items later on. Dining out this evening with friends or colleagues offers the chance to catch up with the latest gossip that you may have missed hearing.

3. SUNDAY. Mixed. If too much of a good thing over the festive period has played havoc with your health and well-being, consider contacting a nutritionist or alternative therapist for practical advice. A regimen of vitamins, or reverting to a healthier diet, should have you back in good form in no time at all. Plans involving friends could be altered abruptly, leaving you without alternative arrangements. If your home is still in disarray after the holidays, this could be an opportune time to start cleaning, reorganizing, and restocking depleted food supplies. Keeping busy will help you avoid arguments with other people in your immediate environment.

4. MONDAY. Constructive. Positive benefits are foreseen as the Moon slides through your opposite sign of Virgo. If you still are harboring negative feelings from tense situations experienced with your partner or roommate last night, it should now be possible to find common ground. Your innate Pisces skill at sensing when someone close is willing to meet you halfway will indicate the right time to talk things through without further eruptions. Open discussion with a friend or with members of a group will resolve any outstanding situations that have caused minor worries. With everyone willing to voice concerns, solutions can be arrived at without incident.

5. TUESDAY. Diverse. Guard against being drawn into other people's problems and issues. If you cannot say no, there is a chance that you will end up involved in a situation that you would rather avoid. Listening to the woes of others should be limited because giving advice that proves unsound is a pitfall you might easily fall into. Checking out the post-festive sales could produce a number of excellent bargains. Your eye for quality is enhanced, and if you remember to negotiate for a better price you should be very pleased with your purchases. Make arrangements to spend leisure time with friends, enjoying social activities together.

6. WEDNESDAY. Distracting. Avoid early morning discussions to avert the possibility of tension arising. Productivity is unlikely to be very high because the cosmic skies are sending mainly disruptive influences. It is important to avoid making major decisions, accepting a financial settlement, or signing a new lease. With Mercury, the planet of information and paperwork, still moving backward until later in the month, delays can be expected with tax matters, collecting company debts, and real estate concerns. The intuitive Pisces could make future gains by tuning in to hunches designed to bear fruit at a later date. Write down your thoughts and ideas, and research ways that these can be developed.

7. THURSDAY. Satisfactory. Pisces folk begin this year with energetic Mars, the planet of drive and motivation, in Leo, impacting your house of health, work, and service. This can be an exhausting period for those who prefer to take things at a more leisurely tempo. Be sure to pace yourself. Take frequent rest breaks if involved in any type of heavy manual labor. Also expect your daily workload at home or on the job to increase significantly. Sort out unwanted household goods and clothing to create more space so that you can purchase items to add comfort and ease to your home life. Satisfaction will increase if you donate unwanted items to a charitable organization.

8. FRIDAY. Fair. Be prepared for an up-and-down day. Don't become too upset if you find that it is harder to please clients, the boss, or those higher up the corporate ladder than you. Do the very best you can and relationships are likely to improve over the next few weeks. Studious Pisces who have been seriously considering further study, travel, or training should use the upcoming weekend to research various ways to achieve these aims. Check with an expert if you need assistance obtaining travel visas, purchasing the best lightweight luggage, or arranging an interesting itinerary for a getaway trip.

9. SATURDAY. Uncertain. Be prepared for the people around you to be more agitated than usual. Those of you on the job could experience frustration with coworkers or clients, but do your best to keep your temper in check. Unreliable information could trigger further delays or could cancel a nearly completed task. De-stress will come through reading, writing, or researching a topic that captures your attention. Pisces bookworms who have read every interesting book at home should consider visiting the closest bookstore or library to replenish reading stock. If money is a concern, an estate sale or thrift store could be an inexpensive source of interesting books.

10. SUNDAY. Bumpy. Family strife or an ongoing drama is possible through much of the day. Pisces folks who have a hard time connecting to in-laws should consider putting off a visit. If not possible without creating family upset, arrange the visit for early afternoon, when planetary influences are a little less likely to create emotional stress. A late lunch with friends is a good option for singles seeking a relaxing activity, especially for those who stayed out late last night. The self-employed Pisces can make productive headway catching up on paperwork and routine tasks later this evening.

11. MONDAY. Fruitful. As the new working week begins, most Pisces people should start off on the right foot. If you have specialized skills and expertise, these qualities can very easily be passed on to other people, assisting those who are employed as teachers or trainers. You will excel at imparting your hard-earned knowledge in a proficient manner. The ability to engage in unusual creative work makes this a fruitful period if you are seeking new methods of generating income. Arrange to share this evening with a relative, lover, or special companion. Love and warmth surround you like a cozy blanket, stirring up emotions that will make tonight memorable.

12. TUESDAY. Promising. Over the next few days the Sun and Venus happily connect with erratic Uranus, bringing a lively, enthusiastic, and unpredictable quality to your daily activities. The tempo of life quickens, and you can expect an increase in social invitations and meetings. Planning a party, wedding, or any special celebration should proceed easily thanks to your flowing imagination and enhanced creative flair. Unexpected assistance could arrive just when you need it most. New ideas can be acted on, and a breakthrough with an ambitious project could add excitement to the day. Leisure time spent participating in an unusual sport or hobby should be very enjoyable.

13. WEDNESDAY. Chancy. Challenges are likely, creating an unsettled environment. You may need to reassess where you are heading and why. With Saturn, the taskmaster of the zodiac, heading into retreat from now until the end of May, delays and problems with monetary payments, company issues, and joint financial resources are foreseen. Throughout this period Pisces business owners should be proactive and reexamine your current commercial practices. Expect a delay with a property or insurance settlement, and don't rely on a positive outcome regarding a tax appeal. Joy comes from sharing happy times with family members and friends.

14. THURSDAY. Good. The possibility of domestic tension arising early this morning is higher than usual. However, if you use your Pisces ability to tune out, you should escape unscathed. This is a great day for work of a creative or artistic nature. Bringing a stalled project to a successful completion should be easy if you are willing to take a leadership role; your efforts won't go unnoticed. This evening plan to socialize with those who share your hobbies or interests. Getting together with like-minded folks can be more comforting than wasting time attempting to convert other people to your favorite pastimes.

15. FRIDAY. Important. If you dare to strike out boldly in a new direction, cherished dreams can begin to formulate. Over the next few days initiate action, begin a new project, and start developing plans that have been sitting on the back burner. Today's eclipsed New Moon in Capricorn, impacting your solar eleventh house of friends, hopes, and aims, provides an excellent opportunity to begin fresh undertakings. Don't delay taking the first step to achieving a long-term goal. Whatever social activity is chosen this evening, find a way to spend time in the company of special friends and companions. Being with them will soothe your soul and make you feel at one with the world.

16. SATURDAY. Quiet. People in your circle could mistake your tendency to drift off into your private world as aloofness. If you feel a need to get away from a noisy environment and find a quiet spot to replenish your batteries and recharge your energy, don't feel guilty. The Moon is currently slipping through your twelfth house of Aquarius, leading you to prefer solitude and your own company. Private concerns and puttering around completing outstanding personal tasks may hold more interest than routine activities. Avoid a boisterous social event tonight, settling for a quiet dinner at home with loved ones.

17. SUNDAY. Exceptional. There are movements in the heavens today as your traditional ruler, jolly Jupiter, takes up residence in your own sign of Pisces and your first house of personality. This is the beginning of a major growth cycle, with optimism and enthusiasm reaching a peak. You can now begin new activities with the likelihood of a positive outcome. Travel, teaching, and learning are areas that will benefit significantly under this auspicious transit. Just be careful of developing an overinflated ego or attempting to do the impossible. Moderation in most areas of life is advised, and especially with your diet. Your waistline is sure to expand if care is not taken.

18. MONDAY. Dreamy. The stars are combining to ensure a great beginning to the new workweek. Pisces folk are in for another treat as lover Venus changes zodiacal signs this morning. It shouldn't be difficult to tell that special person exactly how you feel. Your feelings will come from the depth of your soul. Venus, the goddess of all that is bright and beautiful, enters Aquarius, your twelfth house of things that are hidden, and remains there until February 11. Love can take on a dreamy and inspired glow, with Pisces individuals basking in the joy of nurturing and caring for other people. Those of you engaged in a secret love affair can expect a number of twists and turns to occur.

19. TUESDAY. Easygoing. This is another day when events should fall easily into place, without too much effort on your part. The Sun now visits your twelfth house of Aquarius for the next four weeks, so you can expect a period of feeling more withdrawn and reclusive than usual. In general this isn't a great time to begin new projects unless you plan to complete tasks on your own, without outside help. However, finishing outstanding work can be accomplished easily now. Include more rest breaks in your heavy schedule because you are apt to feel physically weaker or more tired than usual. If you haven't had a vacation in quite a while, this is the perfect time to seriously consider getting away to recharge run-down batteries.

20. WEDNESDAY. Refreshing. Dreams are important to Pisces, and you could find that you are daydreaming or fantasizing even more than usual. Regardless of how insignificant these may seem, write them down because some relevance is sure to be found. Pleasure and enjoyment can be derived from new associations with people who are both creative and innovative. Self-pampering could be in order. A massage or a reflexology treatment could be just what you need to put a contented smile on your face. Those of you struggling to survive on a strict household budget should forgo expensive entertainment this evening and enjoy the comforts of home.

21. THURSDAY. Assertive. This promises to be a relatively easy day if you are prepared to go with the flow. Avoid taking on too many responsibilities. Also refuse to allow other people to pressure you to hurry. Moving steadily along is the way to accomplish most tasks on your to-do list. You might enjoy the challenge of using your talents and skills to complete an important project. Devoting some time to personal financial matters can help to provide a clear picture of your current assets, expected income, and urgent upcoming expenses. When it comes to love and romance, single Fish might prefer to make the rules rather than following conventional methods.

22. FRIDAY. Fruitful. Venus amicably links to structured Saturn, assisting Pisces to continue putting financial matters into better order. A major achievement regarding joint monetary issues is likely, which should put you in a sunny mood. Obtaining a home mortgage or a loan can be the beginning of a new phase of life. This is a day to put paperwork in order and organize files to achieve greater efficiency, which will help to free up more of your time. Singles seeking romance could prefer an older, more mature person. A new love affair has a good chance of being long enduring. Look to the future and don't be ruled by memories of the past.

23. SATURDAY. Erratic. Curiosity and an urge to be on the move might tempt you to head off in a number of different directions, but beware scattering your energy. Thinking too much could also leave you with a jumble of ideas but no concrete answers or solutions. If you can focus and concentrate on one particular area of expression, productivity should be high. Later on tonight there is a chance of an argument with coworkers for those who must be on the job. Enjoy spending time with friends, particularly early in the evening. Don't drink and drive, and slow down if you are behind the wheel.

24. SUNDAY. Delightful. You are likely to be in your own world, so begin the day on a slow and restful note. A late breakfast and then leisurely reading the Sunday newspaper can get you started on a great day. A misplaced or lost treasure could be rediscovered when you are looking for something else. Sentimental memories could come flooding in when a long-forgotten object turns up. An important decision can now be made as practical and realistic influences guide you in the right direction. Trust your past experience and a valuable contact. An early night could recharge spent batteries and restore your emotional well-being.

25. MONDAY. Lackluster. You are unlikely to be impressed by the need to rise, shine, and face the new working week. Cosmic energy won't be very helpful, and you might feel just as tired this morning as you did when you went to bed last night. Whether you are working at home, cooped up in an office, or heading off to a classroom, pace activities to ensure that your physical reserves last throughout the day. Don't become drawn into other people's problems because this is likely to drain your energy even further. Visitors or loved ones could drop by unannounced. Although you might be pleased to welcome them and even invite them to share a meal, it is very likely that they have an ulterior motive.

26. TUESDAY. Tricky. Minor irritations are likely to be confronted all day. Try to avoid chores that require heavy labor or intense focus because it is unlikely that you will do justice to them. Instead consider finishing outstanding minor jobs that have been on your to-do list for a while. An emotional issue with a family member could have you wanting to run away and hide. Sometimes it is better to face a problem head-on, even if tension will be created for a short time. At least the problem can be resolved and everyone can then move on. Your home could be used as a meeting place, which should please you and give you a sense of pride.

27. WEDNESDAY. Variable. The changeable moods of other people could be disconcerting for the placid Pisces. You might need to lower your expectations of what others can deliver in order to avoid disappointment. Add a dash of compromise and cooperation and you should get through the day without too many hassles. Pleasure comes from concentrating on domestic and household tasks if you are at home or on routine but essential chores if on the job. Don't overload your schedule with too many meetings with friends or clients; family activities are likely to provide the contentment you want. A home-cooked meal shared with those you love should finish off the day on a perfect note.

28. THURSDAY. Exhausting. This is another day when you probably wish you could stay in bed. Love and romance are under a cloud, with quarrels and disputes more likely than not. Avoid expressing your feelings openly because you might be upset by the lack of positive response from your mate or partner. Daydreams and escaping into fantasyland, a favored pastime of Pisces folk, could be interrupted by outside influences and unfortunate distractions. Despite strong instincts to nurture the people in your life, expect problems as youngsters and others stretch your patience to the limit. Entertainment that is not your normal variety could appeal this evening, especially a live concert or show.

29. FRIDAY. Busy. There will be a lot happening throughout the day, so beware the risk of overstretching your physical, mental, or financial resources. The Sun and energetic Mars are in dispute, warning the Fish to take extra care with health and well-being. The sign of Pisces is not known to be robust, so tune in to your physical body to ensure that you are getting the correct nutrition and exercise needed to keep you healthy as well as feeling good. Dealing with authority figures might be difficult. A better outcome is likely if you postpone meetings and appointments with higher-ups until later next week.

30. SATURDAY. Emotional. A Full Moon in excitable Leo adds a few dramatics to the day's events. Emotions are likely to run high, which could play havoc with your physical body as well as your mood. The urge to complete a creative project may be strong and would be a wonderful way to use the silvery light of the Full Moon. If you are careful how you handle the emotions of your nearest and dearest, love and romance can be irresistible. Allow creative juices to run freely, and get set for a wonderful time of bonding with your mate or partner. Plan to spend the weekend at home; issues with friends could become emotional and upsetting.

31. SUNDAY. Surprising. A major planetary influence between disciplined Saturn and erratic Uranus could create unsettled feelings. Try to relax and let life wash over you. Avoid causing yourself too much angst. Concentrate on what is important here and now, and leave less significant issues for another time. Expect some bumps in the road to romance through the early part of the day. Be flexible, ready to handle the mood swings of your mate or partner. Unreliable friends or the unexpected high cost of an outing could spoil your day. If you have been relying heavily on the use of credit cards, you may be forced to take stock of your financial situation and implement changes.

FEBRUARY

1. MONDAY. Edgy. Pisces folk are apt to begin the new month feeling listless and slightly unmotivated. With the Aquarius Sun impacting your solar twelfth house of solitude, the universe is encouraging you to sit back and take a rest. Very often you have a habit of trying to swim upstream instead of going with the flow. Your mate or partner could struggle to express feelings, so it would be worthwhile to think less about your own concerns and concentrate on the interests of others. Friends and associates are unlikely to respond well to criticism no matter how hard you try to sweeten it up. An honest, open approach is the best way to deal with whatever is on your mind.

2. TUESDAY. Bumpy. Expect another trying day that is likely to test the patience of even the most placid of Pisces folk. Be careful with all forms of communication, and do your best to keep a low profile. Although your usually good intuition may be a little off, working behind the scenes should be satisfying. Refrain from shopping, especially if searching for good-quality bargains; the chance of receiving value for money seems slim. This is a good time to seek closure to a relationship that is now in the past, allowing you to put old issues to rest and move on. Visiting a sick friend or an elderly person who doesn't receive many visitors can make both of you feel good.

3. WEDNESDAY. Chancy. Plan your day well. More can be accomplished during the morning than later in the day. Financial issues with friends could cause upsets unless handled cautiously. If someone owes you money, or if you are in debt to someone, try arranging a payment plan that suits you both; otherwise your relationship could take a severe battering. To avoid the likelihood of a heated exchange, steer clear of any discussion regarding shared expenses with your mate, partner, or roommate this afternoon. Harmony increases by evening, and you should then be able to enjoy pleasant companionship with family members or with a special companion.

4. THURSDAY. Positive. Things are looking up, and you can look forward to a good day ahead. Finances and business matters predominate during the morning hours. Time spent going over important paperwork, household accounts, and your current budget can be productive. If you are seeking cost-cutting measures, you might be surprised how easy it is to find small ways to save. Later in the day your thoughts are likely to turn toward more adventurous activities such as travel or a hobby that offers a thrill or two. Your natural Pisces ability to sustain a long period of in-depth research can be a big help if you are involved in academic studies.

5. FRIDAY. Disconcerting. The fact that it is Friday and the end of the working week for many might be the only really good thing that today has to offer. Minor irritations and obstacles are likely to prove frustrating and can hinder output. Although positive thinking is a virtue, being overly optimistic can lead to disappointment, which may be the case now. Be prepared for a loan or commercial matter that you thought had been settled to be delayed or canceled at the last minute. If certain duties must be completed during the day, watch the clock. Otherwise you could sit down at the computer for a minute to do some research and end up spending hours on the Internet.

6. SATURDAY. Opportune. The rough times experienced recently are set to improve as the universe sends harmonious vibes to liven up the weekend. Mental agility improves, and your verbal responses should be quick and humorous. An opportunity to travel with friends or colleagues could come your way, opening up new doors. If the thought of speaking in public has always seemed terrifying, give it a go now if the chance arises; you should be pleasantly surprised how easy the right words flow. Writing also comes effortlessly, so make yourself comfortable and begin composing that article, book, or essay. A night on the town with friends promises to provide amusement for singles and couples.

7. SUNDAY. Rejuvenating. It shouldn't take much to convince Pisces folks that all work and no play is unhealthy, especially on a Sunday. Self-employed Fish working from home should complete essential tasks and then spend quality time with loved ones. Gains can be made through self-promotion, buying and selling, or organizing the home office to be more efficient. A situation could seem overwhelming, especially if old memories or current pressures are impeding your thoughts, but try to put it in perspective. Participating in a creative hobby or stimulating activity can recharge your batteries and clear your mind of negativity. Use cash instead of credit cards when shopping, and count the change you receive.

8. MONDAY. Ideal. This is one of those days when retail therapy holds more appeal than usual, and going off to work is likely to be at the bottom of your wish list. Venus, the planet of love and money, merges with your coruler Neptune, increasing wishful thinking and the desire for the good things in life. Be careful, because under this influence overindulging could happen without you being aware, until the time comes to pay for the cost of your spending spree. Your sense of style and glamour is enhanced. If you have received an invitation to a special upcoming event, you should be inspired when searching for an outfit that will make you feel like a movie star.

9. TUESDAY. Productive. A little dreaming can be inspirational. Put in the effort, make plans, and work on accomplishing your cherished desires and goals. Fortunate influences can put you in touch with those who are able to provide helpful advice. Initiate secret or quiet discussions with a trusted colleague or authority figure on the job to ensure that your current career path is the right one. Actions now could lead to an offer in the future, so toe the line and put your best foot forward. Recognition from a group or club should be accepted with humility, but also with the knowledge that your input is important for the success of the association and your efforts are appreciated.

10. WEDNESDAY. Complex. Take care to avoid confrontations with people you see on a regular basis. Your motivation could be low, and life might appear to be moving very slowly and without much excitement to liven up the day. Getting ideas or strategies across to employees or coworkers could be difficult because whatever you say is likely to be misunderstood, perhaps on purpose. Mercury, the planet of communication, enters your Aquarius house of solitary activities and secrets, turning your thoughts to more spiritual and private matters. Confidential concerns could arise. You may be asked to keep certain hush-hush information to yourself, which will be essential but not easy.

11. THURSDAY. Outstanding. The tempo of life is beginning to rise even though the Sun and Mercury remain in your Aquarius twelfth house of solitary action. Socialite Venus is now gracing your sign of Pisces and your first house of personality. It should be easy to attract opportunities and draw other people to you. Take full advantage of this positive period. Your view of the world is likely to take on a rosier glow. Pisces singles could fall in love with love. If you are making a first impression or a more positive impression on someone of importance, you shouldn't have any difficulties accomplishing this. Consider updating your wardrobe, grooming, or beauty regime sometime between now and March 7 when Venus departs your sign.

12. FRIDAY. Interesting. Tempers flare easily today, so attempt to keep anger contained. If you slow down and take a deep breath, the heat should disappear from most situations. Unless the tendency to put pressure on yourself is avoided, the chance of successfully completing all tasks isn't good. However, organize work time more efficiently and your productivity will rise. In romance, intimacy along with soft music and a candlelight dinner for two may be your chosen way of expressing the depth of your feelings to that special person in your life. The chance of solo Pisces meeting a perfect match is excellent now.

13. SATURDAY. Tranquil. A sensitive day awaits those born under the sign of Pisces. A New Moon culminates in your Aquarius twelfth house, urging you to search for emotional peace and quiet. Whenever the Moon is new, fresh plans and strategies can be implemented. In addition, promises that you have made to yourself and to other people have more chance of success. Don't put off what needs to be done, including an apology. Preserving old family photos can be gratifying as you protect memories for future generations. Plan a treat for that special person in readiness to celebrate Valentine's Day in style tomorrow.

14. SUNDAY. Fair. Mixed trends are in force today with a number of planetary aspects forming. With the love planet Venus unhappily linked to both dynamo Mars and serious Saturn, the vibes are not good for those keen to celebrate Valentine's Day with love and all the trimmings. However, if you make a concerted effort you can manage to turn potentially unfavorable influences into happy vibes. Avoid tasks that require practical solutions and logical thinking because your judgment may be impaired. Art, music, and creative activities are more in sync with current thinking, and these can be enjoyed either on your own or as part of a twosome.

15. MONDAY. Passionate. Romantic feelings hit a high note, and for many Pisces love is in the air. Make the most of the sensual atmosphere formed by the combination of saucy Venus cuddling up to intense Pluto. Actions are well directed now. Using the passionate vibes, you can produce and create something artistic. If your talent lies in turning items of natural beauty into an inspiring art from, now is the time to let your creative juices flow freely. Associates or coworkers should see eye-to-eye with you on important issues. Taking the lead in business and commercial practices can produce gains thanks to your enhanced ambitions and drive to succeed.

16. TUESDAY. Lucky. Love and luck mark this day. The sensitive Moon glides through your sign of Pisces and your first house of self and personality, making you a force to be reckoned with. Stay focused and achievements should come easily. However, with Venus merging with your traditional ruler, generous Jupiter, beware going overboard. Moderation is the rule to live by. Otherwise excessive tendencies could cause havoc with your finances and overall well-being. If you are planning a party you might bite off more than you can chew, making cutbacks necessary. A flutter at the casino or the purchase of a lottery ticket could make you a winner. Evening hours are delightful for love and romance.

17. WEDNESDAY. Bright. Regardless of your situation or circumstances, don't settle for second best. When it comes to making choices, put your own needs on the same level as the desires of other people. Be sure to choose options that can be most beneficial in the long term. Physical energy is on the rise now that the Moon has entered your second house of Aries, increasing your motivation and productivity. This is the time of the month to make strategic plans and devise new methods of increasing your income. The urge to shop could be strong for the feminine Fish. Indulge yourself with a few little treats that provide comfort, but stick to your budget. It doesn't take much for Pisces to overspend.

18. THURSDAY. Happy Birthday! The Sun has now moved into your own sign of Pisces, and for all Fish this can be a very empowering month. Confidence, enthusiasm, and energy improve, and it is now time to take your place in the limelight. As your leadership qualities come to the fore, life should take on a more dreamlike glow. Your drive to achieve is peaking, and your contributions in paid or unpaid employment are bound to be noticed by those who can be of help. The chance of good fortune coming your way increases. Update your wardrobe and dress to impress. If needed, cosmetic surgery or enhancements are under favorable vibrations.

19. FRIDAY. Good. There could be a great deal of talking today as the Moon slips through your Taurus house of communication. Discussions relating to personal finances should produce positive results. Pisces who are traveling to a job interview or business meeting can expect to make beneficial gains. Contacting siblings and other relatives at this time can be enlightening as well as providing the opportunity to catch up on family news and gossip. Conflict with coworkers could quickly arise during late morning to early afternoon. Watch your body language, and be especially careful when talking to staff members. Otherwise you could become entangled in a nasty situation.

20. SATURDAY. Tricky. Short-distance travel may be on the agenda. This is a good time to visit cousins or extended family members whom you haven't seen recently. Working Pisces should approach the boss and fellow workers with caution. This is another day when disagreements could arise over employment activities or assigned tasks, adding tension to the air. Trying to change anyone's mind is likely to be an exercise in futility. Bring discussions to a quick end. If it is important that other people understand your reasoning, wait a few days before broaching the subject once again. Look where you are walking or running, and take extra care on the roads.

21. SUNDAY. Slow. A day of rest is in order for hardworking Pisces. Energy could be a little depleted, but only for manual chores or tasks that don't hold your interest. Compromise and adjustment may be required to keep the peace at home. If you owe money to a relative, it might be time to come up with a sensible repayment plan and honor your commitment, before words become heated or tension arises. If you are viewing real estate to purchase or rent, look but don't commit yourself because you are unlikely to receive value for money. A night at home will most likely provide the most contentment, even if you like to party.

22. MONDAY. Low-key. This is not the most inspiring day of the month. You could even feel a little depressed or melancholy. Put those feelings down to current planetary trends, then forget about anything that makes you uncomfortable or miserable. If moving, renovating, or making improvements to your current place of residence is not high on your agenda, perhaps it is time to at least clean from top to bottom. If there is a need to relocate, checking what is available should lead to a few places that spark your interest. Spend a little money on yourself, which is always guaranteed to cheer you up. A new look or color treatment from your hair stylist could also lift spirits.

23. TUESDAY. Promising. Approach the day with optimism and enthusiasm. The connection between the Sun and powerful Pluto helps to override any negative planetary influences. Use your increased energy and drive to your best advantage. Influential contacts can create fresh and perhaps surprising opportunities, especially if you show that you are willing to listen, learn, and take appropriate action. Pisces who are in the process of interviewing for a new job could receive an offer that far exceeds expectations. Take time out of your day to seriously evaluate plans, hopes, and long-range goals. Your ability to create or attract the right opportunities remains high.

24. WEDNESDAY. Sensitive. The urge to socialize, to meet and greet, is high today. However, the stars are not supportive, so it would be wise to proceed slowly when arranging meetings and dates. Cancellations are likely, and someone you had hoped would accompany you to an event might be a no-show. Issues with a male coworker could taint your happiness on the job unless you maintain a low profile. If you share your home with nonfamily members, you might need to examine this arrangement, especially if money problems or shared expenses are a constant source of irritation. Late-night revelers should have a good time, but those going out during the early evening may be disappointed.

25. THURSDAY. Calm. Morning trends are not offering anything of note. However, from lunchtime on, the day should improve. Shoppers should wait until afternoon before seeking out bargains, then make tracks to a favorite store to update a tired and outdated wardrobe. Postpone making decisions regarding children until later in the day because emotions could impede good judgment. Find someone trustworthy with whom to share a secret or confidence that is troubling you but that you have been asked to keep. A problem shared can often provide a more objective perspective. Pisces folk will be happy being at home with loved ones tonight.

26. FRIDAY. Easygoing. You may discover that the day is not as bleak as first imagined. An overwhelming feeling that you need more leisure time could prompt you to cut back on a heavy workload and make some minor changes to your daily regime. Don't neglect health concerns; a problem could escalate if left unattended. Invest more time in exercise; a home treadmill can bring long-term health benefits. Try to add variety to your exercise mix to keep boredom at bay. Looking after your personal well-being can actually be fun. Unexpected good news regarding a job or contract could lift your spirits, but don't go on a spending spree quite yet.

27. SATURDAY. Creative. Escaping the daily routine is a must today for Pisces folk. With thinking Mercury merging with your modern-day ruler, inspirational Neptune, you will be drawn to artistic, creative, or spiritual pursuits. Throughout the weekend refrain from making any major decisions because mental confusion reigns and your ability to focus may be limited. Psychic impressions and dreaming could be frequent, with sudden insights having to be deciphered and made sense of. Those of you on the job should avoid being too flippant when communicating with fellow workers, who are unlikely to understand where you are coming from. Music, dance, and solitary pursuits could fulfill current needs.

28. SUNDAY. Fruitful. Good fortune abounds as the Sun and your traditional ruler, generous Jupiter, combine in your sign and your first house of self and physical body. Take it easy if you are going out to socialize; going overboard can occur very easily under these influences. A Full Moon in your opposite sign of Virgo may bring partnership issues to the fore, and feelings between you and your mate or partner could run high. Pisces who have recently split up with a lover can use this cycle of completion to seek closure and to move on from the past. This is another day when tapping into your creative ingenuity can be inspiring and a pleasant way to pass the day.

MARCH

1. MONDAY. Fair. A fairly ordinary day marks the beginning of the new month. For most of the day you could feel as though you are running around in circles, encountering one obstacle after another and correcting or adjusting errors or tasks performed by other people. A bevy of planets is illuminating your first house of personality. Jupiter,

Sun, Uranus, and Venus are all in Pisces, and Mercury is about to join the party. Nevertheless, you might not want to shine or to be on display. Day-to-day interaction with your partner or another person may not be easy, but right now there should be plenty of opportunity to let them know what you are thinking and what you really do want.

2. TUESDAY. Constructive. If you are willing to make the necessary effort, this is a good time to work on building and strengthening personal and professional partnerships, especially if money has been a source of friction recently. Be wary of assuming more than you should. If you have committed yourself or your team to a project, put that at the top of your priority list. The mysteries of life could intrigue you, which could lead to learning more about metaphysics, the occult, or psychological topics. An obsession to be rid of anything cluttering up your life could find you undertaking a major cleanup around the house or overhauling a current situation in your life that is not to your liking.

3. WEDNESDAY. Surprising. Unexpected coincidences could produce surprises. You may be thinking about a certain person and then be delighted to receive an e-mail, phone call, or personal visit. Attempting anything new could bring on an attack of nerves, but don't allow fears or insecurity to hold you back. As long as the task you set out to achieve is realistic, it can be accomplished. With the duo of Venus and Uranus merging together in your sign, many Pisces singles could be in the happy situation of an unexpected romantic encounter. Enjoy the time together without expectations; love found now could be extremely exciting but also short-lived.

4. THURSDAY. Soothing. Planetary influences are great, so prepare to enjoy a sparkling day. Travel plans might take priority, although circumstances beyond your control could create problems with your proposed itinerary. This is a good day to spend time with a group of people engaged in a cultural or philosophical pursuit. A book club, theater group, or writing seminar might appeal, moving you closer to a current dream or goal. Enrolling in a workshop or training course that explores a favored hobby or furthers your career opportunities can also be a relaxing method of learning as you share ideas with other people who have similar interests.

5. FRIDAY. Cautious. It would be wise to pace your activities and conserve physical energy. Be careful of concentrating too much on work, which could bring complaints of neglect from loved ones. Refrain from taking on too many responsibilities; an overload of commitments may be detrimental to health by increasing stress. This is an unfavorable period to approach someone in authority, especially an employer or supervisor. Better results are likely if you can wait until next Wednesday when Mars moves forward, especially if you are seeking a special favor, paid leave, or a pay increase. An interesting travel film or documentary could provide the perfect escape this evening.

6. SATURDAY. Diverse. You're likely to be popular on the job as long as you are not working the late shift. If that is your shift, extra care with demeanor, attitude, and body language will be required. Clients, customers, or superiors might be a little moody, so stay focused and cheerful in order to avoid unnecessary confrontations and petty annoyances. If you remain detached at work but still willing to share ideas and opinions, you'll gain increased respect. Social activities will run more smoothly during the day than later this evening. Unless you are courteous if challenged by someone in authority while you are out and about, you may find yourself in an uncomfortable situation.

7. SUNDAY. Promising. Financial prospects are beginning to look up as Venus, planet of money and values, enters your Aries second house of monetary matters and personal possessions. Extra income should come your way. However, unless impulsive and indulgent purchases are kept to a minimum, money could vanish quickly. Generosity toward other people may become more apparent as you experience the desire to share your abundance with the needy. If seeking a new home to share, you could find the perfect place by checking out the local newspaper or the bulletin board at your place of employment.

8. MONDAY. Helpful. Although excellent cosmic trends are in force this morning, these positive influences might not last all day. Business associates or a friend could provide the assistance you need to attain a desired goal early in the day, so don't be shy when it comes to asking for a special favor. A second chance to launch a pet project that failed to get off the ground previously might receive more support now. A friend could disappear from your circle due to relocating or a disagreement, or because common interests and values are no longer shared. Don't dwell on this loss; it won't be long before someone else arrives to fill the gap.

9. TUESDAY. Upsetting. Lover Venus and serious Saturn are at odds, creating a somber atmosphere throughout the day. Beware taking on a new job or additional responsibility just for a change of pace. The chances of becoming bogged down and not completing the task correctly is more than likely. Setbacks regarding insurance, a bonus, or taxes could be frustrating. This isn't a favorable period to apply for a loan, credit card, or mortgage. If relationship issues are causing stress, be honest with yourself; perhaps you are as much at fault as your mate or partner. A male employee or employer might be especially demanding and hard to please. At the end of the day settle down with a book by a favored author and relax.

10. WEDNESDAY. Renewing. As a Pisces you may have experienced problems since the beginning of 2010 initiating projects that require action. On top of that, health and daily routines could have created testing conditions that have been hard to accept and even harder to live with. However, beginning today you will have Mars, the planet of drive and motivation, moving forward in Leo, your house of work, service, and health. This frees energy that has seemed bottled up. Unusual and original ideas can set you apart, so don't be shy when it comes to working with other people in a team or group environment. Enjoying the companionship of friends and loved ones can bring pleasure, with discussions lively and stimulating tonight.

11. THURSDAY. Volatile. The cosmic drives lean toward disharmony and discord rather than smooth sailing. With the Moon moving through Aquarius, your house of solitude, obtaining privacy is something that you will want to actively seek. As a Pisces you are sometimes too agreeable and are often guilty of allowing other people to take you for granted. Don't let this happen now, or it will erode your self-confidence and your own needs will not be met. Steer clear of financial decisions; a proposed investment scheme might not be as lucrative as it first appears. Passion is at a high, creating a hotbed atmosphere for lovers. However, jealously is also likely, so take it easy with issues in the love and romance department.

12. FRIDAY. Stimulating. Inspiration and creative vibes remain strong. Spending time alone, especially at home, can be relaxing and refreshing if there aren't too many tasks waiting for action. Projects that have been languishing behind the scenes have a good chance of being successfully finished now. Meditation or spiritual work can be pleasant. Curling up with a good book could also attract your fancy if you feel less energetic. As a Pisces you have a tendency to take on a rescuer role, but this usually doesn't help anyone. It would be wiser to provide assistance by showing others the way to help themselves. A visit to a local astrologer could supply answers to a number of your questions.

13. SATURDAY. Stable. A slow, steady pace is best suited to this morning's vibes. Later in the day the Moon moves into your sign of Pisces, and you will then be ready to come out of your cocoon. Energy increases along with the need for excitement. Aim to do something different than your usual weekend activities. With vision enhanced and a greater ability to fantasize, apply extra effort so that dreams can be implemented and turned into reality. Pay more attention to your wardrobe and personal grooming. Wearing an outfit that turns heads can make people sit up and take notice, and you'll enjoy the attention. Single Pisces should take advantage of the opportunity for romantic moments.

14. SUNDAY. Focused. With the Sun and Mercury conjoined in your sign, this is a favorable period to make the most of your mental capabilities. Tasks that require focus can be more easily accomplished. Pisces who will be speaking in public should be gratified by the response of an appreciative audience. The urge to chat is enhanced, although it might be hard to find folks willing to listen for very long if talk revolves around only you. Clear, quick thinking assists those involved in business dealings and also when buying, selling, or negotiating a better price at a market or department store. This is a starred day to enter competitions and buy a lottery ticket; it might be your turn to win the big one.

15. MONDAY. Rejuvenating. The Moon continues moving through your sign of Pisces, linking up with the Sun later in the day. Your thinking should be quick, with plenty of ideas coming easily to mind. The culmination of a New Moon marks the time to begin fresh projects and implement new plans. Listen intently to an idea outlined by a friend. If it interests you, it could be the beginning of a venture that you can share together. Don't resist the urge to upgrade your image with a change of hairstyle or a few colorful clothing accessories. When you look and feel good, self-confidence rises and moving out of your comfort zone and accepting challenges becomes second nature.

16. TUESDAY. Purposeful. The cosmos now moves to all things connected to personal finances and material possessions. Monetary issues could create a situation requiring you to reassess your priorities and values. If you don't have an organized and structured method of paying bills and saving for that proverbial rainy day, start to change this situation now. You need to know what your money is being spent on; haphazardly hoping that there is enough income to meet outgoing expenses is a recipe for disaster. Loaning money or a prized possession to a business colleague or friend should be avoided. However, be generous in donating to a good cause.

17. WEDNESDAY. Active. The cosmic heavens are busy with a number of planetary influences in force. Notably Mercury enters Aries and joins Venus in Aries, impacting your money house. Plans to improve income can be more successful by brainstorming to find new ways of boosting current cash flow. Variety is the spice of life as restlessness comes to the fore. It may be very difficult to carry out tasks that you find tedious and boring. Focus on jobs or activities that offer excitement, a challenge, something you haven't attempted before. Even time away from your usual surroundings could help soothe your soul and bring a sense of calm. Be guided by your sense of curiosity and wonder.

18. THURSDAY. Busy. Today's celestial influences serve as a reminder that there are limitations when it comes to personal finances. If you are in the process of trying to procure a loan or make a major purchase but so far without success, keep your spirits high and be patient. There should be an opportunity to break through current obstacles soon, and your aims can then be fulfilled. Later in the day running errands, attending to correspondence, or participating in a meeting could find you busier than you would prefer. A few short trips could be added to your schedule. Even though these may be quick, they are likely to be important and essential.

19. FRIDAY. Useful. With the passage of the Moon through your Taurus third house of communication, the need for stimulation and movement remains high. Dealing with other people could be stressful and demanding. Surround yourself with whatever enhances relaxation and assists clarity, such as soothing music, fresh flowers on your desk, and plenty of refreshing water. Writing down your thoughts can be a productive way to trigger inspiration and imagination. Pisces students should make good headway if extra help is obtained from a teacher or tutor. Tonight the couch, the remote control, and a cuddly lover could be all that you need.

20. SATURDAY. Excellent. Today marks the beginning of the new astrological year, also known as the equinox when day and night are of equal length. This is a starred time to work on situations and projects that are vitally important. The Sun moves into your Aries house of finances, income, and assets, increasing the possibility of

Pisces folk generating more money and acquiring more possessions over the next four weeks. A gift from relatives or a pay raise could give you a head start with saving for what you want. Confidential dealings are unlikely to bring promised gains. However, if you lower your expectations, the bank balance is still likely to rise.

21. SUNDAY. Restful. Plan for a quiet day spent around home base. The Sun happily connects to dynamo Mars but is in dispute with somber Saturn, canceling out any major increase of physical resources. This is an ideal period to catch up on domestic chores, fill the freezer with home-cooked goodies, or remove unwanted goods from the attic or garage. If the state of your living arrangements is causing angst, rearranging furniture or purchasing a few colorful pillows or a new indoor plant could freshen up the atmosphere and make a big difference. Schedule periods of rest during the day, take the phone off the hook, steer clear of the computer, and participate in a favored pastime.

22. MONDAY. Reassuring. Work shouldn't seem like a chore. Your better than normal organizational abilities can be put to good use. If there is a need to impress someone, this is the day to act. You may feel entitled to ask for a pay raise. If the opportunity arises, make the pitch; nothing ventured, nothing gained. Self-employed Pisces should begin experiencing the benefit of recent self-promotion or advertising, with clients now clamoring for more services. Energetic Fish could make good headway with home chores and domestic duties. If you are really eager, jump in and begin a thorough spring-cleaning of every room, closet, and cubbyhole.

23. TUESDAY. Easygoing. The Moon glides into the family-oriented sign of Cancer today, continuing the urge to seek bliss around the domestic sphere. With your Cancer fifth house of children and creative expression enhanced, special treats prepared for youngsters could add to your sense of harmony and contentment. Regardless of your current schedule there could be slight confusion and lack of clarity, advising against making decisions that may have long-lasting consequences. Invite family members or your boss for a home-cooked meal, and show off your culinary and domestic skills. It may be a good idea for solo Pisces to stay home and attend to personal tasks tonight because the chance of a romantic encounter is slim.

24. WEDNESDAY. Satisfactory. There aren't too many obstacles in the cosmic skies. Creative Pisces should spend time working on projects that require inspiration. You can complete these to your satisfaction or to the satisfaction of someone who has commissioned your special talents. Avoid shopping for nonessential items after lunch, when the inclination to spend more than the budget allows will be high. The demands or wants of children could pose financial problems for their parents, but you still might need to purchase necessary items for them. Gambling or speculating with a high-risk investment should be avoided. Social activities are likely to cost more than anticipated.

25. THURSDAY. Mixed. If you haven't been taking care of yourself, you could experience health problems, tiredness, or just a feeling of being out of sync with the world. Begin the day with a healthy breakfast, and drink plenty of water throughout the day. Organizing your workload efficiently can assist productivity, especially if you are typical of your Sun sign and perform tasks haphazardly instead of systematically. Postpone plans to approach the boss about a promotion, pay increase, or more perks; the stars are not supportive of this today. A dispute with a brother or male colleague over money matters could mar the day. Keep communications clear so you know what is happening.

26. FRIDAY. Manageable. Expect a day of mixed influences. Practice patience, particularly with fellow workers, and problems should be minimal. If aggravation erupts, the best strategy is to rely on your sense of humor and don't worry. Minor hassles should pass quickly. Concern for other people, and putting their needs first, is normal for Fish when the Moon sails through your Leo sixth house. Serving others is fine as long as you don't become a martyr and allow them to take your good nature for granted. Pisces with a sweet tooth need to resist the urge to indulge; otherwise the dentist bills could make a large dent in savings.

27. SATURDAY. Tranquil. Today should be more peaceful than yesterday, providing the chance to reevaluate where you stand with both personal and professional relationships. As a Pisces you need your own space. This can conflict with the demands and needs of loved ones, especially if you are reluctant to accept invitations and socialize with your mate or partner. Rather than seeming to be a wet blanket, negotiate and work out a suitable compromise. Meeting with a group of people who share a common interest with you should bring pleasure as well as a chance to test your skills and expertise. For singles, a new attraction could produce a smile.

28. SUNDAY. Troublesome. Disruptive conditions involving another person in your life could put you in a spin this morning. Self-employed Fish, or those of you who have to clock in on the job, could find clients, colleagues, or a boss more demanding. Those of you with a deadline to meet might be feeling the effects of increased pressure. If you are unable to honor a promise, it would be better to let people know beforehand rather than later. If you are seeking a new place to rent you may have to lower your expectations or adjust your wish list when the need to relocate becomes urgent. Financial discussions with a partner will probably end up in a disagreement this evening.

29. MONDAY. Tricky. Changeable cosmic influences prevail, and the focus could center on monetary matters. Lady Venus harmonizes with imaginative Neptune and unique Uranus, increasing creative potential and the ability to develop original ideas. However, there is a Libra Full Moon tonight lighting up your financial houses and adding pressure to any concerns regarding partnerships. Avoid getting worked up over the current state of a relationship or your financial situation, as doing so might make it difficult to assess the best available options to take. Leave the past behind if you are still yearning for an old unattainable love.

30. TUESDAY. Sensitive. Emotions remain intense, and an old bothersome matter could come to a head. Instead of issuing ultimatums, deal with the problems calmly so you can start off with a clean slate. This is a time when intuition can be trusted and your creative side can be allowed to shine through. If retail therapy is your activity of choice to fill the daylight hours, take care. Overspending could easily create havoc with the household budget. A loved one might make challenging demands that are unsettling, or someone close could ask to borrow money. If you cannot afford to loan any money, be honest and say so. Business and commercial interests are unlikely to proceed smoothly.

31. WEDNESDAY. Exciting. A bundle of cosmic influences lights up today's skies. Exploring somewhere new and meeting people from other cultures can be enlightening and exciting. Relationships with siblings and neighbors are favored as lovable Venus enters Taurus and your third house of communication. A charming demeanor and sweeter than usual tongue can help overcome any recent difficulties with relatives or someone who lives close by. If you are in the market to buy a computer, phone, or new car, the chance of getting a quality product for the right price is enhanced from now until April 25. Singles who are looking for love should stick close to home.

APRIL

1. THURSDAY. Ideal. On this dreamy day for Pisces, imagination can keep fantasies alive. Logic could let you down, however, so postpone making decisions that need practical application. If you are required to make some choices, rely on your good instincts, which should be right on target. Although interacting with the people around you should be enjoyable, communicating with in-laws may be a different story. To avoid confrontation keep a low profile, or listen without saying too much. Pisces who are eager to take off on an exciting journey should be able to discover affordable travel packages to fit any budget. This afternoon favors reading and researching.

2. FRIDAY. Cautious. Mixed trends prevail. You could feel you have lost your way and now aren't sure of the direction to follow. Doors are slowly opening, but continue to move cautiously because clarity is still not a strong attribute. Chatty Mercury steps into your third zone of Taurus, warning Fish to be cautious in choosing words over the next few weeks. Your mouth could get into gear faster than your mind, and the wrong words may tumble out before you are able to stop them. Remove high expectations of what romance should deliver and enjoy the moments that are presented. Take time out to ponder, and be proud of your achievements to date.

3. SATURDAY. Testing. The feminine energy of Venus is in dispute with masculine Mars, heralding a period requiring care in romantic situations. This could be a day of pure bliss when a strong connection is felt with your lover, or you could fall into the jealousy trap and spoil the day with accusations that may be totally unfounded. If you are called upon to make a public appearance or speak in front of an audience, the thought might prove terrifying. If nerves threaten to upset your composure, taking a few deep breaths will help you carry out the task with confidence and poise. Pisces working on a commission basis should be pleased with gains made.

4. SUNDAY. Guarded. Be careful when communicating in any form, including e-mail or even relaxed conversation, because putting your foot in your mouth is all too likely. Once the words are spoken or written you might have a hard time explaining yourself. If single, remember that love can be found in the most unlikely place, and it could happen now. The likelihood of a minor accident increases, and an influx of nervous tension could cause errors and miscalculations. If insecurity or an uncomfortable feeling surrounds a possible course of action, it would be wise to cancel or delay acting until confidence returns or you have time for further investigation. Spend time with one or more close friends tonight.

5. MONDAY. Focused. It is important to stay centered and balanced. Intense passion continues to pervade the air, spreading fervent feelings among Pisces lovers of all ages. Tension reaches a peak as planetary energies combine, and agitation or even anger could hinder effective communication. A sense that you should be doing something but not knowing exactly what may become overwhelming. Reassess current priorities. If you have any lingering doubts, wait until the choices become clearer. Avoid coworkers or other people who are prone to temper tantrums, and be careful of road rage. Spending quality time with a close companion is very enticing this evening.

6. TUESDAY. Productive. Today's influences are a marked improvement over yesterday's. With the lunar light gliding through the eleventh house of friends and associates, it will be easy for you to maintain a friendly, happy attitude. Your verbal ability is enhanced, making this an excellent time to sell an idea, product, or yourself. Pisces who speak, write, or design for a living should take full advantage of this productive period. If new information comes to light regarding an employment opportunity, reevaluate the undertaking and be ready to act accordingly. Your ability to argue a case or point in an articulate manner increases, and important discussions held now could break a stalemate in negotiations or plans.

7. WEDNESDAY. Constructive. Working with other people will be energizing this morning. Plan a group breakfast or an early team meeting to forge ahead with business strategies or matters involving a hobby association. Later in the morning you could experience a dwindling of physical energy and enthusiasm as the Moon slips into Aquarius, your twelfth zone. This is the part of the month when the universe signals that it is rest time for body and mind. During the next two days replenish spent energy; meditation, gentle massages, or a yoga class could produce the desired effect. Recording and deciphering your dreams can be helpful because they may relate to your unconscious motivations.

8. THURSDAY. Encouraging. This is another day to honor the need to rest, relax, and pace yourself. Confusing influences are more likely than clarity; however, inspired thoughts and ideas can produce significant gains. Working behind the scenes or on a solitary pursuit could be beneficial for those who prefer independence. Follow through on compassionate urges. Carry out an act of charity, donate time to someone in need, or visit the local hospital or nursing home to spread kindness and cheer. Mighty Pluto has now moved into retrograde motion in your Capricorn eleventh zone, urging you to do what's right and to refrain from compromising your hard-earned gains and victories.

9. FRIDAY. Dreamy. Fish are likely to drift through the day, but be careful not to allow an accusation of laziness to be leveled your way. Make sure to pull your own weight. Unless you remain grounded, accomplishments will be few. Talented Pisces can let their imagination run wild, with inspired ideas the resulting reward. This is a good day for dreaming about the future and visualizing where you want to be in a month or a year. If you have some time on your hands, find a way to volunteer in your local community. Being of service to others will provide emotional gratification and come back to you tenfold.

10. SATURDAY. Eventful. Your popularity should rise, and charming those you set out to impress should be easier. The Moon gliding through your sign of Pisces marks the time to step into the light and be seen by others, which can help you advance up the ladder of success. There may be a number of aggravations that require your undivided attention, so keep your schedule flexible to allow changes to be slotted in without causing havoc. A new or ongoing health issue may benefit from a second opinion, especially if conflicting medical views have been expressed. Although an employment situation could become untenable, it would be wise to obtain another job before leaving your present one.

11. SUNDAY. Fulfilling. Confidence remains high, and your social calendar should be overflowing. If you are intent on spoiling other people, you are hopefully also on the receiving end of goodies being handed out. Purchase a few special items for yourself such as a new outfit, shoes, and accessories. Or meet up with friends for coffee or brunch. A facial or a manicure could also provide a lift to your self-esteem. On the romantic scene, an unexpected surprise will require a flexible approach. Be alert if a friend tries to take advantage of your generosity, spinning a story of financial hardship to encourage you to feel guilty and foot the whole entertainment bill.

12. MONDAY. Fine. It should be easy for you to approach the day with enthusiasm and energy. Don't be afraid to ask for favors;

requests are likely to be viewed kindly, with some being granted immediately. Couples could experience a financial concern that adds tension to the relationship unless a suitable compromise is worked out. Unexpected expenses, or the chance to purchase an item that has been desired for some time, could require restructuring personal finances. Single Pisces who have been watching your dollars and cents could now consider investing money in a sound venture that has a good chance of building a future nest egg.

13. TUESDAY. Sentimental. Rely on your good Pisces instincts and the day should turn in your favor. A pressing situation could make you agitated, although it might not be long before everything works out the way you hope. A wave of nostalgia could sweep over you as the echoes of the past filter through today's activities. This may give you the chance for a sneak peek back to where you have come from and then the opportunity to look forward to a brighter future. A school reunion or family gathering that has been a long time in the planning stages could begin to come together in the manner envisioned. Your dreams could be revealing the answer you have been seeking.

14. WEDNESDAY. Renewing. Financial matters are in focus. A fresh New Moon culminates in your Aries second zone, providing an opportunity to set realistic financial goals, to formulate a sound household budget, and to plan other projects. This is the time to discover new ways to increase your income. Good deals and a number of bargains for your home could be tempting, but don't get carried away. On the other hand, take a second look at any quality sales. If you are good at negotiating, substantial savings can be made. Catch up with a brother or sister not living close by, either by phone or computer. Whether you engage in idle chitchat or a more in-depth discussion, the two-way communication can be enlightening.

15. THURSDAY. Easygoing. A lighthearted energy permeates the day. If the weather is good, a walk in the park or around the neighborhood could be relaxing and refreshing. This is a good time to visit friends, catching up and sharing gossip and news. Pisces who are experienced in networking with others should make an extra effort because benefits might arrive in abundance. Take care around the house this morning, guarding against a minor injury or a fall. Walk instead of rushing, and watch where you are going. Drivers need to concentrate instead of daydreaming or talking on the phone. Watching an interesting travel show or reading an absorbing novel may be the perfect way to relax this evening.

16. FRIDAY. Fruitful. Say exactly what you are feeling. Express yourself clearly and concisely, but make sure your comments and remarks are constructive and not unkind. Write down current aims regardless of how outrageous those goals might appear right now. Having the list in a highly visible area will serve as a constant reminder and increase the chances of one day bringing desires to fruition. Pisces intent on furthering your education might research various part-time or short courses that will increase specialized skills and provide an advantage in the employment stakes. Learning a new language may be one way to begin moving up the career ladder.

17. SATURDAY. Fair. Knowing what you want to say or do is likely, but finding the right words or approach could be problematical. It is time to forget the stresses and strains of the working week and unwind over the weekend. Difficulties at home might be a source of annoyance, but issues can be resolved quickly if you give them due thought and consideration. If purchasing a new car, electronic equipment, or a major household item is on your agenda, complete the sale today before Mercury goes into retrograde motion tomorrow. Domestic projects benefit under current planetary influences, and home entertainment or a family gathering should be especially enjoyable.

18. SUNDAY. Pleasant. A bevy of cosmic trends is in effect, and most of these are conveying positive trends. An unexpected task may actually be an opportunity in disguise. Home repairs can be an ideal activity for the house-proud Pisces. Messenger Mercury now begins moving retrograde in your Taurus house of communication and transportation, so be prepared for glitches, mix-ups, and delays. Various malfunctions are likely, but particularly phones, computers, and television sets. Purchase new art, reupholster furniture, or wash the windows to increase the ambience of your domestic environment. Browse the Internet or the mall for quotes on a large purchase you want to buy once Mercury moves forward.

19. MONDAY. Playful. Whenever the Moon moves through your Cancer fifth house, attitude becomes more playful and light. The child within comes to the fore; so this can be a time when creative juices flow freely. The urge to socialize increases, but the first day of the new working week is not the time to turn into a party animal. If there is a celebration to organize, good ideas should come to mind that can make the party a hit with those lucky enough to receive an invitation. If a crucial financial decision is up to you, double-check facts and figures before proceeding with a proposed investment opportunity. Refrain from becoming involved in any purely speculative venture or any type of gambling.

20. TUESDAY. Diverse. Up-and-down celestial trends are in force. The lunar goddess sends mixed messages that could create a number of annoyances throughout the day. The pace of life is about to quicken as the Sun joins Mercury and Venus in your Taurus third house. Over the next few weeks expect to be doing more talking, visiting, and listening. Running errands, keeping busy, and being constantly on the go can become very tiring, so be sure to schedule some leisure time in your hectic agenda. It is a favorable time to interact with neighbors. When new people move in, extend a hand of friendship to make them feel welcome. Solo Pisces could find love locally or maybe just next door.

21. WEDNESDAY. Loving. You should feel right at home thanks to the planets being favorable throughout the morning hours. Romantic vibes are strong, urging a longer stay with your lover. Parents should pledge to spend time with children, even if only supervising homework or making chores fun. Allow youngsters to see that life doesn't have to be serious all the time. Unless you keep on top of your workload, efficiency will decline. Trouble could come through a boss or due to a delayed payment. Devise a healthy workout regime that you can do consistently every day before leaving for work or as soon as tasks are finished at the end of the working day. Try to get a little extra sleep.

22. THURSDAY. Edgy. The stars could create friction and agitation, so go with the flow and expect to make a number of schedule changes and adjustments. Be prepared for nothing to proceed smoothly. However, most situations can be worked out satisfactorily with a little extra effort and thought. Dramatics need to be kept to a minimum; otherwise stress and tension could bring on indigestion, headaches, or another minor ailment. The urge to assist other people rather than performing personal deeds is strong. Volunteering to help out at a local animal shelter could provide emotional satisfaction if you want to serve your community in some useful way.

23. FRIDAY. Varied. The universe is sending a diverse range of trends to keep you on your toes. Love and money are likely to be to the forefront of activities as love goddess Venus is in dispute with your life ruler, nebulous Neptune, but happily links with eccentric Uranus. This isn't the best period to make an emotional decision because thoughts may run wild, bordering on the erratic to the fantastic. A social gathering should provide pleasure as enjoyment of life is enhanced. For Pisces singles, a new relationship needs to be nurtured with care. Although excitement pervades the air and everything might be glowing, rose-colored glasses could cloud objectivity.

24. SATURDAY. Stabilizing. Over the next few days the universe offers a chance for Pisces to seriously consider cutting loose from a restrictive situation. Venus will be harmonizing with serious Saturn. So if you follow through now, an important breakthrough or a new pathway lies ahead and it could be the beginning of a new chapter in your life. The weekend offers a better chance for singles to meet a romantic potential who could become a stable and steady partner. Someone older, more mature, or wealthier might appeal, so keep your eyes and options open if in the market for new love. Couples can share happy rapport without making any special plans.

25. SUNDAY. Conflicting. Contradictory planetary influences prevail. Although verbal communication could be eloquent and powerful, arguments could quickly erupt unless care is taken with how you speak and what you say. Venus, lover of splendor, moves into your Gemini house of home and garden, encouraging you to spend more time beautifying both these areas. Redecorating and entertaining at home base can be both rewarding and expensive if you allow your heart to rule your head. Small touches including flowers, indoor plants, or colorful prints can add to the overall ambience and appearance. If you are single, say yes to meeting a friend of a friend, who may be the right partner for you.

26. MONDAY. Significant. Powerful influences abound, which can create a life-altering situation anytime in the next few weeks. Serious Saturn, representing the old and the structured, is in opposition to excitable Uranus, which is associated with the new and with breaking through outdated patterns, habits, and situations. Personal and professional partnerships may be under pressure. If changes are needed to allow you to move in the right direction, this is bound to happen in some way. The more you understand, the better prepared you will be to face new challenges and tests. If you seek a stimulating hobby, spend time researching new possibilities until you discover one that captures your attention.

27. TUESDAY. Trying. Getting through the day might be a test of self-control. Unless you remain calm, the day's highly charged emotional trends could put you on edge and some of you may be inclined to overreact. A discovery could clear up an old mystery, triggering a change of plans that can produce a real sense of pleasure. Those of you in business might experience some upset. An associate or colleague with whom you have been discussing entering into a commercial partnership could suddenly pull out of negotiations. Catch up on personal correspondence. Your ability to express yourself in a charming manner remains high. Creative work can lead to financial benefits.

28. WEDNESDAY. Sensitive. An emotional encounter could be intense, and you might feel you are walking on eggshells throughout the day. A Full Moon in Scorpio increases tension and the sensitive feelings of people in close proximity to you. Steer clear of disputes with neighbors and close relatives. Drivers should take extra precautions when out in traffic. If you become involved in any altercation, you may be the one who comes off second best. The urge to visit a special destination for the first time, or to revisit such a place, could be the encouragement needed to look into bargain travel deals. See what is being offered, but before making the arrangements, wait until mid-May when Mercury moves forward.

29. THURSDAY. Watchful. Family relationships continue to be more harmonious than usual, although there may be problems within your circle of friends. Borrowing or loaning money from a friend or colleague may strain the relationship. A visitor from a distance, or an e-mail from a friend who hasn't been in contact lately, could put a smile on your face. Unexpected news concerning travel arrangements may require a sudden change of plans. Important information passed on to you could be the development needed to move a legal issue to a final conclusion. The unattached Pisces should proceed slowly if a possible lover appears on the scene.

30. FRIDAY. Sparkling. The universe continues to press your buttons. Don't take on too many chores and responsibilities. If your agenda is flexible and everything is kept simple, matters should turn out in the manner you envision. An urge to entertain continues. Plans for a small or large gathering, a barbecue, or a kids' party held at home should fall into place without too much stress or changes having to be made. Singles intent on impressing a new person should consider a home-cooked dinner for two, complete with soft music, mood lighting, and a bottle of expensive wine. An idea to improve your home might begin to take shape, and final details can be worked out harmoniously over the weekend.

MAY

1. SATURDAY. Bumpy. It is important to pace yourself and not overdo, and that includes dealing with other people. The Moon sliding through Sagittarius, your zone of career and reputation, brings employment issues to the fore even if this is your normal day off. Pisces who are on the job could struggle to please an employer, business associate, or an authority figure because the trends lack harmonious vibes. Pisces employers should not force workers to deal with tasks that they are not ready to handle; doing so could set them up to fail. Get anything with legal implications in writing before proceeding with even simple tasks in order to outfox trickster Mercury, which is still in retrograde motion until May 11.

2. SUNDAY. Confusing. Misunderstandings and confusion could mar the day. With disciplined Saturn in an aspect of friction with your coruler, foggy Neptune, try to stay on an even keel. This may be especially difficult because you might feel that everything is falling down around you. There is the possibility that you could suffer from mild depression at the worst or just feel grumpier than usual. Be sure to keep a to-do list and consult it often over the next few days. If your schedule is full of meetings and appointments, forgetfulness could be unavoidable. If you get involved in some sort of community fund-raising, only take the lead if that is what you want. Don't allow anyone to push you into taking on any role or task.

3. MONDAY. Variable. Be prepared for a less than pleasant experience if you go head-to-head with an authority figure or a parent. Be on guard for coworkers who are intent on dumping their too-hard work onto you. Verbal communication is highlighted, with word choice at a premium. Pisces involved in debating or giving a public lecture should enjoy every minute of time in the limelight. This is a favorable period to share thoughts and ideas with other people. Lunch with a business associate could be revealing; you might find out what ideas or project holds their interest. Diminish stress and pressure this evening by indulging in an activity that promotes relaxation.

4. TUESDAY. Demanding. A number of planetary aspects will increase challenges and difficulties encountered along today's pathway. Your workload could be heavy, creating tension. Take the situation into your own hands and delegate some of the work, or ask your boss to provide much needed assistance. Try to keep an open mind. You can learn a lot by listening carefully. Constructive criticism either from you or directed toward you might improve a difficult situation. Being associated with a group or an organization could be extremely important this afternoon, and you might be elected to a leadership role. A quiet, early night will appeal.

5. WEDNESDAY. Hopeful. Keep energy and emotions on an even keel, and don't blame anyone else if you are a little touchy. A thick fog could envelop you. Issues might become unclear as the Moon sails through your Aquarius twelfth zone of self-undoing and solitude. If unsure of any situations or choices, it would be wise to postpone judgment and let decisions brew for a few days. Steer clear of people who try to bring you down. A meeting at your home could lead to an original exchange of ideas and thoughts, with you taking the lead. The unattached Pisces who is looking for love should find promising suitors in abundance, but only after coming down from the clouds.

6. THURSDAY. Watchful. Not many lunar influences are prevailing today, and those that are in effect are not very supportive. Remain grounded and practical; common sense may be in short supply. Working behind closed doors or at least on your own will suit you. Constantly interacting with other people could feel like a chore. Sudden blessings can come your way, especially if you give to others without thinking of personal cost. This is a great period to visit someone who is ill or confined at home. Spread a little magic by taking along home-cooked goodies, a few new magazines, or a small gift that provides pleasure and joy.

7. FRIDAY. Happy. Today's picture looks rosier, with love and creativity thriving under present conditions. Relationships with the opposite sex, with coworkers, and with your mate or partner should be harmonious as Lady Venus links amicably with dynamic Mars. Business activities that require a creative flair should progress strongly, as will art that requires the use of tools. Pisces love to dance, and those auditioning for a dance part should excel. If you are currently without a partner and are seeking love, or if you are endeavoring to reignite passion in a long-term relationship, this is the day to take action. Turn to your significant other if you need some moral support, and be assured that loved ones have your best interests at heart.

8. SATURDAY. Chancy. The stars are telling contradictory stories all day, but things will begin to look up when it is time to go out and socialize. Ambitions are stirred, although a combative or impatient attitude won't help you achieve your aims any quicker. Sheer determination is required to overcome whatever obstacles you confront.

With the Moon in your own sign of Pisces, bask in the silvery glow tonight. This will help you make a good impression on other people. Put on your best party outfit, and take time with personal grooming. Singles who are looking for romance could be in luck. Couples should make the most of any chance to engage in a love fest.

9. SUNDAY. Useful. Do something just for you. Buy a new outfit, new shoes, seat covers for your car, or any small item that takes your fancy. Speak up if you feel that someone is treating you unfairly or is not honoring a promise. Projects that need to be revised or rejuvenated can benefit now. Later in the day the Aries Moon brings an opportunity to improve financial stability. Monetary transactions of any kind should be handled carefully. Analyze and assess all situations so your interests are protected. The likelihood of an accident increases late this afternoon unless extra care is taken.

10. MONDAY. Cautious. Energy and enthusiasm should be on display, which can help you meet the day-to-day challenges that come your way. However, misunderstandings, mix-ups, or delays will test your patience, so allow some breathing space in your work schedule. Financial issues continue to demand attention. Guard against impulsive action. Otherwise you may be inclined to rush into a situation without considering all possible consequences. Call in favors if you need something done in a hurry, help with a special task, or someone to help reduce your workload. Looking at existing problems from a different angle should provide the insight needed to solve them once and for all.

11. TUESDAY. Improving. You could find your plans continually overridden if you don't learn to say no or stick up for your views. Steer clear of coworkers or friends who engage in idle gossip or are intent on spreading rumors. Too much mental exercise could leave you feeling a little burned out. Messenger Mercury begins moving forward in the sign of Taurus today, helping to bring to an end delays with contracts, leases, and general paperwork. Travel snarls should be less frequent, meetings will be canceled less often, and hopefully there will be an end to what might have become regular computer crashes. Singles can look for love among those who live close by.

12. WEDNESDAY. Beneficial. With the Moon in the money-oriented sign of Taurus, finances are under auspicious stars. Get the calculator out and figure ways to improve your financial stability and security. If you have been involved in a disagreement with neighbors or siblings, negotiating a peace settlement should be easier now.

A friendly smile or a handshake could make all the difference in resolving an ongoing issue. Your ability to communicate clearly is strong, especially this morning, and that would be a great time to hold an important meeting, conduct interviews, or deliver a report. Don't hesitate to sign contracts, purchase a new vehicle, or catch up on correspondence.

13. THURSDAY. Calm. Morning vibes are a little tricky, but the overall atmosphere of the day is fine. A New Moon activates your Taurus third house of communication, triggering the urge to begin new projects and to forge ahead with future plans. This is a favorable period to buy any form of transportation, electronic equipment, or household linens. Pisces taking a test should exceed expectations if required studying has been done. The current influence also supports efforts to get a message across to key people. Pisces individuals attending a job interview should easily impress a prospective employer with your knowledge and confidence.

14. FRIDAY. Busy. A fast pace continues this morning, slowing down as afternoon approaches. Your natural curiosity is aroused, and restlessness could hinder focusing on a particular task. This morning give serious consideration to travel plans or a scholastic program, alert for something you were not aware of yesterday. You may have plenty to say on a particular matter, requiring extra tact and diplomacy to get your message across. Rest and relaxation might be preferred tonight. You could find that family members need you around more than usual. If staying home doesn't suit you, be willing to compromise. Split your leisure time evenly between family desires and personal needs.

15. SATURDAY. Great. Look forward to a pleasant day. The Moon continues to move through your Gemini fourth sector, urging Pisces to spend time with the folks at home. If you haven't seen an older relative for some time, plan a visit now. For Pisces looking to purchase a new home, this is an excellent period to check what is available. Before signing a contract or an offer on the dotted line, make sure you know exactly how much you can afford to pay each month so you don't become house poor. Put on your party clothes and go out on the town this evening. Those who have a reunion to attend should have a memorable night reliving those good old days.

16. SUNDAY. Gratifying. Time spent renovating your home or garden can add value to one of your major assets. Make sure that everyone in the family has some say in the planned changes before going ahead. To guard against extravagance, obtain a number of price quotes from suppliers to avoid prohibitive costs. This afternoon, waves of nostalgia could sweep over Fish, urging participation in sentimental activities such as viewing old photos or rereading letters from long ago. Old-fashion fun shared with children can be joyous. A get-together with family members or friends could bring back a flood of sweet memories.

17. MONDAY. Buoyant. Pisces, be very aware today. Lady Venus and jolly Jupiter, your coruler, are in a cosmic contest, but fortunately the Sun and Jupiter are happily connected, helping to ease difficult trends. Relationships with children should be warm, although Pisces parents could worry needlessly about youngsters. Moderation is required with what passes through your lips; too much rich food and too many alcoholic beverages could make you feel out of sorts tomorrow. Be careful not to take too much for granted. In particular, be sensible when it comes to spending money. Highlights of your day could include planning to attend a number of future social activities and celebrations or perhaps to host one.

18. TUESDAY. Interesting. A laid-back day awaits Fish, or you might just feel like being lazy. Begin working on a creative project that gives you pleasure in your leisure time. Although results could take a while to appear, they should eventually prove well worth the effort. Venus, the goddess of amour, connects positively to your coruler, foggy Neptune, but is in dispute with staid Saturn. So love, romance, and financial matters are under contradictory influences. The talented Pisces could make headway thanks to the current mixture of inspiration coupled with the knowledge that perspiration is also required to produce anything of value. Attend a concert or romantic movie and lose yourself in a world of fantasy.

19. WEDNESDAY. Baffling. Emotions are likely to be unstable as a number of major celestial aspects take shape in the heavens. Romance is in the air. Single Fish are unlikely to miss out on a number of romantic potentials appearing on the scene. If you don't want to face disappointment later on, proceed slowly. Under these skies an exciting love affair could blossom suddenly, then disappear just as quickly. If possible, avoid signing important paperwork, making any major decisions, purchasing electronic equipment, or scheduling meetings over the next couple of days because thinking could be clouded and logic will be elusive.

20. THURSDAY. Supportive. Venus, lover of beauty, is now residing in Cancer, your fifth house of pleasure. This placement heralds an exciting period over the next four weeks for the unattached Fish: a perfect time to attract a lover. Partnered Pisces are also likely to experience an improvement in love. An unexpected gift from a close relative or neighbor could brighten your day. Later this evening the Sun moves into Gemini, your fourth house of family and real estate. This placement will accent matters revolving around older relatives, loved ones, and domestic affairs. New projects or a decision connected with the family home or property should proceed smoothly.

21. FRIDAY. Vibrant. Love and creativity remain favored. With the Moon now in efficient Virgo, detail-oriented projects should benefit. Pisces can use the next two days to accomplish tasks on a small scale that require organization and a practical application. Plan to spend private time with your mate or partner this weekend, reconnecting loving bonds. A getaway trip for a few days could refresh a romantic relationship that has gone a little stale. If this isn't possible, a heart-to-heart talk over a candlelit dinner might be just what is needed to add extra zing and passion. Solo Pisces could discover an interesting love possibility at the local gym or at a family gathering.

22. SATURDAY. Favorable. Partnership concerns are to the fore, encouraging you to pay more attention to your significant other. Even an hour alone with that special person can be instrumental in clearing up an old misunderstanding or a potential issue. Working in a spirit of cooperation with associates or professional partners is likely this morning, which should increase productivity and enhance amicable feelings. Making promises that you might not be able to keep is foreseen early this evening, so be careful. You could also slip up and reveal a confidence, or say something out of turn, if your concentration is lax.

23. SUNDAY. Uncertain. The opposing forces of your life ruler, expansive Jupiter, versus restrictive Saturn, also sexy Venus in dispute with powerful Pluto, are sure to shake things up today. There may be a number of choices facing you, and knowing which to eliminate could be difficult. Problems with taxes, investments, or joint finances could create worries, perhaps even spoiling the day. Love and passion are enhanced. However, there is also the possibility of jealousy erupting within an intimate relationship. If you tend to be flirtatious, take care when socializing in a large gathering so that your partner or someone you just met doesn't get the wrong idea.

24. MONDAY. Manageable. Once you settle into the day, it should begin to improve. Don't rely on advice from people who are not well known to you. Bonds with colleagues should strengthen during this period. However, take it easy if going out with them for lunch or after work; your cash could diminish and your waistline grow. The Moon moving through your Libra eighth sector is a chance to remove anything that has been getting you down or messing up your environment. A good start would be to declutter drawers, reorganize joint finances to improve stability, obtain more competitive quotes for insurance or medical coverage, or start a detox plan for your body.

25. TUESDAY. Stimulating. Keep dreaming about a prosperous and happy future and perhaps soon you will be living it. Relationships are improving, as are professional matters. Passion and desire will intensify. Relating to other people on a deeper level should be easier to do. A number of interesting possibilities may arise, particularly if furthering your education is a priority. Search for academic or training courses that suit your current requirements by contacting nearby colleges or looking on the Internet. Try a different venue for lunch, or have dinner at a local restaurant that specializes in the cuisine of another country.

26. WEDNESDAY. Diverse. Special precautions are required to avoid confrontations as celestial patterns bring trying conditions for much of the day. Plans connected to your family could fall apart, and it would be wise to have alternative arrangements in mind. Current beliefs may be having a negative impact on your day-to-day activities, so a reassessment of your current direction could be beneficial. Don't hesitate if the boss suggests you take a business trip or a training course. Such opportunities are hard to come by and may lead to extra pay and career advancement. Solo Pisces could be lucky enough to find love through an overseas link, at the library, or in a class.

27. THURSDAY. Sensitive. As a Pisces you tend to be a sensitive soul who understands the importance of treading carefully when emotions run high, as may be the case for much of this day. A Full Moon in the sign of Sagittarius increases tension as well as focusing on your tenth zone of professional matters, success, and recognition from others. Authority figures could be moody, so stay under their radar and be respectful. Your strong desire for freedom could create a situation where you find it hard to settle into one task for any length of time. This is a favorable period to make career changes or to consider moving on to another employer.

28. FRIDAY. Major. An abundance of astrological patterns forms, marking a day of possible challenges, unexpected occurrences, and frequent mix-ups. Nervousness or anxiety could create problems, causing mistakes or a minor accident. It might be wise to wait until confidence returns before tackling any important task. If a project cannot wait and must move ahead, proceed slowly and pay strict attention to detail. Uranus, the erratic and excitable planet, has now entered your Aries second house of personal finances and possessions after a long stay in your own sign of Pisces. Over the coming years you can expect changes with your financial position and income, including a higher paid job, self-employment, or a cutback in hours.

29. SATURDAY. Fair. A practical and serious atmosphere converges on Pisces this afternoon as the Moon moves into reliable Capricorn. Until then you could be more impulsive and independent. Interaction may be less frequent, although what you have to say may be of a serious or sensitive nature. Getting your point across is possible as long as you select your words carefully and contain any hint of criticism. There shouldn't be any pressing need to hurry even though ambition is running high. Relax and spend time participating in a favorite pastime, or take part in an activity involving special friends. You deserve a break, and work can wait.

30. SUNDAY. Encouraging. Changes are brewing, but for now it would be better to go with the flow. Try to meet and overcome each test as it appears. With your friendship zone currently activated, interesting folks could suddenly appear to liven up the day. An old acquaintance could reappear in your circle, and it might be up to you to make this person feel welcome. Effort applied on the job or to a pivotal partnership could soon pay off. Saturn, the taskmaster of the zodiac, turns forward today, helping to redefine relationships with other people. This will be especially helpful for Pisces who have been experiencing a rough patch in a marriage or in a long-term relationship.

31. MONDAY. Significant. Another major astrological move occurs today with the advent of your coruler, Neptune, moving retrograde in Aquarius, your twelfth house of solitary matters. Strange, confusing dreams could be frequent, so take note and be open to learning more about yourself. Look inward, deciphering and analyzing dreams. Recognize that the universe could send answers to your questions. Meditate often, join a yoga class, or head off on a spiritual retreat to aid relaxation of body, mind, and spirit. A connection made now could feel fated. Time spent with friends can be both therapeutic and restful.

JUNE

1. TUESDAY. Invigorating. Pisces folk should be smiling as the new month begins. With Venus remaining in Cancer, your love sector, attracting romantic attention should be a breeze. Inspiration and happiness can be found in the joyful things surrounding you. Energy may be lower as the Moon drifts through Aquarius, your house of secrets and private matters. With the weather heating up, this is the time to claim inner peace and recharge your batteries by relaxing somewhere close to water, whether this is the beach, lake, or a private swimming pool. A cool bath, sprinkled with favored aromatherapy oil, might be preferred if you are seeking comfort in your own home.

2. WEDNESDAY. Restless. This is another day when taking a break from routine appears necessary. If you have a hectic schedule to face, make sure that you schedule time out to take a deep breath before planning your next move. Spending the day alone reflecting on ideas and strategies could work, or you might yearn for some distractions and interaction from coworkers or friends. Your ability to tune in to the thoughts and feelings of other people is enhanced and can be used to good advantage. Avoid possible discord by steering clear of touchy or provocative topics midafternoon. Catch up on unfinished tasks before beginning any new project.

3. THURSDAY. Variable. Don't shoot the messenger today. If you receive information that you are not happy about, exercise tact and patience. Some people won't want to take no for an answer, so you will need to stand your ground, which is not always easy for a placid Pisces. By early afternoon power begins to return to you, providing an extra boost of self-confidence. You'll also regain the ability to speak up if necessary or to ask other people for what you need. Spending money to upgrade your image can also enhance self-esteem, adding more charm to your magnetic personality. Let your significant other know how much you care, either through actions or words.

4. FRIDAY. Slow. Pisces folk of all ages should pace today's activities. With the Moon in your sign of Pisces, vim and vitality should be high. However, dynamo Mars is in conflict with your life ruler, dreamy Neptune, reducing physical resources. Although it may be hard to remain balanced and grounded, a long walk could help clear confused thoughts and increase self-control. If you are typical of your Sun sign, you probably love staying in bed; if you don't, try to increase your amount of sleep now. Conflict in relationships is a distinct likelihood, particularly with fellow workers or employees. Be wary of an opportunity offered to you. Even if it is proposed by someone trustworthy, they might not be aware of hidden pitfalls.

5. SATURDAY. Lively. Don't worry about keeping everyone else happy if you are not included on the list. It is time for you to take center stage. With the Moon glowing in your own sign of Pisces, popularity should be increasing. Other folks will enjoy your company and will let you know it. Dig into your nest egg if you are considering a surgical procedure or an expensive cosmetic treatment that you feel would increase your self-confidence. If you are currently unattached, don't sit at home alone; get out to meet and greet other people who share your interests. Love and romance should proceed smoothly, enhancing the chances of meeting someone special.

6. SUNDAY. Major. Aries, your house of personal finances and values, comes into focus today. It is time to perform some accounting procedures so you can gauge exactly where you stand with overdue bills, loan payments, and expected income. Your traditional ruler, generous Jupiter, enters Aries, your house of money. Jupiter here begins for you a year of possible expansion of income and improvement in your feelings of self-worth. For the less disciplined Pisces, this will be a time when the cosmos urges a let-the-spending-begin spree, regardless of how much is in your bank account. Even if you are a frugal Pisces, which is uncommon, resisting the urge to buy items on impulse could be difficult.

7. MONDAY. Interesting. Pisces shoppers should list any intended purchases before heading off; credit cards could quickly be pushed over the limit. Money can be saved by restoring and repairing items you already own rather than buying new products. Doing that work yourself should be gratifying, giving you a real sense of accomplishment once the object is brought back to its original glory. Mighty Mars moves into your Virgo zone of personal and professional partnerships, bringing the possibility of a few bumps and conflicts to deal with until July 29. A concert or event can warm your heart, providing a welcome break from routine.

8. TUESDAY. Stimulating. Look forward to an exciting day of action and adventure. Luck abounds, making this a good day to purchase a lottery ticket, enter a competition, or apply for a promotion or a new job. Be prepared to take advantage of unexpected opportunities as optimistic Jupiter merges with unique Uranus. Any financial worries should be short-lived because the chance to increase your cash flow is heightened. Old faces might reappear, or a few new friends may liven up your life. This can be a good time to speculate; hunches are apt to be on target. Business deals and negotiations should go well thanks to your enhanced ability to instill confidence in other people.

9. WEDNESDAY. Tricky. Deceptive trends are in play, so be on guard. Refrain from making plans that are set in stone because changes are likely to arise and create major issues. Protect your emotions; inner turmoil and confusion can be disconcerting and even overwhelming. Valuable work time could be eroded though interruptions, idle gossip, or having to answer never-ending e-mails and questions. Stand firm and refuse to be distracted. Otherwise you might have to pay the price for scattered energy, having to work overtime to complete urgent assignments, deliveries, or tasks. A family member might not have any qualms about telling a few white lies.

10. THURSDAY. Active. The cosmic skies are busy, and life is likely to pick up as a result. Expect your head to be buzzing with lots of concerns regarding home and family life. An extravagant gift might come your way, adding increased excitement and joy. Clever Mercury zips into versatile Gemini, accentuating your home and family zone. Thoughts are likely to turn to past memories and childhood conditioning. Your drive and motivation to achieve will be strong. You are likely to be in business mode, making decisions involving money and reviewing how to generate more income. Stand up for what you believe in. Don't shy away from telling the truth.

11. FRIDAY. Disconcerting. Talkative Mercury conflicts with assertive Mars, warning Pisces folk to be careful in discussions with other people. Tempers could flare quickly, creating discord and heated debate. Squabbles at home may take the shine off a family get-together if disagreements are allowed to get out of hand. Meetings could be volatile, so it may be wise to cancel any nonessential gathering or appointment. If part of a couple, you might feel that your partner seems focused on areas of life totally different from your concerns, causing confusion, but don't make waves. This situation is probably only temporary and should soon pass. Enjoying the simple things of family life could be pure bliss for those preferring to spend the evening at home.

12. SATURDAY. Social. Taking pride in your home and tending to household duties will be relaxing. Any restlessness can be put to good use by weeding the garden, planting new seedlings, or redecorating a special room in the house. The New Moon in Gemini this morning increases the urge to beautify your environment and increase home comforts for the enjoyment of all family members. If an unusual pastime captures your attention, consider giving it a go and adding a new skill to your repertoire. As the weather heats up, your social life should also be increasing. That special person you have your eye on may be very aware of you, too, so don't be shy about mingling and making conversation.

13. SUNDAY. Fair. Go ahead and indulge in whatever gives you the most happiness and pleasure. It won't be an easygoing day, so you might as well eke out as much fun as you can. Creative pastimes can be a good source of amusement, aiding relaxation. Practicing reverse psychology on kids who are acting up might work, and so will any other form of discipline. Your lover or partner may be moodier or more sensitive than usual, so proceed warily unless you want continual battles during the day. Take someone you admire off the pedestal to avoid future disappointment. Your expectations for love and romance could be very unrealistic.

14. MONDAY. Excellent. Today lovely Venus sashays into your Leo house of work and service, and remains there until July 10. Making your workplace more attractive could be a priority, providing pleasant and tranquil surroundings in which to perform your work duties. Organizing files, purchasing a healthy indoor plant, and removing extraneous items from your desk can make a huge difference to productivity, bringing a sense of calm. Singles can look forward to an increase in romantic possibilities, with more than one request for your phone number. Love could even be found on the job. The chances are good of receiving a pay raise, promotion, or a better commission percentage.

15. TUESDAY. Fortunate. Focusing on work should come easily, which is just as well because there is bound to be plenty of it. Luck and good fortune are in plentiful supply, so you can afford to take a gamble or a few well-calculated risks. A promotion, improved work schedule, or a change of employment duties could be your reward for recently exerted extra effort. An attempt to improve your general well-being can pay dividends. Begin each morning with a healthy, low-fat breakfast, and drink plenty of fresh water during the day. Lessen stress and pressure by working up a sweat; hit the gym, hop on your personal exercise machine, or go for a jog around the park.

16. WEDNESDAY. Favorable. Pisces folks looking to add a furry animal to the family should check the local animal shelter; there should be plenty of pets that suit current requirements. Concentrating on what can be achieved is the way to reach cherished aims. Focus on the positive. Negotiating a solid strategy for family health and medical coverage with your employer can increase security. Singles are likely to give the computer a good workout, with many taking the plunge into the online dating scene. If you are open as well as discerning, a new love potential could come your way. A cool bath with favored oil should assist relaxation before bedtime.

17. THURSDAY. Encouraging. Today's critical approach warns Pisces to be careful. Cooperation and compromise are most likely to win favors from other people. It is wise to cultivate support rather than trying to go it alone, which can make accomplishments harder to achieve. Spending time together with those who mean the most to you is very important. Arranging to meet your significant other for a lunch date away from kids or friends will help to increase loving intimacy. If there are concerns that should be discussed, this is the time to speak up. Verbalize your expectations, needs, and current ideas with your mate or partner.

18. FRIDAY. Promising. Apply a good dose of that wonderful Pisces humor to all of today's activities and you should come through relatively unscathed. By removing an issue from your active consciousness, very often a solution can be found, so don't dwell on problems. Beware of competitors or coworkers out to prove they are smarter than you on the job or when it comes to providing customer service. After the working day is finished, the company of a best friend or partner can restore your energy. A quiet dinner at a neighborhood restaurant might be your choice if plans are flexible.

19. SATURDAY. Complex. A differing of attitude or priorities could surface for those involved in a long-term relationship. Career or professional interests may be taking over your life, creating discord with your mate or partner. If this is the case, be careful. Being always busy increases pressure on your union. If sensitivity to the feelings of others is not shown, you can expect a backlash. Pay close attention to hunches; your intuitive powers are enhanced. Pisces with artistic talent can dream big and allow imagination to run free. Avoid alcoholic beverages or, if this isn't possible, at least try to remain sober and in complete control. Be careful with any type of drugs.

20. SUNDAY. Lucky. Passion continues to rise as the Moon glides through your eighth house of sex and power. Tensions over money or possessions could cause a few headaches, but issues should be resolved quickly if you adopt a sensible approach. Social occasions could occupy much of the day, but put aside some me time so you can dwell on your own deep thoughts and desires. Be active in your search to find love if currently unattached and looking. A bout of good luck could come your way, supporting romantic efforts. Utilize your creative energy constructively by redecorating your living space, work area, or home office. Lovers can enjoy each other's company at home and also when out and about.

21. MONDAY. Happy. The Sun and Uranus clash today, creating a possible period of chaos, disorder, and restlessness. Unexpected situations are likely to upset plans, although the astute Pisces should be on top of things quickly enough to recover and get back on track. The summer solstice is here, with the longest daylight of the year bringing refreshing change and more opportunities to party. The Sun enters your Cancer fifth house, encouraging Fish of all ages to let the fun begin. The urge to entertain family members and friends in your home increases, offering the chance to display hospitality and catering skills. The next four weeks is a favorable period to celebrate with special parties or family gatherings.

22. TUESDAY. Edgy. The general atmosphere appears awkward, and you will need to take suitable precautions to avoid agitation. With the Moon slipping through Scorpio, your house of aspiration and adventure, fuel is added to your creative fire. Jot down the many ideas and thoughts popping into your head. You can then assess these at a later date to see if there is potential to develop them further. Differences of opinion may mar your day, especially if you spend some time with in-laws. Listening to points of view that seem irrelevant or contradictory to your opinions, without speaking up, can be difficult but might be essential to avoid unnecessary discord and tension.

23. WEDNESDAY. Intense. Emotions and desires remain strong until early afternoon, then the Moon slips into the easygoing sign of Sagittarius. If it has been a while since you had some time off to enjoy participating in activities of your own choosing, this is the day to book tickets, pack your bags, and take a well-earned trip. Or buy yourself front-row tickets for a concert or sports event. Attention to detail and the tendency to trust too much to luck could be your undoing as the Sun and your coruler, expansive Jupiter, clash. Take a moderate approach to all activities. Any form of speculation should be avoided. Current planetary influence is a classic example illustrating the motto if it looks too good to be true, it probably is.

24. THURSDAY. Guarded. Current stars are mixed, but career-minded Pisces could find planetary influences helpful rather than a hindrance. If seeking employment or a promotion, progress can be made providing hopes are kept sensible and realistic. Pessimistic thinking and worrying about petty matters could create issues around home base if negative thoughts are permitted to take hold. Don't allow superficial disagreements to intrude. Productivity can be high as creative juices flow if given free rein. If a personal or professional relationship is beyond repair, this is a good time to arrange mediation or to hire a lawyer.

25. FRIDAY. Satisfactory. Tension reaches a peak as planetary energies clash in today's sky, making it vital to remain centered and balanced. Practice humoring other people, but try not to let their authoritarian attitudes get to you. If possible, avoid crowded places and angry people, especially friends who are prone to temper tantrums. Mercury, god of messages, moves into your fifth house of Cancer and remains there until July 9. Expressing your thoughts in an effective manner should come easily, and you shouldn't experience difficulty communicating your needs to loved ones. Pisces creative types can increase output. Those who use mental power to play or create games are likely to benefit from sharper perception.

26. SATURDAY. Sensitive. If you are fired up and cranky, blame it on today's celestial influences. Mischievous Mercury is in dispute with your traditional ruler Jupiter, expanding sensitive feelings and agitation. On top of that, today's Full Moon in Capricorn also increases emotions. A vivid imagination could add confusion to the mix. Watch what you say to other people and how you say it. Foot-in-mouth disease could be rife. Speaking out of turn could lead to feeling a lot worse at the end of the day than when it began. Work on current friendships. Avoid the Pisces habit of allowing other people to be the ones to make contact rather than you also making an effort to keep in touch.

27. SUNDAY. Difficult. Cosmic influences bring a day of rocky patches, tension, and discord. Emotional and mental stress could almost become overwhelming unless steps are taken to remain calm. Social activities could prove disappointing. It would be prudent to steer clear of negative people, noisy venues, or a gathering that could become unpleasant. A situation might arise that forces you to look at current fears and self-worth issues. If you are holding back because of a fear of failure, it might be time to reassess goals and figure out what possible safety nets are available. If you take a long bath or spend time in the spa this evening, negative vibes felt throughout the day should slowly evaporate.

28. MONDAY. Resourceful. Shake off the doldrums. The day should be a little brighter than yesterday. Creative expression is heightened, making this a starred time to recite or write poetry, begin devising a plot for a children's book, or paint a masterpiece. If you are planning a children's party you should have plenty of clever ideas coming to mind to make it one event to remember. Frustration may be encountered on the job, and energy for activities that require manual labor might be in short supply. However, Pisces paid to handle routine tasks shouldn't have any difficulty performing those duties.

29. TUESDAY. Pensive. Inner peace and solitary action may be high on your wish list but could be hard to obtain. Financial disagreements or money-related disputes could create tension within the domestic sphere. Try hard to resolve problems once and for all. Although you might not want to deal with these issues, burying your head in the sand won't make them disappear. Pisces who are in a developing romantic relationship could be feeling vulnerable and unsure of how committed the other person really is. However, don't allow insecurity and fears to intrude into the affair because this could add even more pressure. Instead, let the relationship move along as it is meant to do.

30. WEDNESDAY. Meaningful. Stay cool, calm, and collected. Watch your diet carefully. The urge to overdo with fine food and wine moves up a notch, which could have a detrimental effect on your overall health and general well-being. Pisces in an established relationship could feel the pressure as intensity heightens and jealous emotions emerge. Devote extra time to your mate or partner and, if possible, arrange time alone to strengthen loving ties. Let your lover know that he or she is still number one in your book. Pisces are known to enjoy a flutter at the track or casino, but current trends do not indicate any major wins.

JULY

1. THURSDAY. Empowering. The new month focuses attention on personal matters. This is a good time to consider a complete makeover or at least to update your current image and style. Practical everyday tasks may be more difficult to accomplish. Signing a contract or lease agreement is strongly advised against because your judgment may be off target. Pisces assertiveness is strong, and you will be inclined to say whatever is on your mind. However, explaining yourself properly could be difficult. Feelings can be easily hurt unless your words are carefully phrased. With the Moon in your sign of Pisces, this is a wonderful night to get out and have fun with loved ones or other favorite people.

2. FRIDAY. Sparkling. The lunar goddess continues to light up your sign and your first house of personality and the advancement of personal interests. Taking the initiative can lead to financial gains if you remain open to opportunities coming your way. Be yourself. Wherever you go or whatever activities you participate in, other people are sure to enjoy your company and good humor. Don't sit at home alone. You need to get out and interact with people on either a superficial or deep level; it doesn't matter as long as you are mingling. Love and romance go hand in hand, and the solo Fish might find a companion who fits the ideal of a perfect lover.

3. SATURDAY. Eventful. Throughout the weekend the Moon sails through your second house, impulsive Aries, which puts the accent on your personal finances and values. Don't become overly confident regarding any money matter. A business deal or financial agreement that seems to be all set midafternoon could unexpectedly collapse later on. Pisces entertaining at home should look for food and drink sales if you are expecting a crowd tomorrow. You can provide a virtual feast and display excellent catering skills to your guests without breaking the bank. If you are heading out for a night on the town, unexpected expenses are likely to create a void in your wallet.

4. SUNDAY. Mixed. Attention continues to focus on money and material possessions. If financial concerns are causing upset, try to deal with issues quickly. Don't waste this special holiday worrying about overdue bills or possible future expenses. Vim and vigor should be soaring. If the weather cooperates, a picnic at the beach or lake could help wash away fears and troubles. Time spent playing with children can bring back happy memories as well as creating new ones, and also engender a sense of being young again. Include extended family members if planning a social gathering. Consider folks who are less fortunate than you; donating goods and sharing resources with the needy can bring blessings in return.

5. MONDAY. Low-key. This is a day to work hard and slog away. Chances of impressing the boss or another supervisor are good, although you may not be quick to take advantage of the opportunities. This may be due to too much celebrating yesterday, or it may be that the Sun and your coruler, nebulous Neptune, are creating friction and confusion. Don't make any decisions on the spur of the moment because you are likely to change your mind or regret actions at a later time. This evening, chatting on the phone or on the computer could have you burning the midnight oil. If that doesn't suit your plans, turn off the lights, lock the door, and opt for an early night.

6. TUESDAY. Erratic. Unorthodox Uranus begins retreating though Aries, your second house of financial interests, creating restlessness where money is concerned. Yearning for freedom from debt and more independence regarding income could inspire you to look at new career options and devise ways to improve your overall financial stability. Although insomnia is not usually a problem for the typical Pisces, you may experience sleep problems as your mind refuses to wind down. A little light reading before bedtime should help slumber come easier. A discussion with a neighbor or relative could resolve a problem situation that has been of concern to all.

7. WEDNESDAY. Variable. Expect a fairly average day. If it isn't the lack of punctual transportation that creates stress this morning, it may be car troubles or traffic tie-ups. Issues with people close to you or with faulty household products could add to your agitation. As a Pisces you are always picking up on the moods of other people, so hang out with positive folks. Also keep your sense of humor at the ready, helping to dissipate frustration as quickly as it arises. Although you are usually a good listener, expressing how you feel isn't always easy. Today, however, there is a chance to be more talkative and let others know your opinions and views.

8. THURSDAY. Guarded. Pisces folks need to step warily. Seductive Venus is in conflict with your modern ruler, idealist Neptune, increasing the likelihood that you will only see what you want to see, whether it is there or not. Misrepresentation or deceit abounds, particularly if money or romance is in the picture. Shoppers should steer clear of large department stores unless a practical partner or friend comes along. Paying too much or not receiving value increases under current vibes. Make the most of your creative urges; imagination is heightened and inspiration should flow. As day turns to night, most Fish will be ready to spend time alone with that special person.

9. FRIDAY. Distracting. Restlessness is likely to limit productivity unless plenty of variety is added to your day. Connecting with the past and with those now at home increases in importance as the Moon slips through Gemini, your house of family and domestic concerns. Pisces who work from home could start to realize that exerting extra effort and energy has been worthwhile. Upcoming changes in the household could be disconcerting, especially if a child will soon be leaving the nest. With every ending there is also a new beginning, so instead of fretting about change, embrace it wholeheartedly. Jot down ideas that come to mind; thoughts might be more brilliant and original than you realize.

10. SATURDAY. Interesting. A bevy of cosmic patterns is forming today. Prepare for a number of interesting twists and turns to lighten your load and make life more interesting. Take pride in your environment. If you use your creative talents to enhance the comfort and appearance of your current home, you should be delighted with the results. For those who prefer a more relaxing pursuit, spending leisure time outdoors could be the preferred option. Go to the beach, lounge around the pool, or enjoy a casual lunch on the back patio. Don't go out this evening if social plans are not to your liking. Instead, settle down to an evening at home enjoying a relaxing hobby or pastime.

11. SUNDAY. Diverse. This is another day when the universe abounds with planetary shifts and configurations. Venus has swept into your Virgo seventh zone of close relationships, partners, and competitors. A romance, a relationship, or a financial situation could arrive at an important turning point. Pisces who have been experiencing a rough period may make headway by trying a new method to work through current differences. Inspiration comes as the New Moon activates your Cancer zone of romance, children, and creative expression. Life is too short to be working all the time, so schedule some leisure-time fun and amusement.

12. MONDAY. Accomplished. Surround yourself with positive people and remain above any drama that may be playing out around you. Your planning and organizational abilities excel, helping to earn the respect of coworkers and colleagues. Expressing your feelings to other people should be easier. If a few recent misunderstandings and disputes have added pressure to a one-on-one relationship, now is the time to kiss and make up. A display of practical and thoughtful actions could let your significant other know and see how much you care. A current project might need a few last-minute adjustments before it can be seriously considered a sure thing.

13. TUESDAY. Complex. Today's cosmic influences are creating contradictory romantic trends. Lover Venus smiles at intense Pluto but produces tension with your traditional ruler, abundant Jupiter. Recharging an intimate relationship with passion could work well for those in a loving union that needs an added dash of zest. With partnerships that have been experiencing problems, it may be a little harder to regain that loving feeling, so increase your effort. Keep your line of thinking open, but tread warily around associates and competitors. Self-employed Fish might need to offer a little extra monetary incentive to retain a special client or longtime customer.

14. WEDNESDAY. Fruitful. Diplomacy and tact will be needed throughout the day; compromise might not work well with rivals. Arguments are possible with personal partners. The Moon sailing through your Virgo seventh sector marks an excellent period to engage in a public relations campaign or to contact special clients and build up your customer data base. Negotiating, selling, buying, and promoting special services are under positive influences, with excellent prospects for a good financial return based on efforts exerted. An important ending or change in partnership issues could be a positive turning point. Sign up for a special offer or you might miss out.

15. THURSDAY. Comforting. A good day lies ahead. You are likely to enjoy the hustle and bustle of your busy life. Take the opportunity to move forward with matters of the heart if your love life has been a bit bumpy recently. There may be a few problems that need to be brought out into the open so they can be addressed. This will help you achieve greater warmth and a new understanding with your intimate partner. Keep an eye open for new chances to assist self-promotion. This isn't the time to take a backseat to rivals or even to friendly associates. Pisces team leaders should utilize previous experience to settle any issues with colleagues.

16. FRIDAY. Challenging. The morning begins well, but it could be all downhill from there. At least it is the last day of the working week for many Pisces, and you have the weekend to look forward to. Other people are unlikely to cooperate or to give in to your whims as readily as usual. Avoid jumping to conclusions. Nor should you do or say anything you may have to change later on. Don't accuse a business associate or friend; your suspicions might be way out of line, and apologizing for your lack of grace will then be difficult. Conduct all financial transactions prior to midmorning. From then on conditions are likely to get tougher, and working out a better deal will be almost impossible.

17. SATURDAY. Satisfactory. Alterations within your surroundings could be unavoidable. This isn't the time to do everything on your own because doing so could create a buildup of stress resulting in health problems. Ask someone to help if there is too much on your to-do list. In personal relationships, it might be time to let go of anger or disappointment if holding on no longer serves a worthwhile purpose. This is also a good day to clean out the attic, garage, or basement, removing items that have only been collecting dust. Do a good deed and donate what you no longer want to a local charity. Or if your finances are tight, consider selling goods online to the highest bidder or at a local flea market.

18. SUNDAY. Purposeful. Reshuffling the energy source around the house could be a good thing. Get up early and clean thoroughly to allow a breath of air to freshen the environment. Money problems could bring on a tension headache if you're not doing anything about them. Be proactive and do something positive rather than just worrying. The lack of support from someone you thought would be on your side might require another look from a more objective perspective. Travel could be a problem, especially for those who are shift workers or are on call. When driving, avoid thinking about anything that could distract attention; it is essential to keep fully concentrated on the road and on the actions of other drivers.

19. MONDAY. Supportive. Planetary tension might lead to a showdown. Try to avoid a drama with an employer or a fellow worker. Unfortunately you could easily be drawn into a disagreement, and extracting yourself might prove extremely difficult. Be open to new ideas regarding possible travel destinations. Even if you don't like the suggestions from your traveling partners, check them out before coming to a decision; the ideas might have some merit. If you have been working hard, try to take off early from work and go for a calming massage. Issues with older family members could rattle your partner, and being supportive might be the only way you can help.

20. TUESDAY. Manageable. A confidential issue could complicate a situation. A lethargic attitude might creep over you, even if you are normally very energetic. Pisces who are on the job should concentrate on routine tasks requiring little conscious thought and effort. Even though most Fish are open-minded, you can sometimes be overly judgmental or closed off. Some of your longtime beliefs and values might be challenged. This won't necessarily be a bad thing, especially if you have become too set in your ways. This is a favorable time to establish a vacation itinerary as long as you know how much you can afford to spend.

21. WEDNESDAY. Limiting. As the Moon slides through Sagittarius, your house of professional interests, pressure is building on career matters and on your reputation. If you have been working hard to move up the career ladder, you should be pleased with current achievements and status. Challenges to balance a career and home duties might be more trying for Pisces with young children or caring for children. Consider employing outside help to assist with tasks such as laundry and ironing, cleaning the house, or gardening. Having more time to spend with the family or your partner should outweigh the extra cost involved.

22. THURSDAY. Rewarding. Positive trends are on the horizon. Job opportunities abound, and extra duties may mean more status and power. Pisces who are seeking a new job or a promotion can expect good news. The Sun now moves on into the sign of Leo and the sixth sector linked to health, work, and service to others. If you are anxious to lose or gain weight over the next four weeks, this is an excellent period to begin a diet that can help you achieve your goal. If you feel that your contributions on the job haven't been duly noted, rest assured that the boss is more than likely watching now. Put your best foot forward and make sure your work is up to standards, and your efforts should be recognized.

23. FRIDAY. Slow. Something important to you is likely to come to a halt. Your traditional ruler Jupiter begins moving backward in your Aries house of personal money, possessions, and values, bringing possible delays to these areas of life. Changes in income could occur, and your bank balance might dip instead of increase. Pisces business operators should move slowly, keeping expansion plans and stock to a realistic level. Your leadership qualities are enhanced. If in charge of a team, you should have success with whatever is on the agenda. Stress and tension can be reduced through regular exercise.

24. SATURDAY. Industrious. Diligence and attentiveness are to the fore. Employed or self-employed Pisces, or contract workers, should make good progress. With the Moon in practical Capricorn, continual networking, advertising, and promoting goods and services can help build a solid business foundation and aid financial growth. If you are organizing a school or work reunion, or if you have lost touch with old friends, the Internet should be a good source of sites to help you do necessary research. Meeting friends for lunch or for a swim at the local pool could be a better option than shopping. Creative energy is strong, and other people will appreciate your artistic talents.

25. SUNDAY. Tense. Surround yourself with special friends and loved ones. Celestial tension prevails as your ruler Jupiter, the king of the gods, challenges the might and intensity of possessive Pluto. This isn't the day to throw caution to the wind because an overly optimistic attitude could be a recipe for disaster. The Aquarius Full Moon amplifies emotions. The inflated ego of a friend or lover might be the cause of embarrassment, especially if you are socializing with a group of people. If you have been rushing around nonstop, by midafternoon you will be ready to call it quits and take a well-deserved break.

26. MONDAY. Baffling. This complex day can bring a windfall or a financial loss. Feelings of being stuck in a rut may be hard to overcome, making it difficult to concentrate on routine chores and activities. Be careful of being too obstinate regarding how you think things should be done. Generosity is to the fore, but take care that your good intentions are not taken advantage of. If you are borrowing or loaning money, make sure that the terms are clear and are in writing. Your social circle could experience changes due to an old friend leaving, but don't be sad. Someone new is likely to come along soon and fill the void.

27. TUESDAY. Calm. Peace and quiet will be coveted by many Pisces folk today. The need to turn inward and recharge your batteries increases while the Moon slips through your Aquarius house of secrets and solo pursuits. Take time out to review events that have occurred over the past four weeks, analyzing them to see if there is anything that you can do better the next time around. Communicative Mercury is visiting your opposite sign of Virgo, accentuating the seventh house of marriage and partnerships. There is greater likelihood of increased discussion with your significant other, members of the public, or a business partner. Pisces who speak or negotiate for a living should excel.

28. WEDNESDAY. Heartening. You can count on the day getting off to a bright start. The Moon is floating through your sign, increasing your chance of being placed in a prominent position. Even the shy Pisces could soon be in front of a crowd. Being busy is the best way to overcome restlessness, keeping your mind occupied and reducing the chance of scattered energy hindering productivity. Attend to problems quickly rather than trying to make excuses for yourself or for other people. If your aim is to be noticed, chances increase by dressing to impress, smiling, and presenting a confident demeanor. Your love life should be more rewarding.

29. THURSDAY. Loving. Mentally stimulating activities are favored. You are at your articulate best as your ability to hold in-depth discussions peaks. Analytical and research skills are highly refined, aiding investigative and undercover duties. Energetic Mars is on the move, now residing in your Libra eighth house of joint finances, sex, and taxes. Passion and desire increase, assisting those of you who are seeking new ways to express loving bonds. Consider planning a vacation or a weekend retreat with your mate or partner to improve your love life. Credit cards could experience a workout, with impulsive purchases sending the budget into a spin.

30. FRIDAY. Unpredictable. Caution is highly recommended. The inclination to overestimate your abilities or a situation increases now. Avoid jumping ahead without planning first. If promises are made, be sure they are kept. Read the fine print thoroughly before signing any important document or sale contract. Make an effort to move at a slower pace. The combination of impulsiveness and a tendency to rush strongly suggests that this may be an accident-prone period. Walk, don't run. Also be especially careful if driving on highways. Financial prudence is a must. The urge to take a rash gamble could find you a lot less wealthy at the end of the day than you were at the beginning.

31. SATURDAY. Positive. Ambitions and striving to achieve highlight the day. Your sense of purpose and urge to take on more responsibility should be strong. Don't refuse the chance to take on a leadership role, which could challenge you in ways you have never experienced before. Traditional methods are likely to work best. Containing excitement when it comes to buying superfluous treats for yourself or your family could be difficult. However, if you don't draw the line now the household budget might take a long time to recover. The acquisition of real estate, commercial land, or a first home should proceed smoothly, adding value to your asset base.

AUGUST

1. SUNDAY. Helpful. As the new month begins the Sun is shining its light in Leo, your sixth zone of health, daily work, and service to others. If you haven't implemented a healthy diet, launched a more rigid fitness program, or started eliminating one of your bad habits such as overeating or smoking, begin now. Money matters are the other area of concern. The lack of ready cash may cause a headache or two. Self-employed Fish should put work aside for part of the day and spend time with loved ones because someone important to you might be feeling neglected. Be cautious about what comes out of your mouth midmorning; it will be all too easy to say the wrong thing.

2. MONDAY. Hectic. You may be doing more running around than usual, but this could be of your own choosing. If you are chasing after something that you really want, just make sure it is important enough to keep you from performing other duties, especially if you are supposed to be working. Sometime during the day you may have a phone in one hand, be working on a laptop, and also be juggling kids, a boss, or employees. That's the time to take a few deep breaths, do a few stretching exercises, and drink a tall glass of refreshing water. After a short break you will be ready to jump back into the fray and face an overloaded in-basket. Avoid taking part in neighborhood gossip or siding with anyone intent on dishing dirt.

3. TUESDAY. Testing. Prepare for a number of tense situations to arise. The hard aspect between your traditional ruler, optimistic Jupiter, and vibrating Pluto will create a few tricky challenges. Tread carefully to avoid becoming involved in a messy issue, and be ready to rectify misunderstandings or the misconceptions of other people. The Moon is in practical and stable Taurus, assisting you in taking cautious action and making logical decisions. Quiet discussion without rising to anger is the best method of talking things through if someone does become agitated. If you don't think you can manage a passive approach, postpone any in-depth dialogue until you feel you can remain calm and in control.

4. WEDNESDAY. Problematic. Confusion rules the morning hours, and you could be accused of being in another world or of not paying sufficient attention. Planetary vibes continue to create problems, especially where personal funds and joint finances are involved. This isn't the best day to negotiate a property or divorce settlement. Finish work duties that require lots of discussion and sign papers before lunch. From then on, even though the Moon will be in communicative Gemini, you won't be as inclined to interact with other people. You may prefer to retreat tonight to the comfort of home and family to both give and receive some tender loving care and special nurturing.

5. THURSDAY. Slow. With the amount of rushing around you have had to do over the past few days, it's now time to slow down and rest. A day off work might be in order. Spending more time around the house could be a refreshing respite and also give you a chance to catch up on housework. A do-it-yourself project or renovation could capture your attention. This is a great time to look around your living quarters with fresh eyes and see what changes can be made to improve living comforts. It will be easier today to act the gracious host when entertaining guests because Pisces charm and quick wit should be plentiful. If catering is kept simple, you'll have plenty of time to swap jokes and share happy stories.

6. FRIDAY. Watchful. Issues from childhood or your more recent past could crop up. It would be wise to act immediately instead of brooding about what could be or what might have been. Get any sensitive subject out into the open so issues can be dealt with effectively, allowing you to then move on. If you feel too lazy to sort out problems relating to personal values with a lover or a friend, there may be larger troubles to face later on. Money matters are also under a cloud. Refuse any loan request from an adult child or from your mate or partner unless you are very sure why the money is needed. Finding a balance between your private and public life may be stressful. Keep in mind you can't please everyone all the time.

7. SATURDAY. Interesting. Whatever plans are on today's agenda, make sure there are plenty of stimulating activities. Otherwise you might be overwhelmed with tedium, reducing your ability to remain focused. Make an effort to go out and mingle with other people, but choose amusement activities that won't break the bank. Lovely Venus has slipped into her own sign of Libra, stirring up emotions, passion, and intensity. This is the time to back down if by nature you are jealous or possessive of the significant person in your life, especially a new love; relations could sour very quickly. Pisces currently enjoying a loving union can expect things to heat up in the bedroom.

8. SUNDAY. Lackluster. Inertia or laziness could be more pronounced. Fortunately this is a day of rest, so take advantage of the downtime. Stay in bed a little longer this morning, have a leisurely breakfast, and take your time reading the Sunday paper. Express affection to loved ones, particularly younger family members. Joy comes from taking part in their activities or taking them out somewhere special. Seeking support for a new venture is favorable. Pisces shoppers should easily find good-quality deals at affordable prices. It may be time to reassess what you are seeking when it comes to romance. Solo Pisces could be more attracted to someone who is older, practical, or more mature.

9. MONDAY. Good. Pisces folk are not the most disciplined when it comes to luxuries and the good things in life. If you are watching your weight, you will need strong willpower to keep your behavior moderate and consumption of food and alcohol at a reasonable level. Assistance in this aim comes from the celestial skies as a New Moon in your Leo house of health provides the opportunity to evaluate lifestyle habits and initiate positive changes. Pisces determined to begin a diet can expect to make good progress. A medical consultation over the next two weeks should be very helpful. If you are looking for a way out of a boring job, this is an opportune time to act.

10. TUESDAY. Useful. First impressions can sometimes be misleading, which might be the case if you are going on a job interview. Don't be too quick to form negative opinions; after a settling-in period you could find your niche. A minor health problem could be irritating. If you have been reasonably diligent regarding your overall well-being, any upset or inconvenience is unlikely to last long. Becoming involved in a power struggle with a parent is likely. If this only involves a minor issue, it may be better to give in or postpone a discussion for another day because there are unlikely to be any outright winners. In addition, tension around home base could become unpleasant, adding to stress.

11. WEDNESDAY. Constructive. A much better day dawns for those born under the sign of the Fish. You should be brimming with confidence, particularly if you experienced a few difficult moments over the last few days. This is an excellent period of high productivity for Pisces people, driven by imagination and creative urges. Refining or completing a team project can move briskly ahead. Associates should be cooperative and willing to compromise if needed. This afternoon your mental powers will be at a high level, assisting any effort to negotiate a deal or finalize a transaction that promises strong financial benefits. Regardless of how busy your schedule may be, allow some couple time.

12. THURSDAY. Tricky. Don't let petty matters get you down. Pay attention to your good Pisces instincts and remain out of the line of fire on the job. If you follow these guidelines and keep cheerful, daylight hours should pass without too much hassle. Evening is when life could become tricky. Spending money for emotional gratification on items that please you can be good if you have cash to spare, but this will just add extra pressure if money is tight. If you are pinching pennies, steer clear of financial discussions with your mate or partner; arguments are likely to be the only result tonight. Share a quiet dinner for two with that special person in your life.

13. FRIDAY. Resourceful. You need not worry about today's date because the stars lean more toward positive trends than unhelpful ones. Plan your day so employment duties are finished early. Your significant other might require more of your undivided attention than usual, and you will want to be in the position to do what you can to help. Goals can be achieved if you maintain a positive attitude. Pisces who are hoping to make a profitable business move could be in the right place at the right time, and most plans launched now should produce gains. If seeking employment, scour the help-wanted advertisements for something that sparks your interest and meets current income requirements.

14. SATURDAY. Passionate. Life is definitely looking up. Your ability to see things as they really are improves, conveying assertiveness and a desire to move ahead. Consider taking vacation leave if it has been too long since your last relaxing break. Curb any impulsive financial move. You are in a period when it is important to review your long-term security and stability to determine if there are more productive ways of earning a living. A romantic union that is not strong could struggle as insecurity creates jealousy and possessive tendencies. However, a loving relationship should be heating up, with extra zing added during couple time.

15. SUNDAY. Empowering. If someone's attitude begins grating on your nerves, it might be time for a serious chat. This afternoon the vibes favor contacting loved ones from a distance, holding meetings with business folk from overseas, or setting off on a long journey. Even arranging a group vacation itinerary should proceed without too much dissension. You might want to consider changing jobs because satisfaction and opportunities to move up the career ladder are limited. Update your resume, check the local newspaper and online listings, and ask friends if they know of possible employment positions that offer responsibility, challenge, and the money you want and need.

16. MONDAY. Purposeful. Simplify your life. Projects have a tendency of becoming more complicated and troubles may expand while your coruler, abundant Jupiter, quarrels with structured Saturn. Self-employed or business-oriented Pisces can use this time to implement more efficient processes, cut down on wasted resources, or even make wide-sweeping policy changes. Employees should keep production up to avoid flak from a superior. Partners, either intimate or professional, are unlikely to see eye-to-eye when it comes to spending joint money. This isn't the time to invest in any grandiose plan or get-rich-quick schemes.

17. TUESDAY. Positive. By the time most Fish jump out of bed this morning, lunar aspects capable of creating possible obstacles will have moved on, leaving a positive flow of energy for the remainder of the day. This may cause difficulties if you are required to be in a serious business mood; being grave and solemn probably won't suit your more relaxed frame of mind. Career-minded Pisces can make headway through self-promotion. Contact people who can further your current goals, or ask a superior to increase your responsibilities and challenges. An intimate discussion with your mate or partner could be the beginning of positive change in your relationship as both of you explain your needs and desires.

18. WEDNESDAY. Uncertain. Although today's cosmic vibes are not as helpful as yesterday's, they do signal it is time to get back into the fray. There may be a strong push and pull between work and the needs of those at home. Whatever problems are looming, throwing yourself into current obligations can help take your mind off a possible legal issue, competing with a rival, or partnership troubles. Certain matters might benefit from further examination. Holding back may make it more difficult to remain on course. Reading between the lines is unlikely to provide the correct answers. Your judgment may be clouded, and even your famed Pisces intuition might be wide of the mark.

19. THURSDAY. Variable. The day should begin well for early birds but not as well for those who are late to rise and shine. Mixed trends continue to shake things up, with unexpected situations creating tension. Freedom from routine will be your preferred option, although this could be difficult to obtain. Working on a creative project can give you a lot of satisfaction, but don't expect much encouragement or support. Beware going over the top in a romantic relationship by putting your significant other high up on a pedestal. Being in love with love is a trap that Pisces who are currently without a partner need to avoid. Watch impulsive spending and continue to say no to any proposed get-rich-quick scheme.

20. FRIDAY. Mixed. The Sun challenges your coruler Neptune, warning you to be on guard because deception is rampant. Matters of honesty and integrity could have you up in arms. Your personal interests need to be protected if someone is not staying within legal limits. Sensual planetary vibes are in play as Venus and Mars merge together, making this a great time to splurge on a relaxing massage, a new scent, or an outfit that shows off your best features to good advantage. A little luck could be winging your way. Passion and desire are heightened, and someone special could express how much they care in a memorable way. Mercury now begins moving backward, causing delays with legal paperwork and communication.

21. SATURDAY. Complex. A major planetary connection is in force as disciplined Saturn conflicts with intense Pluto, increasing endurance and self-will. Issues with associates could arise. Pisces who are in a business relationship with a friend should prepare for a number of challenges, which might strain the friendship to the breaking point. Gaining the support of team members shouldn't be difficult. Someone may be willing to help with your heavy workload. This evening take time to unwind with special friends or a favorite companion. An early dinner at an inexpensive restaurant will be relaxing, preparing you to face whatever tomorrow brings.

22. SUNDAY. Fidgety. A sense of restlessness and lack of self-discipline will be strong throughout the day. Take advantage of the chance to stay in bed longer than usual. Cuddle up with your favorite bedtime companion or with a book by a favorite author and stress should be reduced considerably. Pace everything you do while the Moon travels through your twelfth sector of subconscious matters and solitary actions. Find a comfortable chair somewhere in the shade, fill up a water bottle, take along an interesting novel or the Sunday newspaper, and prepare to relax if social pursuits are not organized. Don't be too hard on yourself. If you must criticize your work, appearance, or efficiency, make sure you do so in private.

23. MONDAY. Revealing. A mistake made some time ago could come back to haunt you. Resolve the issue correctly once and for all so the slate can be wiped clean. Taking care of someone can be both inspiring and uplifting, and you can do this very well right now. The Sun enters your opposite sign of analytical Virgo, focusing attention on relationships with people including your mate and one or more business partners. Offers and proposals could be forthcoming. This is an excellent period to enter into an agreement that has been on the table for some time. However, wait until Mercury moves forward on September 12 before signing any new proposition.

24. TUESDAY. Significant. Your intuition is right more often than you realize, so respect this natural ability and take notice of your hunches. Today's influences will more than likely bring a significant relationship into focus, increasing pressure and strain. You are apt to be a little more tense than usual, justified by the Full Moon in Pisces raising emotions and sensitivities. Something major can come to a close when a Full Moon culminates. Over the next two weeks identifying the expectations of a partner and satisfactorily resolving issues should become easier. Energy to complete outstanding work increases. This is also a great time to organize a social gathering.

25. WEDNESDAY. Successful. Seeing the bright side of every situation is easier now as the Moon continues to glide through your sign, impacting your first zone of personality and self. As a creative Pisces with an active mind and ingenious imagination, you can utilize your talents in a positive manner. This will improve your chances of financial benefits. If you know of a better way to perform employment duties, take a stand and show the boss what you are capable of doing. With confidence on the rise, you can dazzle higher-ups with a compelling demonstration and reasons why your methods are both effective and efficient. Pending matters may come up for discussion, but this shouldn't cause problems because the outcome is likely to go your way.

26. THURSDAY. Encouraging. Magnetic charm is to the fore, so if you want a favor go ahead and make the request. This is the right time to look after personal needs, even just giving yourself a small treat. And if you can afford to indulge in a little luxury that won't break the bank, go for it. Trying something different could be productive and will add a little excitement and variety to activities. If changing a habit or pattern of behavior is essential, consider taking a workshop or a course that can help with this aim, such as a self-empowerment seminar, a quit-smoking program, or anger management training. Enjoy a swim or a cool shower before settling down to watch television tonight.

27. FRIDAY. Practical. This is a day to enjoy your money without frittering too much of it away. The Moon is passing through Aries, your house of money, so motivation to increase financial resources moves up a notch. However, over the next few days you are apt to be more impulsive when it comes to spending money. Pisces who are on a strict budget should leave the credit cards at home to avoid overindulging. Include your mate or partner in any decisions regarding possibly purchasing a large or expensive item. Obtain price quotes, research stores offering the best deals, and wait until Mercury moves forward before actually taking the plunge.

28. SATURDAY. Dutiful. This is another day when money may be on your mind. There could be confusion as well as fluctuations, creating tension and stress. Cosmic forces are not sending support when it comes to matters relating to finances. If you are doing the math in order to make decisions, it would be better to wait until you have a clearer picture of what lies ahead. Keeping important feelings to yourself is likely to add pressure to a significant relationship, so include your loved one in issues or situations that will affect you both. Maintain a close guard on valuable possession when out and about, and also be sure that your home and vehicle are securely locked when unattended.

29. SUNDAY. Energetic. A trip to an outdoor market could be a happy excursion if you are looking for retail therapy. Energy and enthusiasm should increase starting midmorning, and any pursuits that require communication should proceed with ease. Writing a report, researching an assignment, or catching up with correspondence can be a productive way to utilize current lunar energy. Take a respite from routine Sunday activities or work and enjoy socializing. Visiting relatives, a child's sports contest, a favored hobby, or a special celebration can be an enjoyable way to pass the afternoon. If agitation or stress gets the better of you, go out for a walk or for a drive in the country to calm down and relax. Keep plans flexible.

30. MONDAY. Organized. After the hectic weekend you will be ready to get back in harness and make productive headway with work or daily chores. The heavens are quiet this morning, so that is the best time to handle anything that must be done quickly and without interruption. If there are processes that need to be restructured, do this early when you are feeling fresh and raring to go. Obstacles and disruptions later in the day could shatter peace and tranquility, creating tension in your immediate environment. This isn't the day to act as the family police officer even if you are the oldest in the family. Loved ones will more than likely resent your actions, responding accordingly.

31. TUESDAY. Opportune. If your environment is orderly, achievements will be greater. Interviewing for a new job or auditioning for a theatrical or television role could be reasonably successful, although the pay scale might not be as high as expected. However, don't let this stop you; the opportunity may be the stepping-stone to something better later on. If you are chairing a meeting of any sort, make sure that those in attendance stick to the point. Otherwise valuable time could be lost in superficial discussions and gossip. Pisces who have recently relocated to a new area should take the time to make new friends and to become better acquainted with next-door neighbors.

SEPTEMBER

1. WEDNESDAY. Satisfying. Messenger Mercury remains in retrograde motion as the new month begins. Continue to check that messages are not going missing, confirm appointments prior to heading out, communicate clearly and concisely, and don't sign any contract until after September 12, when Mercury moves forward. Energy to accomplish what needs to be done around the home base increases. This is the time to add a little more order to your household, especially if you tend to be rather lackadaisical like most Pisces. Improvements already started such as redecorating and renovating can benefit now, but wait until midmonth before beginning new projects.

2. THURSDAY. Renewing. Happy at home is the catch cry for many Fish today. Tending to household duties, going out of your way for family members, and taking pride in your environment can be enough to provide happiness and contentment. This is the perfect time to redesign, reorganize, and restructure current living conditions to increase home comforts and rejuvenate living space. Slip into creative mode, use that renowned Pisces imagination, and begin designing so work can be completed in time for the festive season. Your ability to express yourself clearly remains high, and it is important to speak up and clear the air of any stress that has been accumulating.

3. FRIDAY. Resourceful. Children demanding attention might not be anything new and unusual, but review how much quality time you are spending with youngsters to ensure that they are not missing out. Treat new and prospective customers with extra care and courtesy. They may have more money at their disposal to purchase products than initially indicated, or they may have a large base of friends to whom they will recommend your services. To increase the possibility of success and to promote your business, come up with a new advertising plan or schedule a social function that combines business and pleasure. Hosting a dinner party for VIP people could also guarantee more business coming your way.

4. SATURDAY. Pleasurable. Newfound energy filters over Pisces now as lover Venus happily engages with your coruler, inspired Neptune. Wrangles with your mate or partner concerning financial issues should be easier to resolve, as peace reigns over most activities. Heightened imagination can take you to a new realm; if you can dream it, you can do it. Romantically, you might have to juggle a very busy social life as well as making time for your significant other, but with ingenuity this should be easy to do. Also make time to enjoy being with children or that very special person in your life. Hobbies shouldn't be ignored either.

5. SUNDAY. Helpful. Pisces parents know that children are true blessings. However, you might be wondering why they have to wake up so early on a Sunday morning. Urge them to be quiet so you can try to get more sleep. Pay closer attention to your health over the next two days. There are a number of stressful planetary influences placing increased pressure on both your physical and mental resources. Surround yourself with positive folks, meditate, and clear your mind of negative thoughts. Don't allow stress to induce feelings of being unwell. Make time for exercise and relaxation. For singles, hanging out with favorite people will not only be enjoyable but can increase the possibility of encountering a romantic potential.

6. MONDAY. Exacting. Practice mind over matter if emotions threaten to affect your well-being. Taking a deep breath and realizing that current problems are not that huge in the overall scheme of life can make a big difference to your attitude. Fresh air and healthy food are vital for you, so make sure you get plenty of both. Difficulties that have recently surfaced could make you feel uneasy. If there are issues that need to be addressed, be prepared to do so today because you might not be able to escape possible confrontation. For Pisces who must work this holiday, refusing to continually chat and socialize with fellow workers will increase production and put you in the good graces of the boss.

7. TUESDAY. Mixed. Your practical and efficient mood will help fight today's restless urges. Be wary of colleagues who suggest you take on some of their workload. This may be a ploy to dump difficult tasks onto you, possibly permanently. In romance, a unique chance to forgive and forget past wounds and circumstances should be taken advantage of. Letting go of the past, of those who have hurt or rejected you, can be easier now, clearing the way to establish a new relationship or perspective. Professional interests may be more demanding. Some of your clients probably have no idea what they want, or they may take your services and skills for granted.

8. WEDNESDAY. Vibrant. You are apt to have a lot on your mind as the new day begins. If you feel that you have been unfairly treated or that someone is not fulfilling a promise, speak up and express your discontent in an assertive manner. As the Virgo New Moon now culminates, this is a great time to begin new projects, make fresh plans, or enter into a new partnership. Moving in with a lover shouldn't present any immediate difficulties. A fresh start can also be made with a strained relationship. Spending extra quality time with your significant other can strengthen a committed union. Compromise and cooperation from other people will increase over the next two weeks.

9. THURSDAY. Heartening. Sensual Venus has now taken up residence in Scorpio, your sector of long journeys, academic studies, and philosophical beliefs. As attraction to all things foreign increases, solo Pisces could find love with someone from another country or culture. Those on vacation or working overseas might find that romance comes calling, and some Pisces might be making plans to move abroad to marry or set up home. The classroom or library could also be a potential meeting place for those seeking new love. A business deal or negotiations with an overseas company should lead to extra trade and higher profits.

10. FRIDAY. Profitable. Future security is likely to dominate your thoughts. With the Moon in Libra accentuating joint finances, this is a time to calculate household income and expenses to ensure that you and your mate or partner are living within your means. Applying for a home mortgage, new credit card, or business proposition could bring a thrill of anticipation for those seeking to expand assets and secure fiscal stability. This is a good time to take stock of financial resources, including medical coverage, car or household insurance, a pension plan, and stocks and bonds. Knowing how much you are worth in monetary terms can provide peace of mind if assets exceed liabilities.

11. SATURDAY. Purposeful. Intense emotions and desire are enhanced today as the Moon passes through the sign of Scorpio. Romantically, good things are promised as long as you actively avoid a passionate argument with your mate or partner. If you have been waiting for the right time to increase assets, do your homework now. Taking a course in the art of money management or investments could be good way to safeguard and increase fiscal security. Catching up with friends should be high on your list of priorities. Don't look for an excuse to miss a community meeting, a training course, or an educational seminar.

12. SUNDAY. Lively. This spirited day allows you to indulge in whatever your heart desires. Get ready for more romance and positive changes in your love life. Seductive Venus happily links up with intense Pluto, indicating that a marriage, committed union, or financial situation could reach an important turning point. Transformation is likely to bring positive benefits. Confidence lifts, and Pisces singles should be ready to welcome a new romantic potential. Creative pursuits can increase enjoyment for those who have leisure time to fill. Errors in paperwork, misunderstandings with clients, and general delays should begin to clear up now that Mercury is getting ready to move forward.

13. MONDAY. Eventful. Mercury moves forward in Virgo, your partnership sign. There will be a lot to do today, so start early. Professional interests and career duties are activated. If you focus on climbing up the ladder of status and success, you can capture the supportive flow of celestial influences. Don't shy away from challenges, which will help stimulation and motivation. A financial adviser or debt collector could create a crisis to get your attention. If you have been slack in the fiscal area you could hear about it now.

This is not the best day to obtain insurance because you could pay too much. Defer settling on any type of property transaction. Stay focused if operating any type of moving vehicle.

14. TUESDAY. Rewarding. Romantic vibes are still pleasant, encouraging Fish to harness the positive trends. Plan a special dinner or weekend away with your mate or partner to highlight loving feelings. Confusion surrounding an insurance payout, tax problem, or discrepancy with an inheritance should be resolved, bringing relief that this can be put behind you. Legal paperwork, contracts, and leases can now be signed. Mars moves into Scorpio, your sector of education, travel, and foreign affairs. Mars here advises Pisces to be prepared for possible upsets and conflict in one or more of these areas. Conversely, you should have more energy to pour into areas associated with these matters.

15. WEDNESDAY. Disquieting. Diverse energies are in play, warning Pisces to use intuition in matters of importance. Changes in your working environment might need to be made, especially if you are currently unhappy with duties or employment conditions. It might be time to look for a position that is more conducive to your requirements or lifestyle. Legal affairs may require prompt attention. During the next few weeks it would be wise to defer implementing legal action because chances of a settlement in your favor, without prolonged conflict, are weakened under current planetary influences. Don't push yourself or others too hard this afternoon. Seek compromise and a team solution.

16. THURSDAY. Bumpy. Team effort may be necessary in order to maintain a high level of motivation. If you have to be on the job, get enjoyment from working with and relating to other people; their input should prove invaluable. However, a group project might run into a few problems if joint or unanimous decisions are required. Pisces who have accepted a demanding volunteer role should consider the pros and cons of the position before making a decision to resign. You don't want to jump the gun just as success arrives. Wait until you calm down and the pressure has eased before coming to any definite conclusions. Meeting associates after work could go a long way to restoring good humor.

17. FRIDAY. Harmonious. On this stable day, sharing feelings and discussing mutual goals can strengthen loving ties. Lunar aspects urge Pisces folk to spend time cultivating old and new friendships. Consider meeting up with a few special friends for lunch, sharing the latest news and gossip that goes with being part of the same circle. Networking with others can also increase your chances of career success. Creative energy has a practical tone, and there should be plenty of people who appreciate your talents. Unattached Pisces may be attracted to someone responsible and serious, so plan to attend a venue where single folks who match this description are likely to gather.

18. SATURDAY. Exceptional. A busy day ahead is promised, so expect plenty of interesting and unusual developments to take place. Today also offers a chance to complete unfinished business and to catch up on what has been left undone or neglected. A number of positive influences, including the involvement of your lifetime ruler Jupiter, increases the likelihood of positive benefits flowing through to you. Romance is under auspicious and twinkling stars, encouraging passion to be directed toward the love of your life. A career breakthrough might be imminent. Higher-ups should be very supportive of your long-term goals and current aims.

19. SUNDAY. Vexing. An intimate relationship may be very demanding, resulting in having to make a decision whether to sacrifice your own needs and desires to accommodate the requirements of the other person. Don't allow fears, anxiety, or emotional blackmail to push you into doing something that isn't in your best long-term interests. Working alone or from home will seem like heaven for the self-employed who need to catch up on an ever-increasing workload. Include frequent rest breaks in your day to retain vigor and to recoup stamina. Reading can be restful, particularly a stimulating publication or a how-to book offering new ideas or techniques.

20. MONDAY. Nurturing. Take good care of your personal needs. Surround yourself with positive energy as the new working week begins. Following directions ensures the greatest success this morning. Vim and vitality also rise, and Pisces who need to work late should have plenty of energy to complete outstanding projects and tasks. Try to overcome any shyness; this is the time to shine. Be alert for positive opportunities from key introductions that look promising after dark. Tonight favors socializing. You have the magnetic charm and charisma to impress people of all ages. The unattached could even meet a possible new love or get back together with an old one.

21. TUESDAY. Hectic. Prepare for a highly charged day. With stars like today's it is a good thing that most individuals born under the sign of Pisces are flexible and compliant. Trouble will occur if impulsive behavior is allowed to run riot because this has the potential of creating conflict. Handle any tricky situation yourself without making a mountain out of a molehill. There is opportunity for healing. If you have been struggling with a poor self-image, some counseling or a personal development workshop could be highly beneficial. Lifestyle changes should be implemented now if you are seeking to improve overall wellness and physical fitness.

22. WEDNESDAY. Fulfilling. Later this evening the Sun zips into Libra, your eighth house of shared resources, sex, money, and powerful insights. Over the next four weeks the chance to tap into the more mysterious aspects of life increases. Pisces with psychic ability could find that this facility increases considerably. The stars are also signaling that it is time to balance account books, audit bank statements, and update insurance policies. Indulging in a spending spree can be great fun while it lasts but could seriously damage your credit if a moderate approach is not taken. Dance and sing away stress, but make sure you don't drink to excess or in the wrong company.

23. THURSDAY. Edgy. This is apt to be an emotional day as the Moon slips into Leo, your house of personal finances, and culminates in a Full Moon this morning. Your financial sectors are under stress, requiring a balanced approach in all matters involving possessions, assets, and shared resources. Being conservative is the wisest approach to take. Avoid any proposed get-rich-quick scheme. This is a period when the proverb about a fool and his money being soon parted holds true. If problems arise with an older family member, talk through the situation rationally. Perhaps the issue isn't as serious as someone is portraying. Don't spend joint money without consulting your mate or partner.

24. FRIDAY. Guarded. Financial caution is again advised. Curb sudden impulses and steer clear of retail stores that hold great attraction because your willpower to resist tempting bargains could be severely tested. If you haven't had a yearly astrological update, make the appointment now for an examination of upcoming trends. Diplomacy and tact provide the most effective results for Pisces employed to collect debts and for self-employed business operators seeking payment overdue for services rendered. Making decisions that have positive outcomes could be a little tricky through the morning hours and would be better left until this afternoon.

25. SATURDAY. Stressful. This isn't the day to tackle the big or heavy tasks on your to-do list. Physical energy could be drained. Minor matters that normally come easily might take on giant proportions. Take everything with a grain of salt. Try to remain placid and passive even if aggressiveness rears its ugly head. Other people may try to dominate you through emotional blackmail or endeavor to make you feel guilty. Regardless of such pressure, keep striving toward your goals and accomplishments will come. Your management skills are enhanced. Leadership qualities are to the fore, but beware becoming critical or antagonistic toward those in authority.

26. SUNDAY. Quiet. A day at home would be the best way to achieve peace and tranquillity. Aim to finish projects that are partially completed. A practical mood is in force now. If outdoor activities appeal, going for a walk or taking a drive to sightsee will be relaxing and provide a fresh perspective. You should feel great later on and be very pleased you made the effort to venture out. If your mate or partner voices concerns, be prepared to listen without interruption, criticism, or theatrics; when it is time for you to respond, be frank and open. A hot bath and a warm drink before bed could be the only comfort needed this evening.

27. MONDAY. Easygoing. Excellent trends exist for most of the day. The Moon is in Taurus, your house of transportation and short travels. So this is a good time to purchase a new car, boat, or farm equipment as long as the deal is signed before early evening. Pisces working in the technology or retail industry should experience a boost in productivity and better than average sales. Students in all disciplines can expect good progress during the daylight hours. Confusion or not comprehending lectures or assignments is possible, especially for those taking evening classes. Dancing the night away can be great exercise to help you keep fit.

28. TUESDAY. Smooth. Home is the current hub of activity and where you will probably prefer to remain. Tending to the needs of family members, preparing home-cooked delights to tempt the pickiest eaters, or rearranging furniture might appeal to the home lover. If you are looking for decorating ideas, browse through magazines and do-it-yourself books, or watch a television program to get a feel of current home beautifying trends. Although summer is over, it isn't too late to take off to a destination where warm weather continues. A family conference tonight regarding an inheritance, commercial property, or upcoming celebration should resolve contentious issues to everyone's satisfaction.

29. WEDNESDAY. Ideal. Pisces folks have carte blanche to do whatever takes your fancy today. Lunar trends are scarce, so any problems that happen to arise can be dealt with quickly and efficiently. Purchasing new furnishings or planning home-related improvements that you have been meaning to do for some time can proceed smoothly. If you are expecting overseas guests anytime soon, or during the festive season, take action now so your home is ready to greet visitors. Investing in real estate should bring future gains. This is a favorable time to close a property deal or sign a lease for a new apartment. A visit to a local restaurant that offers foreign cuisine should appeal if you are seeking a hearty and healthy meal.

30. THURSDAY. Dutiful. Expect more responsibility to come your way. An increased workload could require rescheduling appointments or meetings, but this is unlikely to faze the Fish who has been angling for more employment challenges. The offer of a new job could be both a step up the career ladder and a more prestigious position. A vacation romance could take on more meaning, even signaling a complete transformation of your life and a possible move in the future. This is a good time to talk to an older family member about future arrangements. Consult other family members and do some comprehensive research before deciding on a move. A long-distance request won't be refused.

OCTOBER

1. FRIDAY. Demanding. As the new month begins, this is likely to be one of those days when nothing seems to go right. A rumor currently circulating in your circle of friends may cause gloom, but hold off taking any action until information has been confirmed. If you can't wait to find out if there is truth in what you're hearing, track down the facts for yourself. If you are in an established, stable relationship, you may find that your mate or partner disagrees with plans concerning an older relative. Present your view in detail, then talk about options once again; you could be missing something. Be careful with funds, and try to limit what you spend on leisure pursuits.

2. SATURDAY. Pressured. Expect another day when cosmic trends throw a few curveballs your way. Pressure continues to build and might reach the breaking point. With restless energy in play, the best way to handle this is through physical exercise or by getting out and participating in something wildly different from your usual pursuits. Pisces who tend to speak first and think later could blurt out words that weren't meant for the ears of everyone. Bite your tongue hard and remain silent. If you need to vent, find a trusted buddy, an e-mail pal, or some other way to express yourself safely. Pisces who work in sales, publishing, or marketing should take full advantage of current stars to move ahead.

3. SUNDAY. Useful. The Moon is not sending any favors for Pisces folks today, as most of her celestial aspects create obstructions and problems. However, sexy Venus is merging with dynamic Mars, urging couples to snuggle up and spend quality time with each other. Currently single Pisces could settle down with a saucy novel or head off to the movies with friends to watch a romantic comedy. A discovery may clear up an old misconception or trigger a change of plans. Shared finances and business activities will be on your mind as Mercury, the planet of thought, zips into your Libra eighth zone of sex, partner's assets, and loans. Think things through before making any definite fiscal decision.

4. MONDAY. Tense. With current influences in play, some of you are bound to be a little edgy. Constantly remind yourself to take better care of your general well-being. If you have been putting off making an appointment to visit a medical adviser, do it now. Avoid get-rich-quick schemes; they will cost more in terms of time as well as money than any returns you get. Don't be surprised if authority figures are less than helpful. The financial resources of other people become more important to you, especially if you are considering applying for a loan or some other type of financial aid. Pay attention to your good Pisces instincts when it comes to an issue involving a coworker or neighbor.

5. TUESDAY. Trying. This is another day that is likely to test your mettle and patience. Be careful of draining your mental energy by trying to resolve other people's problems. If you have been struggling with debt and seem to be always behind with payments, you might need the services of a professional who can help handle your cash resources. Otherwise the cycle of debt could become perpetual. Avoid borrowing or loaning money, which may become a source of contention with a friend. You can be persuasive, resulting in gains as long as your approach isn't obsessive or overbearing. A desire for closeness and intimacy remains strong, urging Pisces to nurture loved ones.

6. WEDNESDAY. Unsteady. It is a day when the universe is shaking things up a little and shuffling things around a lot. It is time to reexamine your goals and aims to determine if these desires remain realistic and obtainable. Although people may be drawn to your warmth, that still might not convince them to cooperate. If you and your significant other cannot both come to a unanimous decision regarding a mutual issue, it might be wiser to allow your partner to make the choice this time. Hiring a publicist, launching an advertising campaign, or promoting a book should produce expected results. This is a starred time to bring your talents, goods, and services to public awareness.

7. THURSDAY. Renewing. Act on today's increased sensitivity to the moods of those close to you. Surround yourself with folk who emit positive energy to ensure you remain upbeat. Today's New Moon in Libra can bring positive transformation to an intimate relationship. Over the next two weeks you will have the chance to take stock of assets and liabilities to ensure that financial matters are in good order. Pisces with substantial savings but without solid investments may want to utilize the services of a financial adviser to formulate ways to begin building a future nest egg. Recent dreams may be psychic in nature, so pay attention to the clues you are receiving.

8. FRIDAY. Opportune. Planetary vibes are more cooperative today, assisting progress in a number of areas. Intellectual Mercury is supported by stable Saturn, conveying a sensible and diligent approach. Pisces who are in the middle of important negotiations should make good headway, and a contract could be signed. This is an excellent day to begin laying building blocks for your future. Pisces establishing a new business venture should have little difficulty coming up with a logo and name for the enterprise. If you need a little extra inspiration in this area, consider employing a designer to turn your ideas into reality. Fill out a loan or insurance application and complete tax-related paperwork.

9. SATURDAY. Encouraging. The Moon is passing through your Scorpio house of long journeys and higher education, assisting your efforts in these areas. Your desire for adventure increases, encouraging you to explore available options to discover what is out in the wide world to broaden horizons and awareness. Staying grounded in reality might be more difficult. Postpone activities that need focus and mental concentration because mistakes could easily occur. Participating in a creative project could also be difficult due to your imagination not being as active at it usually is. Enroll in an interesting course if more skills are required to enhance your employment resume.

10. SUNDAY. Diverse. Break out of the usual Sunday morning routine. If you are an early riser, stay in bed a little longer; or get up early if you rarely see the dawn. If overindulgence from too much socializing last night has brought on a bout of lethargy, plan restful activities in order to regain your stamina. Leave domestic work for later in the day. From past experience you are aware that this is only a temporary situation and energy should return by midafternoon. A difference of opinion with a friend can be resolved this afternoon, with the friendship returning to the amicable feelings of the past. Provide support to those who ask by relating knowledge and experience.

11. MONDAY. Helpful. Work-related interests are to the fore, encouraging career-minded Pisces to increase productivity. Be on your best behavior even though anger could erupt over the length of time it is taking for a project or goal to be accomplished. Breathe deeply and find some type of distraction that will keep you from becoming obsessed over the lack of progress. Pisces homeowners anxious to place real estate on the market should focus on painting, cleaning, and maintenance work to ensure getting top dollar when the property sells. If you are attending an after-hours function, limit the amount of alcohol you consume so there will be few regrets in the morning.

12. TUESDAY. Disconcerting. Finding a balance between work, home, and loved ones may be a challenge. Trouble could escalate if you have been at odds with a friend, lover, or child. By approaching the issue gently and quickly, a compromise can be worked out before the sparks fly too high. Listening more attentively to what is being said could also help you figure out what is bothering the other person. An inspired plan might come via an associate, but don't get too excited because the concept might not be as easy to accomplish or as original as first thought. A blossoming romance may be disappointing because you are reading something into the relationship that isn't there. Money problems could also create upsets.

13. WEDNESDAY. Satisfying. In general the day should be promising if energy is harnessed in a positive and practical manner. If you volunteer your talents and services, your labors will be appreciated more than ever by those who receive the benefit of your effort. Discussions with a close friend could bring to light an upsetting revelation, and you might need to count to ten to control your anger. Giving this friend a piece of your mind isn't likely to change the situation and may only generate friction between you. Travel plans could require modification if you are required to leave earlier or later than planned. Use extra caution while driving or traveling tonight.

14. THURSDAY. Charitable. Enthusiasm to get things done and to keep other people happy at the same time will keep you busy. New contacts could enter your sphere, possibly through your work. Be open to cultivating new friends, who may be able to open up doors of opportunities that help you achieve a long-range goal. Contact with a large group of people should be entertaining, even if the gathering is work-related. Joining a large organization dedicated to the good of other people can be a wonderful chance for the compassionate Pisces to become involved in a good cause. Even duties that many folk are not keen to take on might provide a rewarding challenge, with lifetime bonds being forged.

15. FRIDAY. Promising. Your mind will be more alert and your wit sharper today. A lecture, media interview, or speaking engagement can raise your profile providing the facts and figures you deliver to your audience are well researched and precise. If you are interviewing candidates for a job, you should find that applicants are of a higher standard, although references still need to be thoroughly checked. Discussions regarding importing or exporting goods are likely to proceed as envisioned. A publishing or broadcasting venture can finally get off the ground thanks to required support. First-time authors could receive good news from their agent or editor.

16. SATURDAY. Slow. The lunar low continues as the Moon moves through Aquarius and your twelfth zone of secrets. Move slowly, pacing your tasks so there is time to relax a little. Pushing yourself if involved with any job that requires physical input could increase the likelihood of errors, resulting in extra stress. A practical approach should be evident. Pisces who are scheduled to speak in public can please the audience with quick-witted comments and ample use of humor. A positive outcome is likely following discussions with an older relative or with someone in authority. Sentimental feelings run deep, encouraging Pisces to contact an older family member or to begin collecting favored objects from the past.

17. SUNDAY. Interesting. Use your good Pisces intuition to advantage. As long as you don't overestimate abilities or underestimate situations, this can be a day when behind-the-scenes activities make good progress. In addition, solitary projects are apt to be successfully concluded, and matters of a confidential nature can be wound up to everyone's satisfaction. Things to avoid include making promises that are hard to keep, jumping into situations without thinking of possible consequences, or signing paperwork before reading the fine print. Gambling should be off the entertainment list because your overoptimistic attitude could find you making bets you cannot afford to lose and probably won't win.

18. MONDAY. Variable. Mixed blessings flow today. The Sun frowns at your traditional ruler, abundant Jupiter, while Mercury links happily with your modern ruler, insightful Neptune. It might be a case of only the best will do for you, but this may prove to be your downfall, especially if money is of concern. Before you know it, excessive optimism could find you overcommitting to an unproven financial venture. Restlessness encourages diversity and letting go of habits, objects, or situations that are no longer serving a useful purpose. You should be in your element tonight as other people are drawn to your Pisces charisma and charm.

19. TUESDAY. Eventful. The Moon in Pisces places you in the spotlight, and you will be in demand socially. Vim and vitality move up a notch, so grasp the chance to utilize this time productively. Begin early and jobs will disappear like magic as each one is ticked off your urgent-task list. Issues that crop up today can be thought through in an efficient manner before action needs to be taken. If someone is nagging you to do something that doesn't fit in with your plans, you have the right to say no just like everyone else. Plan to do something different, interesting, and stimulating tonight, giving you something to look forward to throughout the day.

20. WEDNESDAY. Exciting. There should be a number of good ideas that you can act on. Sort out what has the potential to be successful and you could be well on the way to financial security. Foreign people and places feature more over the next few weeks with the arrival of Mercury, the planet of communication, into Scorpio and your ninth zone of travel, philosophical beliefs, and adventure.

If you are looking for life-altering answers, you should find that your thoughts are clearer and your ability to comprehend more complex topics is stronger. Pisces who are planning an overseas trip can easily organize a travel itinerary that includes the majority of destinations on a list of must-visit places.

21. THURSDAY. Stimulating. Finances are of concern, prompting you to become proactive and devise new means to increase disposable income. Ambition rises, and this is a great period to start a new venture and implement changes that have the potential to raise your standard of living. Moderation is essential but hard to maintain. The spendthrift Pisces needs to beware impulsive purchases even though emotional gratification can come from indulging in retail therapy. The problem involves knowing when to draw the line and stop frittering away money on superficial items. Put off making any decision of a romantic nature at least for the next few days.

22. FRIDAY. Complex. Expect a day of contradictions. Beware becoming involved in issues of a financial nature. Emotions are likely to escalate quickly, possibly resulting in arguments that add more tension to the air. Under the glare of the approaching Full Moon in Aries, think over what you value most in your life. This may be the acquisition of money, although this probably isn't the case for the majority of Pisces people. If a job is no longer providing fulfillment, consider looking for employment that offers more satisfaction even at a slight cut in pay. A project could move forward, or unexpected support might be the reason for a new spring in your step and hope for the future.

23. SATURDAY. Empowering. Current planetary energy continues to disrupt concentration. Focusing on the tasks at hand may be difficult because passing the time in a haze of fantasy and daydreaming holds more appeal. If you are asked to lecture or teach a class, accept the offer. You can present your ideas and thoughts in a way that should be a huge hit with an appreciative audience. The Sun begins the journey through Scorpio, your ninth house of aspirations and adventure. Expanding your mind through higher education or long-distance travel is now under auspicious stars. If either of these is a cherished desire, consider taking action now rather than putting off a decision.

24. SUNDAY. Lively. The increase in tempo promises a lively day ahead. You are bound to be busy, so make sure the day begins with a nutritious breakfast and some wake-up exercise. From then on do whatever provides the most enjoyment and pleasure. A sightseeing trip could appeal. Pisces who are currently traveling should find plenty to satisfy a love of adventure and diversity. Show a friendly face wherever you go and a pivotal friendship may develop with a member of a local club or organization. Publishing and publicity ventures tend to be more successful, with the possibility of critical acknowledgment and possibly an award.

25. MONDAY. Stable. Even the most sociable Fish might be happiest staying home. Try not to regret the fact that you have to head off to earn a living or take care of household responsibilities. Being around relatives and taking a stroll down memory lane could capture your attention and provide the chance to catch up on family gossip, making this a good way to spend leisure time. On the domestic scene a surprise, a troubling household problem, or alterations to a renovation project might require taking a more flexible approach. If you can get some time off, leave work early in order to spend time with the people who share your home and life.

26. TUESDAY. Favorable. Powerful aspects are in force. Support needed to bring a goal to fruition should be readily available, and people in positions of authority are likely to actively encourage your efforts. Your leadership and management abilities are enhanced. Something might come to an end, but with every ending there is the chance for a new beginning and to transform situations positively. Don't get too upset if a relative or in-law beats around the bush instead of providing a straight answer. Patience may be required, but eventually needed information will be provided. Your home will again be the focus of attention, with very few Pisces requiring outside stimulation.

27. WEDNESDAY. Testing. A difficult day seems likely, with a number of adjustments required to help smooth the way forward. If possible, clear your mind and concentrate on practical, routine matters. Output should then remain stable. Purchasing products for the house or attending a party selling home decorations could appeal. If you experience any creative urges, begin a small practical project that can be completed relatively quickly. Peace and tranquillity may be hard to find. If stress begins to get the better of you, a walk, bicycle ride, or fifteen minutes of stretching exercises should be enough to reduce pressure and restore good vibes.

28. THURSDAY. Agitating. A celestial block could be creating havoc, but hang in there. If a positive attitude is maintained, life should begin to improve. Kids might be costing Pisces parents a small fortune, or a series of expensive social events may be stretching your budget to the limit. Slow down and use the famed Pisces imagination to dream up ways to reduce household expenses and entertainment costs. If you control generous impulses, rely on home cooking, bring a brown-bag lunch to work, and look for cheaper amusement, it shouldn't take long for savings to steadily build up in your account. Expect increased excitement and activity in your love life.

29. FRIDAY. Bright. A lighter atmosphere dominates. As love and romantic vibes continue to increase, Pisces will find it difficult to focus on the more routine areas of life. A summer romance might be moving toward a more serious commitment. Those of you in a long-established union could add more zest to life and enrich loving bonds with a surprise romantic weekend retreat for two. If you are eager to celebrate Halloween, review party plans so everything is in place in time for the fun to begin. A hobby or favored pastime can provide an outlet for enhanced creativity. A movie that makes you laugh could appeal to couples, while singles should head to a venue for dancing and mingling.

30. SATURDAY. Watchful. Ducking for cover might be necessary because lunar trends are not helpful for much of the day. Pay attention to signals from your body, and control what passes your lips. A prize pooch or cat might need more nurturing. Set time aside and engage in some serious pet pampering so your four-legged companion knows you appreciate their loyalty and love. Pisces who are on the job should deal cautiously this morning with a boss or other authority figure; this person might be on a power trip, and you don't want to be the fall guy. A romantic interlude with a coworker is possible if you are currently without romance in your life.

31. SUNDAY. Mixed. Protect your health more carefully than usual. Avoid consuming heavy food or alcoholic drinks that could result in an upset stomach. Also don't lift a heavy load that could cause a back injury. Organizing your home office can increase productivity, so make an effort to clean your desk, empty the trash, write out invoices, and file away paperwork no longer actively in use. Confirm social arrangements so that confusion or mix-ups don't derail plans during the early evening. Celebrate Halloween in style, and make it a fun event for the whole family to enjoy. A get-together with coworkers should be especially enjoyable if you make the effort to wear a costume.

NOVEMBER

1. MONDAY. Eventful. As this new month begins, the cosmic heavens light up with plenty of action to keep Pisces alert and aware. You may be forced to deviate from a chosen path. Other changes might be needed to ensure that you are still pursuing the best goal or heading in the most auspicious direction. With love in the air, you could be experiencing strong desires, particularly if you are involved in a budding love affair. Plan a long weekend love fest to continue building on current passionate vibes. Singles can expect a magical experience in the romance department, which may be related to travel, someone in your circle of friends, or a classroom acquaintance.

2. TUESDAY. Lively. The social butterfly within you is poised to take flight. Spread your wings to take advantage of this good time to explore activities or topics that interest you and your mate or partner. Endeavor to find a leisure activity that both of you can enjoy. This should help to increase the flow of communication and strengthen loving bonds. You are bound to heartily approve a review of your written work, acting ability, or lecture style. If taking on a mentoring role is of serious consideration, devote further thought to this now. A whole new world might open up if you decide to share your knowledge and experience. A warm bath and a hot drink before bed should guarantee a good night's sleep.

3. WEDNESDAY. Fruitful. You should now have a clearer perception of the big picture. This is a day to plan for the future, anticipate trends, and prepare for contingencies. Workplace teamwork can advance professional and business pursuits. Ensure that coworkers are motivated and ready to cooperate fully. Money is important to most people, even to the more laid-back Pisces. Today it might seem even more of a necessity because peace of mind is what you covet most. To obtain this feeling that all is right with the world, review your bank balances, credit card limits, and money owed to ensure that you are doing your best to efficiently build financial stability.

4. THURSDAY. Lucky. This is one of those days when you will know exactly want you want but might lack the confidence and skills to find the right words or approach. Take the initiative. This is an ideal time to act and to get things done. You have enough motivation and discipline, along with restless energy, to tackle tasks you have been avoiding. A good measure of luck is also on your side as talkative Mercury and your old-time ruler, abundant Jupiter, combine to increase good fortune and raise self-confidence. Buy a lottery ticket, close a financial deal, book an overseas trip, or instigate legal action; a positive outcome is more than likely.

5. FRIDAY. Helpful. You might be considering further study or perhaps deciding whether to enroll in a course to gain increased expertise in some field. If you are undecided, do some research to gather information. Then make the choice once you have all the pertinent information. Interviews, appointments, and discussions regarding publishing a book, launching a computer game, or attending an overseas learning facility should have favorable outcomes. Thinking Mercury is about to challenge your modern-day ruler, Neptune, so over the coming days it would be constructive to write down key points you want to bring up in a meeting or negotiations. Diligently record all appointments to guard against forgetfulness.

6. SATURDAY. Mixed. Your thought processes can make or disrupt today's plans. Mercury is in dispute with Neptune and Saturn while engaging peacefully with erratic Uranus. There is a very real likelihood of misunderstanding and mix-ups. Other people could read more into your words than you intended. To increase the complexity of the day, a New Moon culminates in your Scorpio house of travel, religion, and academic achievements. Travel will be highlighted over the next two weeks. This is an excellent period to plan an escape to an exotic location or to take off on a romantic getaway. Romance and passion could greet Pisces singles, with likely meeting spots part of sightseeing far from home.

7. SUNDAY. Confusing. It might be easy to get lost in problems and issues, leading to valuable solutions being ignored among myriad thoughts, possibilities, and fears. Confusion may still be clouding your judgment, applying extra pressure and stress. Try harder to focus. With a small amount of exerted effort you can make a profound difference to the actions you take. Neptune, the modern ruler of your natal horoscope, now moves forward in your zone of secrets, sorrow, and spirituality. If you have been neglecting regular practice of yoga, meditation, or other spiritual activities, make more of an effort to return to these methods of keeping faith and increasing relaxation.

8. MONDAY. Constructive. Progress can be made both at home and at work if you can accept external assistance to get jobs done. Don't feel guilty about using funds to lighten your load. A professional with expertise will be able to complete projects in half the time it would take you, and may even do a better job. Information or a reply that you have been waiting for could finally be received. Your love life should be sailing along smoothly. Mercury, the planet of communication, now enters Sagittarius, your house of business activities and vocational pursuits. Mercury here increases the focus on matters relating to career achievements and your current life direction. Meetings and negotiations over the next three weeks should result in a positive outcome.

9. TUESDAY. Excellent. This promises to be an exciting time personally for you as confidence soars and verbal skills increase. If you are not as articulate as you would like, ask a colleague for some tips, or observe the way other people relate to clients and associates. Attending a seminar to strengthen self-confidence, or joining a group that focuses on improving speaking skills and presentation of lectures, could make a huge difference to self-assurance. Your enhanced ability to make a lasting impression on anyone and everyone you meet can be a deciding factor in career growth, encouraging you to go forward and conquer. An exciting encounter with a potential lover is indicated.

10. WEDNESDAY. Accomplished. Something you have strived very hard to achieve is now within your grasp. You should have plenty of time and opportunities to strut your stuff, especially on the job. Challenges are likely to put you to the test, but people who matter will admire your skills and efficient manner of solving problems and getting around obstacles. If you need assistance to complete a large home-based project, offer a party atmosphere as an enticement to get family members or friends to give freely of their labor. This can be a fun way to work as a team while getting the job done cheaply. Be prepared for household products to fail or blow up. The evening may produce a few surprises.

11. THURSDAY. Promising. Don't put up with anything that is merely mediocre. Proving to yourself that you possess a high level of skills and talents is worth the effort. Today's Capricorn Moon could bring contacts into your sphere who will soon be helping you move closer to a special goal. Try to get heavy work done as early as possible. Later in the day, with the Moon entering Aquarius, your two-day lunar low begins. Despite decreased energy and enthusiasm, unfinished chores can be successfully completed. Be patient if family upsets or money dramas arise. Your ability to remain logical receives a boost, and the number of people turning to you for advice or counseling is apt to increase.

12. FRIDAY. Tranquil. With the Moon slipping quietly through your Aquarius house of solitude and endings, this is a time to look inward. Refrain from beginning any new ventures. Instead, complete outstanding tasks and projects so you have a fresh slate to begin domestic chores on Sunday morning or work activities on Monday. Dreaming, visualizing, and contemplating the future can be productive. Intuition and flashes of insight are enhanced, and these can be harnessed productively by the astute Pisces. If socializing doesn't appeal this evening, a long soak in a warm bath could be the perfect alternative, helping you to unwind and prepare for the weekend ahead.

13. SATURDAY. Revealing. Feelings and emotions are likely to freely ebb and flow. Don't be overly concerned about those that hang around. They will soon pass, and you will learn something about yourself by observing your thoughts and reactions to them. Loved ones may think that you are in never-never land, although those who know you well are probably accustomed to your constant drifting off and have no qualms about allowing you your own private space. Opt for a lazy day with flexible plans rather than social activities that are ordered and confining. In celebration of the many blessings that have been bestowed on you, consider donating time, money, or effort to the needy.

14. SUNDAY. Dreamy. Take notice of a vision that lingers in your mind long after waking up this morning. If forgetfulness is one of your failings, write down remembered dreams immediately; the universe may be responding to some of your unanswered questions. An old flame might reappear in your circle, causing your heart beat to flutter once again. Consider your response carefully, keeping in mind that as a Pisces you don't need to settle for second best. Use the power of positive thinking to overcome insecurities and fears. A day trip or a weekend retreat to a health spa may be a wonderful gift to yourself, and the benefits could be felt for a long time.

15. MONDAY. Fulfilling. As this promising day unfolds, make sure to go wherever the action is taking place. The happy dance between the glowing Sun and your coruler, jolly Jupiter, brings good fortune into your sphere. Look your best and get ready to have fun. Today is great for making helpful connections. Other people are likely to be drawn to your radiance and optimistic sense of humor. Your mind should be sharp and emotions stable, enabling you to consider how to contribute more on the work scene or to further career ambitions. Sheer determination can help you overcome any problems and obstacles during the coming days.

16. TUESDAY. Empowering. Believe in yourself. You have what it takes to make this a day to remember. The Pisces lunar high is signaling that this is the time of the month for you to shine. If you have been plagued by a health issue, improvements and a return of vim and vitality are likely now. You can impress other people with your skills and knowledge. Problems of either a short or long duration can be resolved with greater ease. Be daring. Make positive changes to your appearance and grooming. Update your wardrobe, try a new hairstyle or color, or take up a craft, yoga, or sport. Basically, do something for you.

17. WEDNESDAY. Spirited. An early start puts you a step ahead of the competition. There are some issues or decisions concerning your love life that are best put aside for the time being. Your usual Pisces ability to clearly see solutions to problems could be obstructed, which may color your actions and responses. Hoarding money is something Pisces are seldom or never accused of. However, the tendency to be overly generous should also be reeled in, or it may derail financial security. At work, colleagues will be supportive and you should have the opportunity to display your team building capabilities. Use free time constructively for your own development.

18. THURSDAY. Tricky. Physical energy to put into today's tasks is limited. Postpone chores that require heavy manual labor because you will probably run out of steam before the jobs are completed. The universe is supporting an effort to be more sensible with finances, helping you find new methods of reducing debt and restricting temptation to buy impulsively. It's fine to allow imagination to run wild in matters relating to creative ventures, but don't let unrealistic ideas intrude on issues relating to finances. Venus, giver of goodies, goes direct today in Libra, your house of shared resources.

Libra here encourages you to put aside laziness and apply more effort toward building fiscal security.

19. FRIDAY. Optimistic. Propose plans and enter into discussions with those who count. Your coruler, fortunate Jupiter, is now moving forward in your sign and your first zone of personality. Regardless of how down you might have been feeling recently, you should now experience a surge of optimism and faith as the big planet lifts the gloom and promises renewed hope. If a sense of restlessness comes to the surface, a large measure of variety will spice up your life. Otherwise tedium is bound to reduce productivity. Expressing how you feel comes easier. If you have something pivotal to say, other people will be listening.

20. SATURDAY. Exhausting. The busy pace continues throughout the day. Eat a healthy breakfast before going out to act on a series of tasks. There might be a lot riding on how a family discussion is handled. Although communications should be clear, honest, and loving, a dash of diplomacy and tact would be advisable. Take time to think before speaking. Attend to all business and personal correspondence, utilizing your enhanced ability to write and articulate clearly and concisely. This evening you could be inclined to curl up in front of the television and lose yourself in make-believe rather than venturing out to socialize.

21. SUNDAY. Sensitive. Choose confidantes carefully. Some people aren't as willing or able to keep secrets as you are. Express your thoughts and opinions with due consideration to the feelings of others. The Full Moon in Taurus emphasizes issues relating to neighbors, siblings, and those in your community. Emotions may be closer to the surface over the next few days, and people you associate with will be more sensitive to words and actions. News from a relative could bring relief. Writing an assignment, report, or novel can be effectively concluded. However, don't begin new studies or projects because there is less chance that these tasks will be finalized to your satisfaction. Enjoy visiting older relatives or neighbors.

22. MONDAY. Diverse. A tug-of-war between work and family life could require more juggling than you can cope with now. If feelings of not being able to cope adequately threaten to become overwhelming, enlist your mate, partner, or a relative to provide assistance. Demand more respect if other people are taking your generosity of spirit for granted, but don't become too bossy with loved ones. Career matters are highlighted as the Sun now glows from your Sagittarius tenth zone of business, reputation, and authority figures. An honor could be bestowed on you based on the high esteem in which you are held. A promotion or increased responsibility could also raise your status.

23. TUESDAY. Good. Emotional events of the past could play on your mind. Allow your thoughts to wander, visiting the good and the bad moments, and rejoice that what you now have is meant to be. Learn from previous mistakes made by you, your parents, or other family members, then move on with the knowledge that you won't go down that path again. If you are currently living away from loved ones, take time out of your busy schedule to regularly keep in touch with a quick e-mail, text message, or phone calls. Your eye for household bargains increases, and spending money on home improvements will raise the value of one of your largest assets while boosting home comforts.

24. WEDNESDAY. Disquieting. A mixed bag of planetary influences greets Pisces. Loved ones are high on your list of priorities as the lunar goddess sweeps through your Cancer house of the sweeter things in life. This is the time to indulge both your nearest and dearest, as well as yourself, in a few pleasures and treats without feeling guilty. A creative outlet that allows you to express your talents or skills could be more fun now and will be a perfect way to release built-up stress. Pisces singles who are in a blossoming relationship could experience moments of insecurity if the other person cancels plans set for tonight. Be practical when it comes to money, and steer clear of the casino or racetrack.

25. THURSDAY. Inspiring. Excellent aspects from the Moon, Jupiter, and Uranus put the accent on Pisces self-expression. Inspiration can be found in areas that provide pleasure, so allow your inner child to come out and play. Be wary of beginning too many projects at once, resulting in scattered energy and nothing worthwhile being completed. Your ability to concentrate is reduced, increasing the likelihood of overlooking important details. Obtain as much information as possible before coming to conclusions. Guard against a tendency to make decisions with insufficient data. Romantic relationships benefit from the current vibrations, encouraging you to plan a cozy evening for two.

26. FRIDAY. Fair. A minor health concern that has been a drain on your vitality should begin to improve. As a Pisces you are very good at taking care of other people but often neglect your own health, so be sure to look after your personal well-being. The athletically inclined should be more diligent with safety through the afternoon hours, when an accident or injury while participating in a favored pursuit could occur. Weather permitting, a brisk walk or a light session at the gym could get your heart pumping and increase blood circulation. Asking the boss for a favor, a pay increase, or a promotion is likely to fall on deaf ears. Save your breath for a more propitious time when a more positive result is likely.

27. SATURDAY. Positive. With your intellect stimulated and creativity peaking, take advantage in whatever way is appropriate. Impulsiveness could occur all day long. You may be inclined to take risks that you would normally advise other people against. Be sure your schedule has some downtime available, and add a dash of spice to daily activities to reduce boredom that limits productivity. Use extra energy to complete an employment proposal, business offer, or negotiation; the results may amaze even you. Try to improve your health by incorporating good habits into your daily routine. If you are confined to a desk all day, find novel ways to stretch muscles, arms, and legs.

28. SUNDAY. Challenging. The day is set to get off to a bright start. A trip to a crafts fair could be worthwhile for those seeking a gift for a special person. An associate or powerful friend who is in a position to help you attain an objective could begin putting strategies into place. Later in the day it would be wise to avoid arguments at all costs, but particularly with a boss, spouse, or business partner. Pisces folks visiting relatives should also be more cautious when speaking with an older person. You could experience challenges due to a possible age-related disagreement, especially if your current partner isn't a family favorite.

29. MONDAY. Edgy. Moderation is always a must when your lifetime ruler Jupiter is in dispute with other cosmic energies. Today the focus is on communication, making it essential to watch what you say and how you say it. The tendency to spill the beans or put your foot in your mouth increases, spelling trouble unless you are disciplined and controlled. This isn't the day to allow ego tendencies to run wild or to promote yourself. Pisces who are on the job should be extra careful because the inclination to promise more than can comfortably be delivered is likely to create stress and pressure. Avoid contentious topics this evening, or be prepared for an argument with lasting repercussions.

30. TUESDAY. Encouraging. If the weather isn't conducive to getting up early, stay in bed longer, especially if there is someone for company. Informative Mercury takes up residence in your Capricorn eleventh house, increasing the possibility of receiving benefits from associates or a government agency. Professional advancement could lead to a lucrative promotion or a profitable business deal. Communicating views and long-range goals to those in a position to provide counseling, advice, or help can play a part in the career-minded gaining new responsibilities and increased income. To generate more contacts, get involved with a new association, group, or club.

DECEMBER

1. WEDNESDAY. Idyllic. You can look forward to a satisfying day regardless of what is on your daily agenda. As the Moon glides through your Libra house of monies from others, this is a time to take precise aim at your goals. You'll be amazed by just how much can be achieved. Clinching a deal could be a breeze because you will know what to say and the right moment to say it. This is a fortunate period to take steps to protect and build your assets. Obtain financial insight if you have money to invest; look for investments that will provide the best returns. Your romantic side could make an appearance. Pisces who write poetry, compose music, or paint on canvas should experience a boost of creativity and extra flair.

2. THURSDAY. Inspired. This is an excellent day for work of an imaginative and creative nature. The artistic and talented Pisces continues to a have a creative edge. Your intuition is strong, helping you to keep up to date with what is occurring in the marketplace. Don't panic if money problems are causing stress because such worries should be short-lived. Mental energy and the power to attract people who can help advance career goals or academic studies are enhanced. A community appearance, panel discussion, or public relations effort can bring positive exposure, possibly turning into major profits. Pisces going on a group tour can look forward to a great vacation getaway.

3. FRIDAY. Hectic. The action tends to be fast and furious today. Even the dreamy Pisces needs to take it easy because current celestial influences have the potential for an accident or injury. This is the day to slow down, whether you are walking or driving. Don't run for a bus or train, or try to zip through a traffic light before it turns red. Discussing core beliefs, philosophical views, or political opinions would be better left for another time. Your ability to express yourself succinctly is limited, and you could end up in a tangle of words and jumbled thoughts. Avoid issuing any ultimatums. Deal with emotional or sensitive situations in a cool, calm, and composed manner.

4. SATURDAY. Expansive Passion and intensity color all of today's activities. As a Pisces you are known to close your mind to things that you don't want to see, hear, or believe. Your ideas and views may be challenged. Instead of standing up for beliefs that you may no longer hold, do some research and open your mind to fresh thoughts and opinions. If you are scheduled to take exams for an academic degree or a hobby pursuit, you should do well if you apply effort to your studying. The travel bug might bite. If you will have some time off during the festive season ahead, look into a holiday package deal that could widen your horizons and bring new people into your sphere. A trip away might also be what you need to reduce stress.

5. SUNDAY. Motivating. Major planetary patterns are forming in today's skies. The conjunction of talkative Mercury and powerful Pluto in Capricorn increases your verbal and written communication and also adds more depth and feeling than usual. Pisces writers and those who conduct research or analysis can increase productivity thanks to enhanced ability to dig deep for hidden facts and figures. Public speakers should impress the audience with expertise, presentation, and the ability to speak with great conviction. The New Moon culminates today in your Sagittarius house of career and current standing in the community. This allows you over the next two weeks to develop new business goals and organize career plans and public responsibilities.

6. MONDAY. Beneficial. If you have been stuck in a rut during the past few months, prepare for changes to take place. Chaotic Uranus is about to move forward in your sign, impacting your first house of personal interests, vitality, and opinions. This could lead you to experience a change of views and attitude. Public visibility is increased with the presence of the Sagittarius Moon, which sits at the top of your natal chart. So expect to be noticed by those in authority.

Added responsibility could come your way. If you are seeking more challenges in the working environment, promote yourself and make contact with people who can provide assistance or guidance. Take immediate action rather than procrastinating.

7. TUESDAY. Invigorating. Adopt a sensible and practical approach. If you use your energy in a realistic manner, your efforts will be rewarded positively. Concentration increases, enabling you to advance in a concrete and direct way. Money investments should produce some healthy gains. Pisces who are considering entering any of the financial markets could find the right course or broker to guide your efforts. Dynamic Mars, the planet of motivation and drive, starts to activate your Capricorn eleventh house now. So now you may pour your psychic resources into groups and associations with which you are currently involved. A leadership role may be offered, raising your profile in a positive manner.

8. WEDNESDAY. Enjoyable. The tempo of social life increases, something you will probably relish. Look forward to opportunities to catch up with friends and meet new people. Outings, parties, and gatherings should be fun. Conveying instructions and messages to team members won't be a problem. Pisces who are part of a group project shouldn't experience any difficulties understanding what is required. Just don't bite off more than you can chew during this potentially busy period. Good ideas abound, but it is vital to filter out what could be a winner from what doesn't have much hope of getting off the ground. Romantic desire and intimacy are enhanced. The Pisces single could meet up with the love of your life.

9. THURSDAY. Rejuvenating. Spend the next two days conserving energy as much as possible while the Moon is slipping through Aquarius and your twelfth zone. This is the time to implement self-healing and to recharge run-down batteries. Psychic influences reach a peak, and it is wise to steer clear of folks who are inclined to be negative and maudlin. Your compassionate Pisces nature will attract those who require assistance or empathy. Listening, understanding, and finding solutions are second nature to Fish. Finish off neglected tasks, engage in solitary pursuits, and work on activities behind the scenes. Don't put off contacting a friend or neighbor who recently moved.

10. FRIDAY. Fair. Life might appear to be progressing in slow motion as your inclination to hibernate continues throughout the day.

This doesn't mean that you will shun interaction and socializing, just that your preference will be for quiet and more relaxing activity rather than a noisy gathering. Displaying a sympathetic nature comes naturally. However, avoid taking on the problems of other people. Trickster Mercury moves into reverse, remaining that way until December 30. You now have the opportunity to revisit long-term goals, humanitarian efforts, and your involvement with certain groups and organizations. Take the time to review the effort and commitment you have been making, and cut back if necessary.

11. SATURDAY. Restful. Sleeping late is in order this morning. Your energy will remain under par until later in the day, suggesting that less strenuous pursuits should be on your agenda. Relax and rest, especially if you have a heavy social evening ahead. Although as a Pisces you like to please everyone else, another lunar cycle begins after lunch as the Moon sails into Pisces, which is the signal to begin pleasing yourself for a change. The cosmos then will shine on you, and other people will be drawn to your extra charisma and charm. Implement plans, let go of worries, start the festive shopping, or make an appointment for a massage or facial. Social activities are promising, and singles could meet a potential lover.

12. SUNDAY. Smooth. Your popularity grows and you are looking good on all fronts as the cosmic light continues to shine your way. Although Pisces are the chameleons of the zodiac, this is the time to just be yourself without trying to be something you're not. Confidence soars with an assurance from someone important that you are on the right path. If you want a favor, this is the time to make a request. Festive shopping should be fun, and you can make good headway with gift purchases and catering requirements for the upcoming holidays. Be sure to look for special presents for guests arriving to visit you soon. Or book your own journey abroad.

13. MONDAY. Purposeful. Take a deep breath and prepare for an intense day. Mercury, Mars, and Pluto are making strong connections with each other, increasing your mental capacity and the ability for deep and penetrating thinking. This powerful combination can be used to actively pursue goals, persuade others to support your ideas, and explore the deep recesses of the psyche. Selling, speaking, and writing are areas where advancement is likely as your sharp wit puts you ahead of the competition. Patience with friends and associates could be limited, and it will be important to understand their motives and where they are coming from in order to avoid a confrontation. Games or puzzles requiring mental application will help you avoid obsessive thinking.

14. TUESDAY. Expressive. The ability to express yourself clearly remains strong. Promoting your achievements, skills, and expertise shouldn't be a problem. Although rising to anger quickly is out of character for the passive Pisces, you might have to deal with some explosive urges throughout the day. If you are waiting for the right time to increase your assets, consider taking action now. Pisces who plan on heading to the stores for retail therapy should first write a list to limit the amount of money squandered on impulse buys, which are always tempting at this time of year. Loaning money to a friend is not recommended because it might be a long time before the loan is repaid.

15. WEDNESDAY. Satisfying. Making time for yourself could be very tricky because other people are likely to claim your attention. Your sense of timing may be off, and avoiding a power play could be difficult. Unresolved personal issues could be weighing heavily on your mind, but it would be wise to push these aside until later. It is more important to meet employment problems head-on and resolve those issues first. Comments from someone you respect could lead you to think about current career options, encouraging a more realistic approach toward current goals. Rising costs could challenge Pisces who are in business. Be sensible if shopping for festive items.

16. THURSDAY. Accomplished. Honesty is the best policy, and that includes being honest with yourself. If you are a Pisces who likes the good life a little too much, perhaps it is time to look at ways to cut down and become more moderate in your habits and behaviors. Important details could be overlooked in a rush to get finished. Be careful in choosing friends and associates now; they could be to your detriment in the longer term. Do your best to remain focused because too many distractions could hinder progress. People skills are important. If you feel that you are lacking in this area, consider enrolling in a course that provides skills and group experience.

17. FRIDAY. Stabilizing. With the Moon in practical Taurus, you should be realistic and sensible, making this a good time to finish last-minute shopping. Your ideas are apt to be more visionary, allowing you to keep within a budget but find plenty of gifts that family and friends will enjoy. Whatever activities are planned for the day, don't neglect networking in some capacity. Important new information could come your way, but be sure to confirm its accuracy before taking action. Bounce ideas off friends, and listen to the advice of older people if guidance is needed. Sudden arguments could occur with forceful types, but use your mediation skills and peace should be restored quickly.

18. SATURDAY. Frenzied. The cosmic skies are a bevy of activity. Retrograde Mercury slips back into Sagittarius. Expect to be busy and on the go, which you will appreciate since restless trends are in play. Contentious issues need to be viewed from a different angle in order to be resolved; a diverse approach could be the best and only way to achieve results. Finish routine chores early so the rest of the day is free to carry out pursuits and activities of your own choosing. Allow inspiration and imagination to run free. Group harmony could quickly dissolve as unexpected situations cause upsets. Socializing can be fun. The urge to chat is enhanced, but be prepared for a friend to act out of character.

19. SUNDAY. Rewarding. Expect to be on the move again today, even if your preference is to remain around the house. With the holidays almost here, consider visiting family members who are going away, are confined indoors, or who have mobility problems. Spread a little cheer, and also take along a few inexpensive decorations or gifts to make the visit more enjoyable for everyone. Pisces cooks can increase pleasure of the day by baking festive goodies to eat and to give away as gifts. If you do not have children or grandchildren nearby, spend some time teaching neighborhood youngsters to bake family recipes and to carry on traditions. Your communication and mental skills are enhanced.

20. MONDAY. Focused. Today calls for concentration because of an increased inclination to say what is on your mind before thinking things through. You could even be your own worst enemy. Sarcastic responses are possible, but you are not likely to win friends or influence people with such an approach. If you are having problems with a friend, both of you need to calm down and take a break from each other. Even dealing with routine matters may be challenging. Flashes of insight can arouse excitement, but beware scatterbrained ideas and activities. Channel your energy into home activities, decorating, or cleaning so that you will be ready for the influx of festive guests.

21. TUESDAY. Seattered. An abundance of cosmic patterns are now forming in the heavens. However, this might be one of those days when you are as busy as a bee without accomplishing much at all. Although creative juices are flowing and intuition peaks, you may be inclined to scatter your energy, overlook details, and generally run around in circles. Emotions are highly charged as the Full Moon culminates in Gemini, your house of family affairs and domestic property. Someone currently in your household, perhaps an older child, could decide it is time to look for new lodgings. Or Pisces seeking a new place to live could close the deal on a new home or apartment. News might be received of a promotion, which could also mean a change of location.

22. WEDNESDAY. Sparkling. Yesterday the Sun took up residence in your Capricorn house of friends, income from business dealings, and hopes and wishes. Extra rewards for professional efforts are likely over the next four weeks. A promotion or larger than expected performance bonus is in the cards. Increased activities with friends and involvement with a group or association could add joy and fulfillment. You may feel a little deflated, and this means that you need to be more mindful of minor details in order to keep errors from occurring. Don't be too quick to confide in other people; you might not know someone as well as you think you do.

23. THURSDAY. Uneven. Unexpected or unforeseen situations may arise, but the astute Pisces can deal with most obstacles and situations. If you have felt under pressure for a while, you can now relax as you finally see the fruits of your labor. A vigorous pursuit or an exercise regime could also help take the edge off any stress that has been building up over the last few weeks. Purchase last-minute groceries to stock the pantry for the upcoming holiday celebrations. Aim to be free to work around the house tomorrow. Pisces who have been slaving away at work or at home should take a break this evening and relax.

24. FRIDAY. Uplifting. Your attitude will play a large part in how you manage to complete today's tasks. Tact and diplomacy need to be on display. Pisces who work in the retail or service industries might have to cope with a number of customer complaints and grumbles throughout working hours. Social activities at home could occupy a lot of your time. Your innate imagination and awareness ensure that you will instinctively know how to please family members and guests with gifts and food. If you won't be attending a religious service, going caroling, or visiting family, opt for a relaxing bath and an early night in preparation for a hectic day tomorrow.

25. SATURDAY. Merry Christmas! Although the lunar influences are not overly helpful, you can still look forward to a great day. The hours of effort and all the exertion you have put into baking, cleaning, and general hospitality should make this day a success, with all of your guests appreciating your efforts. Even Pisces who don't celebrate this holiday can have a happy gathering with family and friends, sharing hospitality and reminiscences. After the rush of the day, sit down early this afternoon for a well-deserved rest and enjoy yourself. Other people should be more than willing to take over and assume at least part of the role of host or hostess.

26. SUNDAY. Social. A rewarding day is assured, with cosmic trends brighter. As a Pisces you are often very compliant, which at times can be to your detriment. However, today you shouldn't have any concerns in this regard as the Sun and powerful Pluto merge together in Capricorn. You might find yourself in a position of power, requiring decisions to be made or actions taken. Open your eyes to all possibilities. An opportunity could come knocking, and your significant other will probably be very happy to support your efforts. For couples, a change of routine could work wonders in adding spice to life. Those on the dating scene might decide to look further afield for new faces.

27. MONDAY. Active. If you are back on the job you could be bombarded with a lot of work. Be on your best behavior because the boss or another superior might be lurking close by, and may even be taking notes. Shopaholics heading for the post-festive sales should find plenty of bargains. However, be discerning with the use of credit cards. Don't fall into the trap of buying items because they are cheap and on sale rather than because you need them. A quiet dinner by candlelight should set the mood for those in love or in a budding relationship. Pisces in a long-established union should make an effort to spend a quiet evening at home, alone together.

28. TUESDAY. Slow. Once you recover from this morning's sluggish trends you'll feel more inclined to meet and greet the day. Spending time with those you love should be of benefit. Take youngsters to visit extended family members even if it has only been a few days since their last visit. Review the year and get ready to draw up your list of New Year's resolutions and goals, including financial aims and plans. Be honest in writing down what you could have done better and what lessons you learned throughout 2010. Postpone any delicate negotiations and discussions until tomorrow.

Late in the afternoon is the best time to conduct financial transactions, whether buying or selling.

29. WEDNESDAY. Agitating. Expect a tricky day ahead as the challenge between fiery Mars and serious Saturn creates inconsistent emotions and stubborn attitudes. Self-discipline slumps, physical energy declines, and melancholy could appear. A fear of letting friends and associates down could find you taking on extra tasks, increasing your already heavy workload and stress level. Even your best efforts are likely to meet with obstacles or delays. Problems with authority figures are also a real possibility. Being adaptable will be more difficult as irritation reduces productivity. Unless you hold a position of power and can delegate, don't rely on receiving help from other people.

30. THURSDAY. Cheering. Things are looking up now that mischievous Mercury is about to move forward in Sagittarius, your career house. If business and professional plans have been stalled during the last three weeks, you can expect an improvement now. Paperwork, leases, and negotiations should begin to flow, computer problems will become less frequent, and those waiting to hear of a promotion, pay raise, or new job should be put out of suspense. Important paperwork can be signed. Change your routine in some small way; variety is the spice of life, and you could do with some now. A legal proceeding might not be resolved as expected.

31. FRIDAY. Bright. Plan on wearing a new outfit and looking your best for tonight's entertainment. If you are taking off on a cruise or the vacation of a lifetime you should have a great time. For singles, the chance of finding romance at an exotic location looks promising. Party plans should proceed smoothly. Invite colleagues along with family members and friends to share your hospitality. Put on your dancing shoes, and wherever and however you decide to celebrate, do so with style and grace. If you are traveling a distance to a party or other gala event, arrange alternative transportation or book a cab to ensure that no one is tempted to drink and drive.

PISCES
NOVEMBER–DECEMBER 2009

November 2009

1. SUNDAY. Vexing. Expect to be slightly more agitated and volatile over the ensuing day. Don't try to process why you feel this way, just go with the flow as the phase will soon pass. Care is required in conversation. You could accidentally put your foot into something that upsets other people. The habits of those with whom you share accommodations are likely to annoy you. A financial matter could catch you off guard. But it shouldn't pose too much trouble if you attend to the problem immediately. Before spending money, avoid possible embarrassment by checking out available funds on credit cards and in the bank.

2. MONDAY. Mixed. Annoyance and irritability follow you around again today in the form of complaining loved ones and close companions. But it isn't all bad. Loving Venus positively connects to your coruler Neptune, which can bring romance to the fore although harmony may be in short supply. Ignore the crankiness of others, and you should escape their negative vibes. The Full Moon in Taurus places the spotlight on Pisces communication, and that is an area where you want to be articulate. This Full Moon phase is an excellent period to write the last chapter of a book and to conclude a thesis or other important report.

3. TUESDAY. Expressive. It is a busy day when you have people to see, places to go, and things that must be performed. The Moon in Taurus or in Gemini signals a period when your ability to communicate is on a higher level than usual. The Moon visits Taurus all day and then enters Gemini at midnight. If you haven't said hello to your neighbors recently, make an effort to be sociable. Drop in for a chat if you are on a friendly basis. You never know when assistance will be required from people who live close by. Pisces creative urges remain juiced. Now is the time to produce something of value or design something that is out of the ordinary.

4. WEDNESDAY. Fair. Home and family life is highlighted now. If money is tight, that could be a concern for Pisces commuters or one of your loved ones. Buying a new car may deplete funds in savings. Today your coruler Neptune, the planet linked to inspiration and delusion, begins moving forward in Aquarius after a period of retreat. A behind-the-scenes situation should become clear as Neptune goes direct. Activity could occur around an illness, either one you are suffering or one of someone close. If you have been waiting to admit an elderly relative to a care facility, delays around this move should now disappear.

5. THURSDAY. Pleasing. Home, family, and real estate matters are again to the fore. Some Pisces may be in the throes of making your home ready for the upcoming festive season. Those of you who are expecting overseas visitors or a large family gathering over the holidays will begin making arrangements to accommodate guests in your abode. Home entertaining can be enhanced by the addition of beautiful items that convey comfort, ease, pleasure, and aesthetic delight. If studying overseas is one of your dreams, send in a completed application now while your motivation and enthusiasm are enhanced. Trading with people from abroad should be profitable.

6. FRIDAY. Tricky. Soft-pedal any agitation around the home front and in the employment arena. Confusing influences make a mark on the day. Pisces folk could have a tendency to make things up as you go along, especially if you don't know the answers to questions. Endeavor to remain composed and to calm the ruffled feathers of irritable others. That way you should find it easier to cope with stress and pressure. Acting with love can be rewarding. This could be as simple as spending more time around the dinner table or preparing a favorite meal for loved ones. Those of you single are in for a happy night of attraction and flirtation at a social gathering.

7. SATURDAY. Exciting. News from a family member living afar could spawn fresh plans for a visit. There may be some obstacles to overcome, but with a little Pisces ingenuity it shouldn't be long before you have all the i' dotted and the t's crossed. Take care in discussions with friends. A penchant to tell things as you see them might be offensive if your pals are seeking a version that fits what they want and not how things actually are. Venus, goddess of the beautiful times in life, swings into Scorpio, your house of travel and education. Head to the relevant research source and book your next overseas journey or cross-country trip.

8. SUNDAY. Fine. Too many distractions could hinder Pisces students unless you hide away in a private space and stick to the books. For most of you today the world of nature and of cultural experiences will assume importance. Whenever possible, take a trip out of the city. Relax amid the greenery, walk in the gardens and parks, admire the scenery, breathe fresh air. Your vim and vitality could be slightly down, so choose gentle pursuits rather than amusement that requires great effort. Nostalgia could overwhelm you. This is a fine time to display photos or put on a slide show for family and friends.

9. MONDAY. Fortunate. Good things can happen now. Sexy Venus combines with intense Pluto, maximizing the loving vibes both for Pisces singles and those in a committed union. Luck is on your side, and anything is possible. A holiday romance will brighten the love life of the Fish on vacation. Meeting your soul mate is a distinct possibility. Good food, fine wine, and excellent conversation will be enjoyed by the social butterflies among you. Money from a business transaction could be more than envisioned. Mixing business with pleasure is bound to meet with success. The time is right to approach an employer for a salary increase or a promotion.

10. TUESDAY. Diverse. A lively day is ahead, but there are also a variety of pitfalls that could trip you up unless you are careful and wary. The main problem is the conflict occurring between the Sun and your coruler Jupiter. Pisces generosity is enhanced, but this can also equate to going overboard with grandiose ideas and promises that cannot be honored in the time allocated. Those of you setting off on a trip may experience a few dramas, which would be exacerbated if you complain about delays, service, or other petty issues. Students should stick to a word limit when writing an original paper or a factual report.

11. WEDNESDAY. Bumpy. Complex influences are on display. Mercury is happy with excitable Uranus but cranky with your coruler nebulous Neptune. Be prepared for news that could give you a jolt. But be sure to write the message correctly because memory cannot be relied on. Getting others to believe what you have to say may be difficult if a tendency to waffle or prattle on takes over. This isn't the day to carry out detailed work or tasks that require intricacy and precision. Your concentration may be in short supply. Personal business may have to be delayed until later in the week.

12. THURSDAY. Powerful. There is a possibility that some of you could become the voice for a team effort today. Stop doubting your ability. Grasp the chance to shine in the spotlight when the opportunity arises. As a Pisces your ability to mobilize everyone for a common purpose is a natural instinct. So most of you are perfect for a leadership role. Original ideas and innovative procedures are likely to come to mind. These will elevate your profile with peers and superiors. Recognizing what is truly important in your life is a gift. You might now see that a significant other provides support in every way possible. Show appreciation.

13. FRIDAY. Productive. If you are tired of the same old same old at work or around the house, then it is time to remove the clutter. Get out the bags and boxes and start filling them with out-of-date files and papers. Pack clothes and items that are out of style or no longer comfortable. Donate these usable secondhand goods to a local charity. Don't forget to throw away old foodstuffs and medicines. Do your bit for the environment. If the right questions are asked, you will receive the right answers. Dress to impress. You could be featured in the media, an event that will be to your advantage now or in the future.

14. SATURDAY. Surprising. Expect the unexpected in today's situations and scenarios. Pisces enjoying a holiday romance could be in for a shock when your lover wants to expand the affair into a long-range relationship. Any social activity that has an overseas flavor will provide excitement and stimulation. Those of you taking an exam should do well as long as you have prepared well in advance. A college reunion or graduation should be a pleasure to attend. The Fish in charge of an educational conference or seminar program can expect accolades for a job well done. This is a great time to research interesting vacation locations.

15. SUNDAY. Uneasy. If you had an enjoyable day yesterday, you could come down to earth with a thud today. Cosmic energies are likely to create unsettled feelings and angst. Confusion and restlessness could have you thinking that all you ever do is cater to others with little appreciation coming from anyone. Although there are some hiccups and obstacles to plow through now, an overly sensitive mood could be your undoing. Be wary of entering a business partnership or financial agreement with a friend or an acquaintance or of risking shared assets in a group project. Deceptive trends abound, promoting schemes that appear too good to be true.

16. MONDAY. Renewing. Pisces folk presenting an argument, writing an article, or proposing an advertising campaign can have sweet success today. Talkative Mercury has just entered Sagittarius, your house of career and business. Keep your eyes and ears open, as you could come across the perfect plan or idea that provides a boost to your professional aspirations. Your ability to navigate business negotiations will also hasten your progress up the ladder of success. A Scorpio New Moon heralds the opportunity to plan a long-distance journey, to apply for overseas study, or to join a religious group. During the next two weeks make plans to expand your horizons and broaden your outlook on life.

17. TUESDAY. Strategic. Pisces concentration and focus are enhanced today. Big plans can be born, so don't be afraid to put pen to paper and be inspired. Approaching the boss for a salary increase or extra responsibilities should meet with a positive response. Your professional standing is rising, and with it more money will come. Some of you will be applying for a loan to consolidate all debts into one. Reducing overall monthly payments would be worthwhile. However, be careful when it comes to taking on more debt. It is never wise to put your assets on the line. An invitation to an occasion of special significance will thrill you.

18. WEDNESDAY. Lucky. Positive energy continues to fuel your career and business life. This is a great time for Pisces folks to begin thinking about future life direction, especially if you haven't yet made up your mind as to what pathway to take. Those of you who are just filling in time on a job should be making plans to follow your dream. Research positions that can provide the emotional satisfaction you are seeking. Upgrade your resume, check all the want ads, register with agents, and ask family and friends to help in your search for suitable employment. An honor or an award could propel some of you into the public arena.

19. THURSDAY. Prickly. Romance could be touchy today, and you might face a number of shocks that will be uncomfortable. An awkward emotional situation will require a cool and calm approach to avoid upset and tears. Insight and understanding about this situation will come, just wait awhile. There is a caution to protect your hard-earned savings. Splashing the cash around on trivial items you really do not need could deplete your budget. A legal ruling may be the court of last resort, but this isn't the time to start proceedings against debtors or others with whom you are in dispute. Any contentious financial matter requires further input to avoid possible loss.

20. FRIDAY. Tough. Pisces who work within a team environment could find the going difficult. The Moon is not very supportive and may create a few hurdles for you to overcome as the hours pass. Participants in a group meeting might agree to implement fresh ideas, but these may come to nothing later on. If you hold a position of power in a club or association, you should show respect to everyone to avert discord and tension. And if you are organizing a festive function, be sure you plan for all age groups. When out socializing this evening, don't be surprised if you feel alienated from the rest of your friendship circle.

21. SATURDAY. Soothing. A restless spirit could hinder progress. Include plenty of variety and stimulation in the day's proceedings, or not much will be accomplished. If relaxation is your preferred activity, catch up on your reading and movie watching from the comfort of home. A yoga class could also be of interest to Pisces wanting to calm the mind. At midnight the Sun will be on the move and will visit Sagittarius, your house of fame, recognition, and professional advancement. During the next four weeks, the effort you put into a business or a vocation should be rewarded with achievement and success.

22. SUNDAY. Revealing. Be open to new experiences and possibilities, even if these appear to be a little overwhelming. A social function that includes professionals in your field would be a good choice for the career-minded Pisces to attend. Someone close may reveal an unexpected confidence. Be very careful before agreeing to keep quiet about everything told to you. Being party to this secret may draw you into some unsavory entanglement. Protect your good health by avoiding heavy-duty tasks that create pressure and strain. If you are looking for someone to share your life, keep your eyes open now and you could be pleasantly surprised.

23. MONDAY. Unpredictable. With the Moon in Aquarius and Mars in Leo, it is a day of contrasts. And when Venus and Jupiter meet in the heavens, moderation is a must. Today Venus and Jupiter are in dispute. Avoid any dealings that could lead to legal action. Steer clear of any situation where you might be sued or held responsible in some way. Pack a healthy lunch if you are on a self-imposed or forced diet because the temptation to overindulge is greater now. Pisces career and business matters are promising. You can put forward a powerful argument that will convince people to back you. Prepare to spend more than you bargained for while sightseeing or traveling abroad.

24. TUESDAY. Opportune. Pisces professional life is under auspicious stars right now. Opportunities arise that include new contracts and connections that will help you expand your business. Remain alert. You might notice a niche in the market that others haven't yet discovered. If you have been too close to a personal issue, your ability to see clearly arrives now. Finding shortcuts for time-consuming tasks may be a priority, and you will make headway here. Interviews and meetings conducted from midday on have a great chance of proceeding in your favor. A new agreement will provide fresh motivation for a group enterprise.

25. WEDNESDAY. Encouraging. The positive trends continue. People are recognizing your talents and charisma, and let you know. Appreciation will be shown by an employer or a colleague. The Fish in a relatively new union will find that a deeper love blossoms unexpectedly. Partnered Pisces might be on the receiving end of a delightful surprise. Single Pisces could meet an exciting lover. But be wary of reading too much into the affair because passion and desire may depart as quickly as these emotions arrive. Those of you experiencing a personal problem should leave your troubles at home. Don't involve coworkers in your private business.

26. THURSDAY. Varied. Mixed trends exist. With the Moon still in your sign of Pisces, effort expended on the job should pay dividends, possibly boosting a depleted bank account. However, sultry Venus and your coruler idealist Neptune are at loggerheads. This could cloud your judgment about financial proposals and love affairs. Don't even entertain the idea of becoming involved in get-rich schemes. Today's stars warn that a fool and his or her money will soon be parted. The glamorous Pisces has the power to turn heads your way now. But refrain from placing a lover on a pedestal. Doing so might set both of you up for disappointment.

27. FRIDAY. Happy. Your sensitive side remains on show, greatly benefiting those you love the most. Tell them how you feel. Honesty and openness will further enhance and cement loving ties. Take time out to cruise the shopping mall with friends. Book a table for two at lunchtime and treat your significant other. Pisces parents need an occasional time out from the kids. That way you and your mate can focus on each other and your mutual goals and aims. Refrain from making large purchases after midday. Receiving value for your money appears less likely then. Guard your wallet and personal possessions while shopping in a crowded store.

28. SATURDAY. Uplifting. The celestial influences are favorable for Pisces folk. Make a commitment to be of service to others. Become a member of a group specializing in humanitarian causes. Such experiences will be emotionally fulfilling, and you will relish the challenge. Your innate ability to empathize with people in need guarantees that you would be valuable in any venture that provides care and service to others. Today is a much better day to head for the shops. The discerning Fish will discover quality goods priced just right to save you money. Don't waste today's sociable stars. Go out, circulate, meet, and greet.

29. SUNDAY. Variable. A mix of cosmic energies is at work now. A good sense of humor and the ability to remain flexible can carry you through most situations that arise today. The anxious feelings of others can be eased if you remain lighthearted, and this should restore their equilibrium. Steer clear of situations that could become volatile. Don't visit areas that are known to harbor a criminal element. Ask someone to accompany you rather than walking alone. There is an element of good luck prevailing. A small wager on a game of chance at a casino or racetrack may net a pleasant windfall. Touring spiritual sites will delight the Pisces traveler.

30. MONDAY. Challenging. A demanding day is more than likely as informative Mercury challenges erratic Uranus. Some Pisces may receive unexpected news regarding a business or employment deal that you thought was in the bag. Negotiations might not go your way. So if possible, it would be wise to avoid them altogether today. Wait until the stars are more supportive if your enterprise depends on getting this contract. Turning off your mind could be difficult, making it hard to concentrate on one thing at a time. Add plenty of diversity to your schedule in order to stimulate your mind. Record inspirational and original ideas for future reference.

December 2009

1. TUESDAY. Stirring. The mood is about to change as the last month of the year begins. Uranus, the awakener, has woken up and is now moving forward in your sign of Pisces and your solar first house of personality and ambitions. Uranus here will shake things up, reactivate personal aims, and provide motivation and encouragement for you to begin going after the things you hold dear to your heart. You might be tempted to change your appearance as the seasonal celebrations approach. Reconsider expensive cosmetic surgery if you still have doubts about it. A makeover far less radical can include hairstyle, hair color, and zany costuming.

2. WEDNESDAY. Successful. The boom in Pisces career advancement continues to amaze and satisfy. Venus, goddess of love and money, has just settled into Sagittarius, joining the Sun and Mercury there to maximize your solar house of fame and fortune. This should be a wonderful time of the year for your professional interests, and one you will not forget. A bonus, promotion, or pay raise seems very likely now for those of you who have put in considerable effort. Business negotiations and financial transactions should proceed smoothly. You can expect viable contracts and lucrative deals that increase your earnings.

3. THURSDAY. Charismatic. Charm is definitely an asset for Pisces folk now. It is one of the attributes that can help you progress quickly in your field of expertise. An offer or an award will convey due recognition for your contributions, delighting you and your extended family. This is a favorable time to finalize details for an office party or community celebration. You know what is needed for everyone to have an enjoyable time. Catch up with friends and neighbors by phone or visit. The unattached Fish has a very good chance of meeting someone who makes your heart beat faster and who will become a constant companion.

4. FRIDAY. Fruitful. Plans to move forward with a business expansion should meet with success. Employed Pisces will be lucky in terms of career advancement. An authority figure could notice your input and compliment your effort and expertise. Now your professional reputation and standing will get a nice boost. Love is in the air. An older or more mature lover may appeal to you. Some Fish may announce an engagement. Others of you are ready to move into a permanent relationship with a lover. The decision is imminent. Current planetary patterns indicate that it is a great weekend to walk down the aisle.

5. SATURDAY. Bright. Mercury, the communication planet, moves into the sign of Capricorn today, putting into prominence your hopes, desires, and friends. Long-range goals and group projects will benefit now. Mercury clarifies your strategy for achieving your desired direction in life. Issues of personal freedom, independence, and autonomy could rise to the surface and will need to be addressed. You can expect increased activity in your social life and more interaction with people in your friendship network. An honor could be bestowed on you by members of a professional affiliation. Some Pisces will be chosen to head up a group.

6. SUNDAY. Constructive. Direct equal time and attention to health and home life now. In any exercise program make sure you warm up first. Over enthusiasm could lead to muscle strain, then in turn lead to expensive chiropractic work and therapeutic messages. If a new pet is on your wish list, it is a great time to make a choice. Those of you who are purchasing a pup, kitten, or goldfish for a child should determine which kind of animal would best suit the home environment and age of family members. On this leisure day you will find joy in baking, cooking, and preserving.

7. MONDAY. Perceptive. Thinking planet Mercury connects positively to intense Pluto but is in conflict with sober Saturn. These contrasting planetary influences may make life a bit difficult. Your thoughts could be powerful but possibly gloomy. Nevertheless, logic and analytical ability are your allies today. Being articulate, you can present a compelling argument. But you may be reticent about speaking out for fear of hurting someone's feelings. If you are called to duties that are beyond your skills level, ask for assistance. Teamwork will lead to a favorable outcome for everyone.

8. TUESDAY. Thorny. If it has slipped your mind that the festive season is fast approaching, it is time to act. On top of an already hectic lifestyle, you now have more details to straighten out so that you are not left rushing around at the last minute. Prepare and send greeting cards and invitations. Arrange a menu for parties. Shop for special gifts. Avoid giving opinions to people close to you, particularly friends and coworkers who ask your advice. Your comments could be more critical and cutting than usual. Issues with roommates arise again. If you have been suffering in silence about their sloppy habits, speak up now or forever hold your piece.

9. WEDNESDAY. Uncomfortable. Pisces diplomatic skills may be missing for the moment. Avoid confronting people over petty issues. If you did not speak up when the time was right, your spiel can wait awhile. Cooperation and compromise are unlikely outcomes anyway. If you persist, you will become further upset and frustrated. Minimize complications by refusing to make judgments even when someone challenges and tests your patience and resolve. Keep building on your personal and professional relationships. These will provide the emotional comfort and support you need to move into more demanding areas.

10. THURSDAY. Fine. A better day than yesterday arrives. The happy combination of the Sun and dynamo Mars raises your energy and drive and throws opportunities your way. Career kudos can be expected. A tantalizing opportunity to do something you have always wanted to do may be presented. Grab the opportunity. Go after whatever realistic goal or dream is in your sights. Your worth to a company is valuable. A senior partner or boss could shed positive feedback on your achievements and provide guidance that will enable you to keep moving up the ladder of success. Be wary of sharing confidences with a friend.

11. FRIDAY. Fair. Changes to prearranged plans will frustrate you if it is too late to make other arrangements. Write everything down that is important and you need to remember. Preoccupation with all the things on your agenda could cause forgetfulness, which in turn can create future hassles. A financial mix-up or misunderstanding may catch you unawares. A regular source of money might show signs of drying up. Keep your eyes open for developments that could raise your profile either as an entrepreneur or as an employee. If you have a plan that can generate higher profits or better income, approach a financial backer. Your local banker might respond positively.

12. SATURDAY. Lucky. Unexpected good luck is on your horizon today. The luck may be minor or major. But whatever it is, make the most of it. Jump at any opportunities that can expand your awareness and assist you to learn new skills. If opportunity comes knocking, don't be impulsive. But certainly take a long and serious look at what is on offer. A meeting of the minds is a stimulating experience for Pisces eager to combine socializing with education. Surprise someone you love. If money is in short supply, do something that is inexpensive but still demonstrates that you want to please. A family reunion is a wonderful way to reconnect with people who have been off the scene for a while.

13. SUNDAY. Active. Family members living at a distance might be on your mind today. If you haven't yet bought gifts to send afar, or mailed greeting cards, or composed festive e-mails, put these tasks on your to-do list now. Preparations to host visitors for the holiday season should begin now while you have leisure time. Organizing the guest rooms could take the whole day. Some Pisces will be happily occupied packing bags and getting ready to drive or fly away on a long journey. If you are studying for final exams, don't cram. Take a rest every now and then, and hope you have done enough to pass with flying colors.

14. MONDAY. Mixed. Restless influences mix with potentially auspicious stars to present a complex day. Career developments may be unsettling. But be patient. Whatever happens should turn out to be beneficial, even if you cannot imagine this outcome now. Your in basket could be filling up very fast, and you may decide you have reached your limit. Don't do anything impulsive. Instead, ask for assistance. Or advise a superior that the workload needs to be shared. Rebelling or raising your voice will get you nowhere. Good news arrives, although you may not be in a position to tell of your happiness yet. You may be asked to remain silent for a while.

15. TUESDAY. Uplifting. A lucky day dawns for the Fish. There may be a very special spiritual and dreamy quality that encourages you with any form of creative venture. People are sure to seek your wise advice. Those of you in various counseling fields should be pleased with the guidance you dispense to anyone who requests your services. Schedule a consultation with an astrologer. Visit a New Age fair. Any revelations you gain will unlock your subconscious. You should use such knowledge to your advantage. Pisces singles may connect with someone new. Let your hair down and enjoy the happy spirit surrounding you.

16. WEDNESDAY. Enthusing. The tempo of social life rises as the countdown to the holiday period moves closer. A New Moon in Sagittarius puts the focus on your career path and life direction. If your current employment duties or conditions are no longer providing challenge or fulfillment, then now is the time to take action. Throughout the next two weeks there should be more career opportunities up for grabs. So remain alert and be ready to move. A past achievement could be honored. Some Pisces may receive a measure of fame. Any involvement with the media, even a brief appearance, might be the vehicle that opens new doors for you.

17. THURSDAY. Heartening. Pisces are again in luck as the universe continues to send positive and constructive trends to assist your progress. Love and romance are in the frame now. If you have the time to remove yourself from the hustle and bustle of life, this is a wonderful period to be exclusively with your lover. Take a trip to a cozy retreat. Go about town and treat yourselves. Catch up on all the little things you haven't been free to talk about recently. A larger than expected bonus will make it easier to entertain generously and graciously over the holidays. The single Fish attending a work party may find romance blossoming with a colleague.

18. FRIDAY. Hectic. A whirlwind day is likely ahead for the Fish. Even those of you who prefer to move slowly may be on the go and under pressure. However, the lunar trends are friendly for much of the time, indicating that you will find the experiences enjoyable rather than strained. Pisces shoppers should locate a number of bargains to gladden your heart. Socializing is a must if you like to interact with diverse individuals. Your brain requires mental stimulation and your body responds well to physical movement. Dinner and dancing with family, friends, or colleagues could be just what you need to unwind after a busy week.

19. SATURDAY. Dreamy. Fantasizing and wishful thinking may mark much of this day. You may be inclined to take it easy. The Moon is in Aquarius, your twelfth house, from this morning to Monday evening. So this weekend is the time to rest and recharge rundown batteries. Get yourself in top shape for the social activities and workload of the coming week. Your creative juices are flowing, so it is an excellent time to decorate the tree, office, or apartment. Someone may be delving into your background. If you are not willing to share your life story, just drop enough casual information to keep this busybody off your back. Better still, tell them to mind their own business.

20. SUNDAY. Tranquil. The energy for the day may prompt you to meditate and reflect on what has happened in your life recently. It is a perfect day to linger in bed and dream about whatever takes your fancy. If you have someone to share your dream and bed, all the better. Romantic vibes are high through the happy link between saucy Venus and generous Jupiter. Defer decision making and practical chores now. Enjoy lazing around, quiet socializing, informative chat. Mars, planet of action and initiative, turns retrograde in Leo today, and may slow down anything that involves a health or employment condition.

21. MONDAY. Excellent. Inspiration and creativity continue to flow, providing a lovely atmosphere for most of you to work in. With an abundance of planetary patterns forming now, you can expect life to be busy and interesting. Energy can be productively used to retrace your steps and put things right that may have gone off track. Today the Sun joins Mercury and Pluto in Capricorn, your house of hopes, wishes, and goals. Over the next four weeks the Capricorn Sun encourages Pisces to dream big and forge new long-range goals. A boost in career income is foreseen. Build up savings from extra earnings and windfall profits.

22. TUESDAY. Quiet. A fairly peaceful day seems assured. The Moon is flitting through your own sign of Pisces. So you are placed in a position to shine and to let your presence be felt in a positive manner. Surprises are heading your way. Your social calendar should be bursting at the seams, announcing a variety of professional events and social functions. Frazzled nerves could play a part in creating minor disharmony at home, especially if you have frittered away joint funds. Clear your agenda and aim for a peaceful evening. Listen to relaxing music, play with youngsters, read, and chill out.

23. WEDNESDAY. Happy. The tempo continues to rise as the crowds spill into the shopping centers and the holiday fever swells. Spending money could begin in earnest, but you should know by now exactly what to buy and how much to pay. You usually select gifts that are beautiful and arty rather than practical. As a Pisces you have superb taste when it comes to things of a creative nature. Don't forget to nurture yourself today. Take time out for a beauty makeover. Add some delightful accessories and jewelry to your wardrobe. Do what makes you feel good. The best treat would be enrolling in a crafts course that would hone your skills.

24. THURSDAY. Festive. Take the weight of your feet now. If you have been something of a workaholic of late, return to party mode.

Gentle Pisces folk will surprise yourselves and others as the Capricorn Sun connects with powerful Pluto in Capricorn, your house of friends and cherished desires. You might need to quell any aggressive tendencies, although assertive behavior can be utilized positively. This is a wonderful period to think about and write down your goals for 2010. Make time for this task. If you are celebrating Christmas Eve with newcomers and strangers, your social graces are bound to turn a stiff gathering into a spirited and stimulating party.

25. FRIDAY. Merry Christmas! Regardless of your religious or spiritual affiliations, this is a day when you can gather with family and friends and enjoy one another's company while sharing hospitality and banter. At home devise a roster of chores for loved ones in order to give you a break and to conserve your energy. Some Pisces will be entertaining on a grand scale. You should relish being in the spotlight and playing the adored host or hostess to appreciative guests. Venus visits your Capricorn house of friends and social interactions, maximizing the magical spirit of this holiday and granting you some special favors.

26. SATURDAY. Social. If the party mood continues, go with the flow but be careful driving and even walking in crowded places. Sales at your favorite stores may attract you. You have an eagle eye for bargains today, and you should be pleased with your purchases. Pisces returning presents for credit will experience goodwill from the store owners. Information gatherer Mercury is now retreating in Capricorn, your house of friends and of income generated from business. Mercury will be retrograde in Capricorn until January 15, 2010. Defer expensive acquisitions, be extra careful before signing contracts, and don't go into business with a friend.

27. SUNDAY. Easy. A local event could turn out to be a memorable occasion, so take a camera and recorder along. If your vim and vitality are running low right now, rest up. If you don't have to be anywhere special, enjoy some downtime. Focusing on your hopes for the future can bring inspirational ideas and thoughts to mind. As this year's end approaches, think about your resolutions for next year. Discard goals and aims that no longer fit in with your current desires. Replace the old with fresh hopes that are realistic and will keep you motivated. Avoid wishful thinking.

28. MONDAY. Inspiring. Meetings and social events will tap your inspiration and motivation. Those of you who are organizing an

end-of-year party or gathering should do a fantastic job with just
the right amount of entertainment and information to thrill everyone. Your ability to educate and to communicate is enhanced. You
can convince team members and close companions to go along with
you. Confidently speak out in public. Love and romance are there
for the taking, so soak up the passion and embrace your significant
other. The solo Pisces can look forward to some heady interludes
when the right partner comes along.

29. TUESDAY. Uneasy. A strange day for intimate relationships
unfolds. Lovely Venus is still cuddling up to intense Pluto but is not
happy with disciplined Saturn. These planetary patterns could cool
off some of the heat in a love affair and pose a serious and more responsible overtone. Today's energies may also pose limitations when
it comes to creative thinking. If possible, postpone putting the finishing artistic touches to an upcoming celebration. Concentrate more
on the practical and financial aspects. A night at home may be in order for Pisces hoping to replenish energy lost during the past hectic
week.

30. WEDNESDAY. Sensitive. Pisces defenses are down and emotions may be close to the surface today. Remain under the radar. Go
about your daily concerns as quickly and efficiently as you can manage. Casual acquaintances could be insensitive. However, it would
be wise to keep quiet and refrain from retaliating. Perhaps you are
reading something into their words that is not there. If you crave
companionship, invite a close friend to visit at your home this evening. Keep conversation light. A long soak in a hot tub followed by
an early night will get you rested and ready for the hectic celebrations that start tomorrow but may not end until 2010.

31. THURSDAY. Unpredictable. This could be a weird day and
night for many Pisces. Although the Moon is racing through Cancer,
your solar house of pleasure and fun, there is a Full Moon culminat-
ing in Cancer. Emotions are highly charged under a Cancer Moon.
So you need to take extra care when interacting with cranky folk
prone to a quick temper. A sharp tongue could also cause upsets. Be
tactful in discussions with coworkers, companions, and especially
children. Tiffs could easily develop, creating tension and strife. An
evening home with family members and close friends might be the
best choice. Happy New Year!

WHAT DOES YOUR FUTURE HOLD?

DISCOVER IT IN *ASTROANALYSIS*—

**COMPLETELY REVISED THROUGH THE YEAR 2015,
THESE GUIDES INCLUDE COLOR-CODED CHARTS FOR
TOTAL ASTROLOGICAL EVALUATION,
PLANET TABLES AND CUSP CHARTS,
AND STREAMLINED INFORMATION.**

Maria Duval, the famous clairvoyant, is making you this unusual offer:

Choose from the 33 wishes below those you'd most like to see come true in your life NOW!

Maria Duval

Maria Duval, the famous clairvoyant and medium, is making you this strange and truly amazing offer. She is ready to help you to realize your Secret Wishes, the wishes you cherish most, FREE OF CHARGE. All you have to do is choose from the list of 33 Secret Wishes below those you'd most like to see come true in your life, and then leave the amazing "powers" of Maria Duval to do their work…

Please note: offer limited to only 7 Secret Wishes per person.

Then what is going to happen?

As soon as Maria Duval is in possession of your "Special Form for Fulfilling Your Wishes", she is going to perform, on your behalf, a ritual known only to her which should allow your Secret Wishes to come true. You will have absolutely nothing special to do, other than to follow the very simple instructions that she is going to send you in a large, discreet envelope.

Only a few days after receiving your big white envelope, you should see the first beneficial effects of this special help. Then your life will take a new and quite astonishing turn!

You can expect some real "MIRACLES!"

That's right, "miracles" are going to occur in your life once Maria Duval has performed (free of charge) this very special ritual that should allow your Secret Wishes – whichever they may be – to become a reality in your life. You probably won't be able to believe your eyes, but each of the wishes you have asked for should come true.

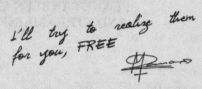

I'll try to realize them for you, FREE

Choose your 7 wishes <u>NOW!</u>

- ❏ 1. Win a lottery jackpot within a few weeks
- ❏ 2. Win a big prize ($10,000.00 minimum) on an instant-win scratch card
- ❏ 3. Win at the horse races
- ❏ 4. Immediately win a sum of money (indicate the amount you'd like to win on your special Form)
- ❏ 5. Have a monthly income of $10,000.00
- ❏ 6. Win everytime I go to the casino
- ❏ 7. Have enough money to buy a house
- ❏ 8. Sell or set up my own business
- ❏ 9. Get enough money to never have to work again
- ❏ 10. See my kids do really well in their studies
- ❏ 11. Get a new car
- ❏ 12. Travel around the world
- ❏ 13. Have enough money to help out my family
- ❏ 14. Make sure that my children and/or grandchildren have a happy life
- ❏ 15. Become the owner of properties that I could rent out
- ❏ 16. Succeed in an important exam or competition
- ❏ 17. Be the friend of wealthy people
- ❏ 18. Never have any more money problems
- ❏ 19. Buy a boat
- ❏ 20. Go on a cruise
- ❏ 21. Be and stay healthy

- ❏ **22.** Have a country house
- ❏ **23.** Get promoted at work
- ❏ **24.** Find a job which is enjoyable and pays well
- ❏ **25.** Find true love at last
- ❏ **26.** Be madly loved by someone
- ❏ **27.** Marry the person I love
- ❏ **28.** Attract men
- ❏ **29.** Attract women
- ❏ **30.** Be on TV
- ❏ **31.** Make new friends
- ❏ **32.** Have more time to do things that I like
- ❏ **33.** That my children have a substantial monthly income

So that's it! Have you chosen your 7 wishes? Then quickly complete the original of the Form below and return it without delay to Maria Duval.

FREE
PARTY LINE

Make new friends, have fun, share idea's never be bored this party never stops! And best of all it's FREE!

Never Any Charges!
Call Now!

712-338-7722